Sociology of Education

Theoretical and Empirical Investigations

Sociology of Education
Theoretical and Empirical Investigations

Lynn M. Mulkey

Hofstra University and
The Board of Education of the City of New York,
Office of Research, Evaluation, and Assessment

Harcourt Brace Jovanovich College Publishers

Fort Worth   Philadelphia   San Diego   New York   Orlando   Austin
San Antonio   Toronto   Montreal   London   Sydney   Tokyo

E000 30 40 018 9 001

Editor-in-chief   Ted Buchholz
Acquisitions editor   Chris Klein
Project editor   Steve Norder
Production manager   J. Montgomery Shaw
Book designer   Jeanette Barber

Credits: Grateful acknowledgement is made for permission to use the photograph of school children and their teachers from the Nazareth Day School, 216-218 15th Street, New York City; Sister Georgianna Manning, former director.

The organizational chart is presented through the courtesy of the New York City Public Schools.

Address for Editorial Correspondence: Harcourt Brace Jovanovich College Publishers, 301 Commerce Street, Suite 3700, Fort Worth, TX 76102.

Address for Orders: Harcourt Brace Jovanovich, Publishers, 6277 Sea Harbor Drive, Orlando, FL 32887. 1-800-782-4479, or 1-800-433-0001 (in Florida).

ISBN: 0-03-032343-6

Library of Congress Catalog Card Number: 92-073501

Printed in the United States of America

2 3 4 5 6 7 8 9 0 1 039 9 8 7 6 5 4 3 2 1

For Anna

Levy-Bruhl says with truth that in primitive consciousness, the consciousness of the individual depends upon the consciousness of the group. But this is not the final truth about humans. Society is a special reality, a degree of actuality. To regard humans as exclusively social beings means slavery for them. The slavery of the human to society finds expression in organic theories of society . . . Society is presented as though it were personality of a higher hierarchical degree than the personality of the human. But this makes a human a slave.

Adapted from Nicolai Berdyaev, *Slavery and Freedom*

Contents in Brief

PART II
Describing and Explaining Education from a Sociological Perspective   63

About the Author

Lynn Mulkey is a graduate of Columbia University (Ph.D., 1985) with a specialization in sociology of education. Her area of specialization emerged from studies with Bernard Barber in the sociology of knowledge, R.K. Merton and Harriet Zuckerman in the sociology of scientific knowledge, and Sloan R. Wayland in the sociology of knowledge and education. While she has been exposed to the gamut of sociological theoretical formulations and their accompanying methodologies, she has been most influenced by Émile Durkheim, Talcott Parsons, and Robert K. Merton in the tradition of functional theory. She is practiced in a number of modes of observation (survey, evaluation, experiment, field, and content analysis) with special expertise in evaluation research and she enjoys teaching both undergraduates and graduate students. She was recently a Fellow of the National Institute of Mental Health and Visiting Assistant Professor in the Department of Sociology at the University of California, Los Angeles, and has a regular appointment as an Assistant Professor of Sociology at Hofstra University (Hempstead, Long Island, New York). She has taught classes in sociology of education, research methods, sociological theory, and others. She also is employed by the New York City Board of Education's Office of Research, Evaluation and Assessment (110 Livingston Street, Brooklyn), as an evaluation research consultant, where she supervises and conducts large-scale federally, state, and locally mandated and funded assessments of the effectiveness of educational programs implemented in New York City public schools. She has authored numerous journal articles and reports and, in general, likes to talk about the utility of sociology for understanding education.

Prologue

Thawt E. Knowsitall just graduated from college. He says he has acquired the wisdom and knowledge of the ages, has had that accomplishment recognized by the presentation of a diploma, and is ready to go out and face the world. Thawt conveys one of American culture's most enduring tenets about what it means to be educated. The accomplishment belongs to the individual. This book, however, argues that the accomplishment does not belong as much to Thawt as we might think, and will divert from traditional interpretations of the significance of being educated by directing the reader to another point of focus in viewing the world. The sociologist does not locate the determinants of success in the individual, but in the conditions which surround the individual. It is the characteristic of the groups to which a person belongs that channel her or his propensities and behaviors. For the sociologist, the blame for failing to be educated or credit for achievement belongs mostly to others rather than to the individual. The expectations or shared rules (agreements) that characterize a group impede or facilitate becoming educated. Thawt will become an engineer because society has structured his accomplishments by making provision for males to learn the knowledge and skills necessary for this type of work. The economic condition of his family did not exclude him from experiences that affected his motivation to become an engineer.

The sociological perspective, I hope, will have implications, especially for those who make educational policy. By having insight into the arrangements which permit us to become "who we really are," we can redefine old arrangements or intervene with new arrangements toward fostering a more equitable distribution of educated individuals. Our classrooms, for example, can be characterized by disciplinary strategies that foster autonomy versus dependence, or they can structure girls' estimations of their prospects so that many do not choose subordination. Women politicians are not less aggressive, women lawyers are not less ambitious, fathers are not less nurturing, unless social structures (society's expectations) make them so.

Preface

This book is intended as a sociological analysis of education. When *The New York Times* (1989)[1] contained news on declining enrollments in graduate programs in sociology and the shutdown of the sociology department at Washington University in St. Louis, my thought was that regardless of whether people choose to study how *social forces* affect their survival, the significance of these forces in their lives is not diminished. The utility of sociology for making possible a distinctive understanding of human behavior has compelled me to write this book. In this preface I want to identify some of my major assumptions. The assumptions concern two themes; the first theme is the contribution of sociology as a unique way of accounting for how people behave and to employ the cognitive tools of the discipline in an analysis of the phenomenon commonly referred to as *education*. Sociology is used to explain education and education is used to explain sociology. The second theme is a view of sociological understanding, a way of thinking about the world, as itself a step in the development of what it is to be human. Individual freedom is available only to those who see the social determinants of their behavior.

Let me please add that when I say the second theme portrays sociology of education as inseparable from and paramount to an aspect of human development, I mean this theme is analagous to movement from "crawling" to "walking." Most sociologies of education (or of anything) devote their time and attention to documenting and explaining the world of "crawling"—social determinism. This project introduces, documents, explains, and emphasizes the role of sociology in making possible the world (activity and understanding of the activity) of "walking"—individual freedom. The consequence of "walking" is ultimately and reciprocally needed for an adequate sociology.

A New Approach

Sociology of Education: Theoretical and Empirical Investigations is a response to a comment made by Robert and Ann Parelius in their book on the sociology of education: ". . . there is still room for improvement, particularly in tying the growing body of empirical findings back into theoretical paradigms so that general principles of social life can be established. A glut of discrete findings, with no organizing framework, can be as useless as the untested speculations of the armchair theorist." (Parelius and Parelius, 1987).[2] The purpose of the book is not to present new research in the sociology of education, but to present a meaningful framework for organizing the vast array of theoretical and empirical work in the subfield. The contribution of the project is, therefore, its *emphasis*. I have developed an overarching, integrative, and comprehensive scheme (a paradigm, a metatheory) (Mulkey, 1990; Ritzer, 1991).[3] Given my intention to introduce a new approach, rather than new material, I have relied upon many colleagues who have written before me, both for their reviews of the literature in certain areas and for many of their ideas. The work of Kathleen Bennett and Margaret LeCompte (1990),[4] Jeanne Ballantine (1989),[5] Rodney Stark (1989),[6] Earl Babbie (1992),[7] Maureen Hallinan (1989),[8] Sarane Boocock (1980),[9] and others has been immensely helpful, but even more importantly, necessary for me to do my work.

Philosophical Assumptions

I have had to take a certain epistemological stance to accomplish the task of integrating theory and research in the sociology of education. I am aware that some sociologists will be uncomfortable with my use of the concept *principles of sociology*. I feel comfortable, however, in taking a position that allows me to make the claim that there is a set of universal laws when we talk about social phenomena. I refer to these as the *principles of sociology*. That is, to me, sociology is fundamentally about six universal ways that explain why we act as we do. With all its subtlety and complexity, human behavior may ultimately be understood by a single tidy set of social principles. Wherever there are humans, they socialize, organize, stratify, socially control, institutionalize, and change social structure. At this level of determinateness (level of individual consciousness, or awareness of reality), these conditions function over and against our will and make voluntary behavior impossible. The explanations of how these social forces operate are the many sociologies or theories. Like physicists who attempt to explain the universal phenomenon of light by positing wave and particle theories, sociologists attempt to explain social forces. The laws are already there, but we have not fully explained them.

I create a *reality* as well as describe and explain it. I have chosen a focus which I feel gives students the chance to see the central significance of sociology. Karl Von Frisch (1951),[10] in his classic documentation of the social life of the honey bee, *The Dancing Bees*, and George F. Oster and Edward O. Wilson (1978),[11] in *Caste and Ecology in the Social Insects*, point to the source of controversy. The relation of the individual honey bee to other bees or the relation of the individual African weaver ant (*Oecophylla loinginoda*) to other ants (the group) is part of the genetic programming of the organism. In human beings, the inherent programming for social organization is distinctive; Gerhard Lenski and Jean Lenski (1987),[12] in *Human Societies: An Introduction to Macrosociology*, explain that human organisms have the most enhanced capacity for cooperation. The rules for interaction are not inherent in human genes; what is inherent is that the organism will make rules and then follow them. Humans respond not to the world but to the meanings they give to the world; sociologists debate over the relative contribution of fixed and arbitrary aspects of social meanings. *Culture* (meaning systems) has been substituted by social scientists for the idea of human *freedom*; two persons, for example, will give a different meaning to the same event and there are so many permutations in the way individuals assign meanings that sociology seems to be an indeterminate scientific activity.

Views of the tenable differentiation between social structure and culture range from the *relativist* position, in which the rules are totally arbitrary and are the

product of the mind, to the *positivist* position, in which the rules exist independently of the mind (Haferkamp, 1989). Social determinants (prescriptions for
behavior) are conceptualized by sociologists as *in, between,* or *external* to the
individual.[13] How much human behavior, they ask, belongs to the individual, and
how much belongs to other people (society)? *Freedom* is a word they find helpful
for designating the degree to which individuals can claim their actions as uniquely
their own, despite their need for the collective.

Sociologists of the *positivist* perspective on freedom view individuals as passive
representations of society. Émile Durkheim (1964),[14] for example, points out that
the suicide rate reflects the conditions of the group rather than highly personal,
idiosyncratic motives; population density and high degrees of differentiation (division of labor) limit the establishment of meaningful ties between individuals.
Symbolic interactionists (G. H. Mead, 1934;[15] and Herbert Blumer, 1962[16])
emphasize that the individual (self) is a process rather than a fixed entity. Human
predisposition interacts with society's expectations and in the transaction, persons
acquire a core sense of self and a behavioral repertoire. *Social constructionists*
(Berger, 1963[17]) see that the self is no longer a given entity that moves from one
situation to another but is, rather, based on the thread of memory, continuously
created and recreated in each social situation that the person enters. It is social
structure that imposes on the individual the definition of a continuously existing
person who is the same at twenty, forty, and eighty (Bell, 1979).[18] *Gand theorists,*
such as Jeffrey Alexander (1982),[19] claim that any given act is multidimensional
and can be viewed as combining internal (voluntary) and external (coercive) determinants of behavior.

All four of these sociologies ultimately view us as dependent on society for
who we are and what we do. In one way or another, they leave persons relatively
determined by the group. That is, there is a common denominator to the conceptualizations, an assumption, that has consequences for an adequate definition
of what sociology is about. All four perspectives assume that the individual is
solely a social self, a social construction and a necessary construction, one without
which the individual cannot function; moreover, this social self operates on the
basis of self-preservation, self-interest. The logical dilemma here is that there is
no freedom or self-governance for a being that depends on external affirmation
of itself, for a self that is constantly oriented to sustaining itself.

The way out of the contradiction between individual freedom and the preservation of the social self is to posit that freedom is not found in society. The
several sociological perspectives can be integrated into a clearer statement of what
it means to be an individual in society by showing that ultimate freedom is found
at the end of a *developmental* sequence that begins with an awareness of society
as cause and the individual as effect, and ends with an awareness of the individual
as cause and society as effect. The subject is virtually *outside society*, until, through
a dialogue with philosophy and religion, it is brought back into the social realm
(Mulkey, 1990)[20] so that the fully developed human being is *in the world, but not
of it.* In this way, being social means, being *first* the effect of society, and *second,*
making society an effect (see Mulkey, 1992, "The Relation of Principles to Theoretical Logic in Sociology: A Re-Examination of a Field of Study"[21]).

This book therefore introduces sociology as having two equally important
roles by emphasizing its significance for both the study of the social determinants
of human behavior (in the context of education) and for the complete realization

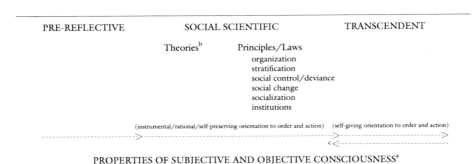

PRE-REFLECTIVE   SOCIAL SCIENTIFIC   TRANSCENDENT

Theories[b]   Principles/Laws
organization
stratification
social control/deviance
social change
socialization
institutions

(instrumental/rational/self-preserving orientation to order and action)   (self-giving orientation to order and action)

PROPERTIES OF SUBJECTIVE AND OBJECTIVE CONSCIOUSNESS[a]

A Metatheoretical Model of Social Determinism (Collective Order) and Individual Freedom (Voluntary Action)

[a] *Consciousness* is used here to denote various states of awareness (what the individual perceives as *real* or *a reality*). *Mind*, an instrument of sensation (visual, auditory, tactile, olfactory, and gustatory) emotion, volition, and thought *transmits awareness* via the brain. Inherent in the cognitive domain of consciousness is the capacity for memory and a *social* predisposition, that is, the capacity to acquire language and to cooperate through rule-making and rule-following activity. (Neurophenomenology, for example, endeavors to explain the predisposition or innate structural antecedents to cooperate as *essences*, basic forms of cooperation devoid of cultural conditioning, by reference to invariant neurognostic structures which constrain both cognitions and perceptions—see Warren TenHouten's "Into the Wild Blue Yonder: On the Emergence of the Ethnoneurologies, the Social Science- and Philosophy-Based Neurosciences," *Journal of Social and Biological Structures*, 1991, 14:381–408.) The manifestation of these inherent and invariant structures is indicated in the figure as *principles* and *laws*. Principles refer to the law-like, cooperative, rule-making and rule-following predisposition of individuals that, when objectified in collective form, appear as types of behavioral prescriptions (social structure; society). The principles comprise a level of scientific precision or determinateness; they appear universally in all human groups as categories of behavioral directives. These essential elements of social life are the social structural determinants of consciousness and the social self (personality). Simultaneously, social self consciousness is externalized in collective form and objectified as society. Society is cause, the individual the effect; society is a macro-determinant of human behavior; the social self is in the world and "of it." Society is order and determinism, law, morality, and the regulation of self-interest. Society affirms rather than confirms *Self*. *Theories* explain the nature of the operation or dynamics of principles. *Consciousness*, also as it is referred to here, includes the direct awareness of *Self*. The individual is able to *transcend* the social self (abandon all mental and internalized conceptions of self) and experience (realize) a *prereflective* state of awareness of *Self*—the Self, alienated in the consciousness of the individual in the formative process of social self-objectification. (See Maurice Merleau-Ponty's *The Phenomenology of Perception*, translated by Colin Smith, London: Routledge & Kegan Paul, 1962. Like J.P. Sartre, he viewed freedom as the capacity of consciousness to transcend its "situation," to another level of awareness. Also see Peter Berger's "Religion and World Construction" in *The Sacred Canopy: Elements of a Sociological Theory of Religion*, New York: Doubleday, 1967, and Morris Rosenberg's "Self-Objectification: Relevance for the Species and Society" in *Sociological Forum*, 3:548–65, 1988.) The significance of acknowledging, after socialization, the Self that exists antecedent to the social self, is for the subject's freedom from social determinism. The subject is thus "in society, but not of it" in that she or he is free to "express" Self through social structure rather than "equate" Self with it. The transcendent property of consciousness represents the evolution of cooperation as the evolution of individual consciousness. It refers to a process of realization as opposed to an investigation, a search for self through cognitive

of individual human freedom. The figure depicts how sociology, as a science, is itself a level of awareness (a consciousness), a reality, and is in this way a phase in the complete development (evolution) of consciousness, to that place (in consciousness) of individual human freedom. The real Self or subject in the world is experienced outside society as an awareness of self or being that is independent of a social self. Self is (exists) before society defines a social self; there is no need to depend on society for identity becuase it is available before we are socially defined. There is a part of being human that is not socialized or transformed into social identity; this residual state of unsocialized self is eventually realized in individual consciousness so that persons are freed from identifying totally with their social roles.

For example, in contrast to the idea proclaimed by Descartes, "I think, therefore I am" is the idea that "I am, therefore I think" (Berdyaev, 1938, 1944).[22] Society becomes an avenue for the expression of Self; there is nothing to get, only to give. This awareness results in the ultimate form of cooperation and perfection of society (Royce, 1968).[23] Joseph Campbell (1990)[24] discusses in an epilogue, "The Tiger and the Goat," that social structures are the forms through which one radiance of eternity shows itself; you can regard the appearance of the miracle of life in all these forms. He says the function of sociology is to teach us about how we act as goats in the world, until we come to the progressive realization that we are tigers. We are free to be tigers when we no longer identify ourselves totally with the coming and going reflections afforded us by society. When we

---

activity of the mind. At this level society is the object and the individual the subject, and social change results less from changing social structure and more from changes in one's view of it. At this phase in the developmental continuum of consciousness, G.W.F. Hegel's characterization of consciousness as "absolute reason" is more accurately typified by Thomas Acquinas's (1985) habit of equating love with being or Teilhard de Chardin's (1960, 1964) "amorization" of absolute reason. In other words, love is simply a disinterested reason, or reason stripped of self-interest. The shift in consciousness marks a departure from ego sociology and the finding of oneself "in the normal distribution." Here, sociology means the breaking down of social-self defense, a "sociotherapy" of exercises in desocialization, a transformation that results in the individual's being in society, but not of it. Consequences of the transcendent orientation to cooperation are for individual psychological well-being and for the actualization of the ideal community (representations of levels of consciousness are found in societal forms such as communism, socialism, democracy, and so on). In this state of Self-awareness, the subject is free from, or impervious to, material and social threats to its annihilation. At this stage on the continuum of awareness, thought is non-recursive, non-linear, and acts back on society with consequences for social structure.

[b] See George Ritzer's *Sociological Theory*, New York: Knopf, 1988, as an exemplary documentation of the many explanations of social principles. Functional, conflict, symbolic interactionist, and others are the typical fare or jargon.

[c] The vector pointing left indicates that "transcending" society has consequences for society. Mainly, when persons realize the "prereflective" Self, social structure represents the relations of a "loving" community espoused by Josiah Royce in *The Problems of Christianity, Vol. II: The Real World and the Christian Ideas*, Chicago: Henry Regney, 1968, in contrast to the law as an external regulation of self-interest.

find this freedom, we are in society to act out a sense of ideal community rather than to fight to defend fictitious selves. Society in any of its forms, across time and level of technological sophistication, becomes the effect, as opposed to the determinant, of our behavior.

Peter Berger's *Invitation to Sociology: A Humanistic Perspective* (1963)[25] also discusses how sociology can uncover the infinite precariousness of all socially assigned identities and how it is at odds with other sociological viewpoints that equate persons with their socially assigned identities. For Berger, the concept of *race* does not elicit responses that are *racist* or *liberal*, but is questionable as a category in the first place; the real problem, he says, is how to be a human being. Essentially, the human in the socialized state forgets the true nature of being, often described as our godlike nature, the nature that makes the social self possible at all. Our social selves obstruct our vision of our true self and nature often described as our godlike nature; it is trapped inside our consciousness as social role. The human has forgotten that she or he has invented this response and that once she or he was God. When we are stripped of all names and all identities, we are not stripped of ourselves. The liberated individual is precisely one who no longer confuses identity with social role. What has happened is that sociologists, for the most part, in their investigation of how we are and to what extent we are associated with others, have defined the social self as the only self, and in taking this stance, they have lost sight of the second contribution of sociology as itself a step in the complete realization of individual human freedom.

The human capacity for adaptation through cooperation and to affect and perfect society is actualized when the person comes to see the world as a context for the development of his or her independence from it. Independence here means that the human perception of well-being and selfhood is not dependent upon external conditions. Persons are more than their roles and in seeing that they are free to make society a reflection rather than a determinant of human potential.

One last discussion of social determinism and individual freedom is from Richard Sennett and Jonathan Cobb's (1972)[26] classic work, *The Hidden Injuries of Class*, which considers development from a social scientific understanding of the social self to a transcendent awareness of self. They claim that persons do not come to exercise control over their situations, transforming the conditions of their life, but instead simply move from one set of circumstances to another. Circumstances—the structure of society, roles—remain, but people move, leaving situations, classes, and structures as they are. Thus, someone like James, the college student, who does not seem to feel particularly inadequate or insecure, plans to deal with the contradiction between his expectations of college life and its reality by moving from one major to another, staying in school but creating a slightly different life-style in order to survive with some sense of personal growth and dignity. Simply because he can see himself moving in society, he individually looks for another situation, rather than transforming the one he is in. He does not transcend his social role; he is identified or equates himself with it. At this level of awareness, society is powerful enough to wound people at a very deep emotional level, the level where the wounds are inflicted on dignity, and the power to shut society out would have to be a transcendental, almost miraculous power.

Sennett and Cobb go on to explain that personal consciousness is something other than a storage locker or receptacle for social information; consciousness, they think, is an active human power that empowers the individual to rearrange the information society furnishes about the nature of human dignity. The arrangement of consciousness, which divides the self in terms of the *real me* and the *performing me*, defends against the pain a person would otherwise feel if she or he had to submit the whole of herself or himself to society. The demonstration of worth now has become a demonstration about inner capacity in the person greater than his or her tangible works, about a virtue which permits him or her to transcend situation after situation, mastering each, but attached and identified with none. There is no need to prove oneself, rather the need to gain an awareness of the innateness and completeness of that essence of social being. This self has achieved *ontological security*, a feeling that the self can survive whatever it encounters in the world; in having this awareness of self, self changes the world. The person who transcends society (the experience of the self as social self) is one who is inwardly free to deviate from societal norms. Yet nothing within compels that person to do so; she or he may choose conformity or nonconformity with equal ease and according to her or his larger interests, the new standard of self-giving that replaces defensive social self-interest (Bell, 1979).[27]

A Sourcebook of Principles

Part of my intention for writing this book—to present a distinctive way for thinking about who we are and what we do—is to provide a sourcebook of principles, which are useful for making sense of what goes on in education. We extract from the world about us, using the conceptual tools of the discipline, by eyeing the regularities in how we are constrained by others in our behavior. Students attain a new consciousness (Berger, 1963)[28] about how we, at once, both affect (by making rules) and are affected (through the rules we make) by other people. The absence of this awareness means we are more likely to be influenced by the world than we are to influence it. For example, Elizabeth Cohen, Rachel Lotan, and Chaub Leechor (1989)[29] demonstrate how *classrooms* learn. Classrooms are conceptualized as collectives with variable properties, such as the *differentiation of instructional technology, delegation of authority,* and *interdependence of work arrangements.* Class members' achievement is seen as an outcome of the operation of these variables. In other words, the same children in a classroom typified by one type of curricular material and management rules would perform differently if the classroom was typified by another type of curricular material and management rules.

Features

Part I (The Nature of Sociological Inquiry) is designed to acquaint readers with a distinctive way to understand what being human is about. **Chapter 1 (Conceptualizing the Social Realm: Six Principles of Constraint)** introduces the concept *social* as the subject matter of sociology. **Chapter 2 (How Do We Know? Casual and Scientific Inquiry)** introduces sociology as a scientific enterprise; presented are the fundamental characteristics and issues that make science different from other ways of knowing things. The lessons of these chapters are applied in later chapters when attempts are made to make sense of the human behavior we call education. **Chapter 3 (One Sociology, but Many Sociologies: Theories Explaining Principles of the Social Realm)** takes each of the six principles of constraint that later serve as organizational schemes of the book and acquaints readers with the various causal schemes set forth about how the principles of institutions, socialization, stratification, organization, social control and deviance, and social change determine behavior. **Chapter 4 (Many Sociologies and Many Sociologies of Education: History of the Sociological Study of Education)** presents the emergence of the subfield of sociology—the sociology of education—by discussing major theoretical explanations of sociological principles as they operate in the context of education.

Part II (Describing and Explaining Education from a Sociological Perspective) applies sociology to education. Chapters 5 through 10 are each devoted to a discussion of one of the six principles of the social realm and how the principle is manifested in the context of education. The theories that sociologists have put forth as their best hypotheses about how the laws of the social realm work and the empirical investigations on various issues that illustrate each principle are presented. **Chapter 5 (The Institutions: Patterned Interactions to Meet Basic Human Needs)** examines issues relevant to education as an institution. **Chapter 6 (Socialization: Becoming Human by Learning Society's Conventions)** discusses curriculum and pedagogy as major issues of socialization in education. **Chapter 7 (Stratification: Rules for Acquiring the Desirable Things in Life)** is concerned with equality of opportunity—educational and occupational attainment according to gender, race, ethnicity, and age—as the main issue of stratification in education. **Chapter 8 (Organization: The Arrangement of Individuals into Large and Small Groups)** details the nature of organization and treats formal organization issues concerning the school as a bureaucracy and informal organization in the case of the *hidden curriculum.* **Chapter 9 (Social Control and Deviance: Getting People to Conform)** examines theory and research as they pertain to classroom discipline as an issue of social control and deviance in the context of education. **Chapter 10 (Social Change: Change in the Rules for Living Together)** investigates the nature of social change and identifies the operation of this principle in education in the form of educational social movements. **Chapter 11 (Enduring Questions: How Does Education Influence Your Life? Can You Influence Education?)** is the *phoenix emerging;* it addresses the ultimate issue in any sociological analysis—how much is the individual responsible for his or her actions and how much is society responsible?

L.M.M.

Notes

[1] Daniels, L. "Some Top Universities in Squeeze Between Research and Academics," *The New York Times.* May 10, 1989, sec. 1.

[2] Parelius, J. and A. Parelius. *The Sociology of Education*, 2nd Ed. Englewood Cliffs, NJ: Prentice-Hall, 1987, p. 15.

[3]Mulkey, L. "Consequences of Too Many Sociologies for Teaching Sociology of Education," *Teaching Sociology*, 1990, 18:356–61. Also see George Ritzer's "The Recent History and the Emerging Reality of American Sociological Theory: A Metatheoretical Interpretation." *Sociological Forum*, 1991, 6 (2):884–97.

[4]Bennett, K. and M. LeCompte. *How Schools Work: A Sociological Analysis of Education*. New York: Longman, 1990.

[5]Ballantine, J. *The Sociology of Education: A Systematic Analysis*, 2nd Ed. Englewood Cliffs, NJ: Prentice-Hall, 1989.

[6]Stark, R. *Sociology*. Belmont, CA: Wadsworth, 1989.

[7]Babbie, E. *The Practice of Social Research*, 6th Ed. Belmont, CA: Wadsworth, 1992.

[8]Hallinan, M. "Sociology and Education: The State of the Art," In J. Ballantine, ed., *Schools and Society: A Unified Reader*, 2nd Ed. Palo Alto, CA: Mayfield, 1989, pp. 21–47.

[9]Boocock, S. *Sociology of Education: An Introduction*, 2nd Ed. Boston: Houghton Mifflin, 1980.

[10]Von Frisch, K. *The Dancing Bees: An Account of the Life and Senses of the Honey Bee*. New York: Cambridge University Press, 1951.

[11]Oster, G. and E. Wilson. *Caste and Ecology in the Social Insects*. Princeton, NJ: Princeton University Press, 1978.

[12]Lenski, G. and J. Lenski. *Human Societies: An Introduction to Macrosociology*, 5th Ed. New York: McGraw-Hill, 1987.

[13]Haferkamp, H. *Social Structure and Culture*. Hawthorn, NY: Walter DeGruyter, 1989. The "in," "between," and "external" distinction in the individual's awareness of what is real, are reinterpreted so that all three aspects are three forms of one consciousness, as, for example, water, steam, and ice. The three substances are not separate even though they are perceived as separate. The "world" perceived as materially and socially (things and people) external to the individual are really still perceived by mechanisms internal to the individual.

[14]Durkheim, E. *Suicide*. Glencoe, IL: Free Press, 1964.

[15]Mead, G. *Mind, Self and Society* Chicago: University of Chicago Press, 1934.

[16]Blumer, H. "Society as Symbolic Interaction," In Arnold Rose, ed., *Human Behavior and Social Processes*. Boston: Houghton Mifflin, 1962.

[17]Berger, P. *Invitation to Sociology: A Humanistic Perspective*. Garden City, NY: Doubleday-Anchor Books, 1963.

[18]Bell, I. "Buddhist Sociology Some Thoughts on the Convergence of Sociology and the Eastern Paths of Liberation," In Scott G. McNall, ed., *Theoretical Perspectives in Sociology*. New York: St. Martin's Press, 1979.

[19]Alexander, J. *Theoretical Logic in Sociology, Vol. I: Positivism, Presuppositions, and Current Controversies*. Berkeley, CA: University of California Press, 1982.

[20]Mulkey, L. "Comments on a Critique of a Classic," *Teaching Sociology*. 1990, 18:510–15.

[21]Mulkey, L. "The Relation of Principles to Theoretical Logic in Sociology: A Re-Examination of a Field of Study," Working paper. Los Angeles: University of California at Los Angeles, Department of Sociology. 1992.

[22]Berdyaev, N. *Slavery and Freedom*. New York: Charles Scribner's Sons, 1944. Also see Berdyaev. "The Ego and Solitude: Solitude and Socialability," 3rd meditation. *Solitude and Society*. London: Centennary Press, 1938.

[23]Royce, J. *The Problem of Christianity, Vol. II: The Real World and the Christian Ideas.* Chicago: Henry Regney, 1968.

[24]Campbell, J. "The Tiger and the Goat," In Phil Gousineau, ed., *The Hero's Journey: Joseph Campbell on His Life and Work.* New York: Harper San Francisco (division of Harper Collins), 1990.

[25]Berger, *Invitation to Sociology.*

[26]Sennett, R. and J. Cobb. *The Hidden Injuries of Class.* New York: Vintage Books (division of Random House), 1972.

[27]Bell, *Buddhist Sociology.*

[28]Berger, *Invitation to Sociology.*

[29]Cohen, E., R. Lotan, and C. Leechor. "Can Classrooms Learn?" *Sociology of Education,* 1989, 62:75–94.

Acknowledgements

I've always been somewhat unclear about where to begin when it comes to acknowledging the many persons who have, in one way or another, contributed to the development of this book. In fact, it would take a detailed history of ideas to document how various individuals have influenced the evolution of the work. I feel compelled to start the accolades by singling out Peter Berger and Joseph Campbell; when I met them in the literature, their *humanistic* social science was exactly what I was coming to realize myself. When I met Harold Garfinkel at UCLA (in post-doctoral study), I learned things that made it "so I can't go home again." I learned that sociology *is* a reality more than it describes reality. Charles Harrington and Ronald Miller deserve credit as being indispensable in the development of my project; they hired me to do research and educational evaluation.

I suppose I should continue the applause by thanking my students, who, in their quest for knowledge and good grades, sought from me clarity on the subject matter of sociology of education. Then I am especially indebted to Chris Klein, sociology editor for Harcourt Brace Jovanovich, for his belief in the contribution of this project, and for his incredible patience whenever I'd tell him that I can't organize inspiration. I also liked his balanced and uncompromising sensitivity to the demands of both the sociology market and authentic scholarship. Steve Norder, project editor, and Linda Wiley, assistant editor, provided expert guidance in helping me speak the project into existence. Also helpful in the book's production were Mike Hinshaw and Elaine Eldridge as copy editors, Jeannette Barber as designer, and Monty Shaw as production manager. I *appreciate* Maureen Hallinan's *appreciation* of this book (from her review) as a "masterful job of providing a strong theoretical foundation for basic and applied research in education . . . and a comprehensive and integrated theoretical analysis of the discipline of sociology of education." Other reviewers who had insightful comments, besides Maureen Hallinan of the University of Notre Dame, included Dana Dunn, University of Texas at Arlington; Floyd M. Hammack, New York University; Brian Powell, Indiana University; John G. Richardson, Western Washington University; Richard Rubison, Emory University; and Philip Wexler, University of Rochester.

Then there are a selected few whom I choose to acknowledge explicitly because of their more direct participation in my agonies and ecstasies of creative work. Mom and Dad have given me the fundamental, continuing, and greatest occasion for exploring the boundaries of the individual in relation to others. Along the life course, various persons have been influential in what I now call my conversions of consciousness; David Cernic, has, in the present stage of my life, influenced my finding and emphasizing the individual in my sociology. Most of all, I would like to attribute my re-examination of the field of sociology (and sub-field of sociology of education), not to the influences of my position in social structure, but rather to the same forces that make my eyes see, the sun rise and set, the almond tree blossom and to that place in my awareness where there is no mother, father, sister, brother.

Contents in Detail

PART II
Describing and Explaining Education from a Sociological Perspective 63

Chapter 5

Institutions: *Patterned Interactions to Meet Basic Human Needs* 66

Chapter 6

Socialization: *Becoming Human by Learning Society's Conventions* 84

Chapter 7
Stratification: *Rules for Acquiring the Desirable Things in Life*   124

Chapter 8
Organization: *The Arrangement of Individuals into Large and Small Groups*   162

Chapter 10

Social Change: *Change in the Rules for Living Together*   217

Sociology of Education

Theoretical and Empirical Investigations

Part I of this book acquaints you with a distinctive way to understand what being human is about. Chapter 1 introduces the concept *social* as the subject matter of sociology. Chapter 2 introduces you to sociology as a scientific enterprise by discussing the fundamental characteristics and issues that make science different from other ways of knowing things. The lessons of these chapters will be applied in later chapters when we attempt to make sense of the human behavior we call *education*. Chapter 3 takes each of the six principles of constraint that will serve as organizational schemes of the book and acquaints you with the various causal schemes set forth about how the principles of institutions, socialization, stratification, organization, social control and deviance, and social change determine our behavior. Chapter 4 presents the emergence of the subfield of sociology—the sociology of education—by discussing major theoretical explanations of sociological principles as they operate in the context of education.

CHAPTER

1

Conceptualizing the Social Realm

Six Principles of Constraint

When sociologists say they study *social* behavior, just what do they mean? The term *social* refers to a concept, a mental image used to organize the myriad of specific experiences we have. We form concepts in order to group similar things and to distinguish among the dissimilar. The concept *human being* groups nearly 5 billion creatures into a single category and distinguishes them from billions and billions of other creatures (Babbie, 1988). Sociologists formulate the concept *social* to refer mostly to how living together with other people *constrains* how we think, feel, and act. Others around us, the various groups of people to which we belong, or more specifically, the behavioral expectations which distinguish a group of people—two friends, a family, a classroom, a state like New York, a country—determine our behavior, make us conform, or influence what we do. For example, think about how the behavioral expectations that characterize a classroom constrain members of that group. A sociologist might ask, more specifically, "How do the rules of classrooms affect the school performance of children in those classrooms?"

In using the concept *social*, sociologists also ask *how much* our behavior is affected by our association with other people. In other words, they ask if there is such a thing as an *individual* apart from other individuals. The word *constraint*, as it is referred to in the preceding paragraph, might imply that we as individuals might violate the rules of the group if we had the opportunity. Instead, constraint connotes a paradoxical relationship between the individual and others. The preceding photograph represents how sociologists see what being human is about. It shows that we can make sense of what an individual person is and does only by seeing that person in relation to other persons. The sociologically interesting thing about the photograph is how the behavior of the children shown is less unique, arbitrary, and personal and more the result of constraint imposed by others. The very spacing of individuals between each other, the designation of those who will stand versus those who will sit, and the fact that almost all members of the group are smiling are responses to behavioral agreements made about how persons should arrange themselves into groups. The whole defines the parts and the individual emerges from, yet is inseparable from, others. Sociologists have identified *six principles of constraint* or ways in which others influence our behavior. We now turn to a discussion of the generic properties of these constraints and how they determine our actions, but even more importantly, how they make being human possible at all.

Later, in Chapter 11, we will see that while sociology is a scientific study of the social determinants of human behavior, it is also an *idea* (Babbie, 1988), a way of thinking about the world, that itself has consequences for the *realization* of individual freedom. Sociology's devotion to systematic investigation of *groups* obscures its genuine concern with the individual; one can be individual only by taking others into consideration. The inevitable question of sociology, then, is how much are we free to act individually, and what does it mean to be an individual? The traditional focus on groups stresses social determinism and diminishes the significance of sociology's second, but ultimate role of fostering the realization of subjective freedom. Freedom to be fully individual is available only to those who understand the social determinants of their behavior.

Outline

ociology is a way of finding out about why people behave the way they do. Two skills are required for an adequate understanding of human behavior from a sociological perspective. The first skill is having a certain awareness or way of thinking about the world. The sociologist must be able to identify a *social* behavior with the same precision that, for example, an oncologist has in identifying cancer cells. The second skill is to be *scientific* in our observation. This chapter explains the meaning of *social* and then describes several major types of social behavior. In the following chapter, we will discuss the scientific aspect of sociology.

Experiencing the Social Realm

Sociological Awareness

The most profound and essential insight of the sociologist is the awareness of the fact that we do not live in a world as individuals *alongside* others as much as we are individuals *because of* others. Common sense, however, tells us that what we do is, for the most part, predictable, not arbitrary, and the product of our own personal willpower. We decide what happens to us and we can usually recognize and control the forces that influence us. We think we are in charge of who we are and what we do. Americans especially value the right of the individual; we have the right to life, liberty, and the pursuit of happiness. We feel as if we choose whom we love, what we eat, what we wear, and what we think.

The sociologist comes along and says that we are not in charge as much as we think we are, and we are deceived by conventional wisdom which tells us, "Be who you really are." We would like to believe that our taste in music and art, our choice of an occupation, where we go to school, or our choice to commit suicide, fall in love, marry, pick our nose, belong to a health club, run a marathon, abuse a spouse or child, have a baby or an abortion, put peanut butter on our mashed potatoes or take drugs, is uniquely our own. Other people, however, have in some way determined what we want, what we feel, what we believe, and even what makes us happy! Often, what we think we want is what we have been taught to want.

In other words, we do not often wonder much about why we do what we do; we assume our actions are our own and other causes of our behavior are usually not in our immediate awareness. We don't, for example, think much about "why elephants do not give birth to butterflies, mushrooms do not grow as tall as oaks, and pigs do not produce chlorophyll" (Lenski and Lenski, 1987). Or, for example, we take for granted how time, especially how we designate days of the week, and how literacy, simply knowing how to make sense of the symbols of the group or society into which we are born, regulate our lives. Even though we are constrained by forces beyond our personal control, as in the case of our need for oxygen, without which we cannot live for more than minutes, our awareness is predominantly of our individual identity and freedom to act and choose what we do.

The sociologist declares then that, if we look at ourselves in a new way, we will observe that much of what we do is the result of *forces* beyond our personal control and free choice. Social forces act on us with the same regularity that gravity acts on us, and in seeing this, we can ultimately come to experience what it means to be an individual—being aware of the difference between a social self and a prereflective self. This means we become aware of our reliance on the group (other people) for our survival, or as Peter Berger (1963) says, "Once we see the machinery by which we are moved, we are free to modify the nature of the machinery."

Testing Your Sociological Awareness

To test our sociological awareness or consciousness, let us think about how as students we might be sitting in a classroom. We look around and notice that all the students in the classroom are wearing articles of clothing. The temperature is in the mid-eighties, but not one person in the classroom is naked. Why? No gene or inherent, instinctual programming dictates that people wear clothes. People have agreed to arrange themselves in such a way so that they are all wearing clothing, and more profoundly, everyone is obedient to the rule. The rule is a *social fact* (Durkheim, 1958), a characteristic expectation of society, which then becomes a part of the individual's moral consciousness so that she or he feels uncomfortable if she or he does not wear clothing in this setting. You might also notice that while everyone is clothed, no two persons are wearing exactly the same thing. This is the "personal" range of freedom in this case.[1] What a person does is mostly explained by forces outside of personal will, and to some degree by personal choice. We refer to these major forces as the *principles of the social realm.*

We are most interested in the *principles* of the social realm and how they affect our behavior. We will become especially sensitive to interpreting what people do by seeing them always in relation to other people. To repeat, the sociologist's distinctive understanding is about how other people influence our becoming and being individual.[2] We discuss human association—the *basic properties of social phenomena*—and then we identify the *six principles* whereby social phenomena determine our behavior.

Describing the Social Realm: Properties of Social Phenomena

Sociologists describe social forces and how they operate to show us how what we do is very much affected by other people. The sociologist recognizes limits other people place on our freedom (what we claim as uniquely our own reasons for being and doing what we are and do). This brings us to a fundamental definition of the word *social*. We will conceptualize a **social** phenomenon as **any way in which other people influence our behavior through constraints on how we are to think, feel, and act.** Social phenomena are rules for behavior that:

- Are part of a *system* (society);
- Are observable facts that exist in their own right, *sui generis*;
- Constitute *structure*;
- Are *constraints*.

The *social realm* consists of six regular ways in which *social phenomena* influence us. We refer to these social forces as **sociological principles**—the principles of:

- Institutions;
- Socialization;
- Stratification;
- Organization;
- Social control and deviance;
- Social change.

Principle is used to refer to what Abraham Kaplan (1964) defines as a law—a universal generalization about classes of facts. For example, the law of gravity states that bodies are attracted to each other in proportion to their masses and inversely proportionate to the distance separating them. A law summarizes the way things are; it is discovered rather than created by scientists. A law does not explain anything; explanation is a function of theory and theories are created. A *theory* is a systematic explanation for the observed facts and laws that relate to a particular aspect of life (Turner, 1974). When sociologists speak of the *principles of sociology*, they claim that social forces act on us with the same regularity and determinateness that gravity acts on us.

Part of a System

The first property of a *social phenomenon* is that it constitutes an aspect of the *system* (a set of interrelated parts). For example, the individual members, the cell or violinst, can be understood only in light of the part they play in the whole, the organism or symphony orchestra. If you look at the individual, you know something about the whole. A *system*, as a set of associated components, is inherent in the etiology of the word *social. Social* is an adjective, derived from the Latin word, *socialis*, from *socius*, meaning companion, ally, associate, or akin to. The word *society* is a noun, also derived from *socius*. According to those who study animal behavior, the human species (*Homo sapiens*) is a social species, meaning simply that individuals *associate* with one another for their mutual benefit. Association for mutual benefit is referred to as *cooperation*, a process whereby a social species enables its members to solve their problems by acting together as a *system* instead of acting individually. The societal mode of life is common in the animal kingdom in the same way that protective coloring is common; they are important adaptive mechanisms that are vital to the survival of the species (Lenski and Lenski, 1987).

One important distinction between the systematic nature of social behavior in the human species and in other social organisms is that the human species is not genetically predisposed in the same way bees and baboons are to cooperate for survival. Humans have a greater flexibility in how they cooperate. In bees, the behaviors of the queen in relation to the drone (the behavioral arrangement) are governed solely at this level of instinct. Certain behaviors appear in all normal members of the species under identical conditions. For example, all drone bees in all insect colonies will act identically toward the queen bee; what is instinctually programmed in each individual bee is a reflection of the systematic design for cooperation. In the human, the level of precision we can obtain in our prediction of what individuals will do in relation to others follows a different *level* of instinctual programming. Humans act instinctually to develop their sociality so that they respond not to the world but to the *meanings* they give to the world; sociologists debate the relative contribution of fixed and arbitrary aspects of social meanings.

Culture (symbolic meaning systems) has, for social scientists, come to represent freedom—culture, it is thought, *frees* each individual from the slow process of physical evolution by offering a flexible and efficient means of adapting to changing conditions. We do not have to wait for our bodies to develop fin-like and wing-like structures to swim underwater and fly. We devise scuba gear and airplanes.

The vast number of permutations possible in the way individuals assign meanings makes sociology appear as an indeterminate scientific activity. While the rules are not genetically specified except that they will pertain to prescriptions for passing on the rules (socialization) and for accomplishing valued tasks (organization, institutions, stratification, social control, and social change), they are grounded in a fundamental predisposition of the individual's interest in self-preservation. All other organisms depend on the process of biological evolution to adapt to their environments, but humans employ culture to adapt quickly to different conditions. The substantive aspect of culture is not genetically transmitted; there is no gene that tells us how to *satisfy* basic drives. Alternatively, the *satisfaction* of our drives is learned through cultural experience even to the point where we can learn to override our drives completely. For example, the meaning the group assigns to physical death determines whether or not a person will commit suicide.

Culture is thus a surrogate for instinct as a means for responding to the environment, but it frees us, in one sense of the word freedom, from depending upon the slow process of physical evolution by offering us a flexible and efficient means of adapting to changing conditions. We make our own rules and patterns of behavior; the rules must be passed from one generation to the next as culture. In this way, sociology is more about the individual than it is about the group, because it is only by learning one's part in the whole, the rules of the group (shared agreements [Babbie, 1980]), that an individual can be human and survive. In the same way that you can visualize an animal's liver and heart performing in relation to each other to maintain the whole system, think of a school as a system. It is more than a collection of people; it is the unique arrangement of persons in relation to each other that distinguishes the school from other groups of persons (a group characteristic) and the well-being of each member is insured only when each relates to the other according to specific but collective expectations for conduct. The behavior of persons is not arbitrary, but in behalf of self-preservation, individual behavior is dictated by basic types of shared expectations (for example, socialization and organization). Through socialization, persons develop social identity, the individual expression of the group's characteristic design for interrelationship—society is embodied in personality.[3]

Other important characteristics of the systematic nature of a social phenomenon are whether it is *purposive* or *non-purposive, functional* or *coercive,* and whether it exists at the *macro* or *micro level.*

Purposive, Non-Purposive and Functional, Coercive

People share prescriptions for how an individual is to behave in the group. The rule-like constraints on our behavior can be intentional (manifest [Merton, 1968]), purposive rules, or sometimes unintentional (latent). The school, as a group, for example, might be purposively designated to function to transmit the language and knowledge essential for survival in the society, but schooling also has consequences for keeping children occupied until they are old enough to work or enough jobs are created to employ them.

Furthermore, both intentional and non-purposive social behaviors (or how people act together to promote the survival of all of society's members) are always within the context of *ecological* constraints (for example, the presence of others in a particular physical environment). How we arrange ourselves in relation to one another is, for example, constrained by the presence of others when the population density is high, especially when natural or technical resources are limited.

Also worthy of our consideration is whether the rules of the system are sustained through *coercion* (the power of one group over another) or simply through *function* (what the rules do for the whole system). People have various behavioral responsibilities in a system, but who ends up with the most powerful and highly rewarded position (function) in the system might have less to do with who is best suited for that position (on the basis of merit) and more to do with power. In the latter case, the school may represent a set of agreements that is maintained by those who have more power in that system.

Macro and Micro Levels

Social phenomena as part of a system (society) are observed at both *macro* and *micro levels.* The associations among members of the group can be thought about as one society in relation to another or one person in relation to another.

Facts that Exist in Their Own Right

Society exists, as a *fact* (observable with the senses), *sui generis,* independent of or external to any one individual (Durkheim, 1958). The rules or agreements that people make take on a life of their own. To illustrate this notion, let's think about society as a symphony orchestra. The symphony exists in its own right and cannot be found at the level of its individual members. Although each musician plays notes, the characteristic sound of the symphony cannot be located in the notes played by one musician but is a property of all the musicians together. The individual parts that make up the symphony reflect or represent the whole. By learning the characteristics of the whole society, we will know something about the individuals embedded in it. In other, words knowing that a fish lives in water helps explain why a fish has gills and fins, and knowing that a child grows up in the context of the ghetto helps explain why that child drops out of school at twelve and has a baby out of wedlock.

Features of the group, not individual characteristics, explain why people act the way they do (Durkheim, 1951). For example, an increase in suicide rates in a group suggests that the cohesion in that group is weak and its members are not safeguarded against existential crises. In order to explain regular differential rates of suicide in various religious or occupational groupings, Durkheim studied the characteristics of these groups and their ways of bringing about solidarity among their members. Some groups are characterized by agreements that allow their members to interact frequently by sharing beliefs and feelings. The *societies* that have relatively higher suicide rates all have in common a relative lack of cohesion. People who are well-integrated into a group are less vulnerable to the contingencies of human existence. Some groups permit more cohesive arrangements among their members than others. For example, family members share a great deal of who they are with other members in the family; but if while checking out at the market, I leaned on the cashier's shoulder and started to recite what a rough day I had (my feet hurt, and I didn't feel like shopping, but I ran out of cat food), I would quickly be told to shut up and would be labeled, at best, as eccentric. Durkheim saw that in groups where we are, in a sense, cut off from interacting with others, we are not integrated into the group. The same individuals would be influenced to behave differently if they were members of a society with another set of prescriptions for interaction.

To emphasize how a property or characteristic rule of the member's group acts as a determinant of behavior, let's consider a newlywed couple who are living in the home of the husband's parents. The new wife complains to a co-worker that her mother-in-law is a real problem because she wants to know exactly when the bride and her spouse are going and coming. She says her father-in-law is lazy and expects everything to be done for him. A psychologist might explain these events by attributing the problem to the daughter-in-law. In the psychologist's view, she could not adjust to the fact that they were *still living at home*; the daughter-in-law is biologically weaker and emotionally unstable, and therefore she cannot tolerate living in the same home as her in-laws. Sociologists would not, however, try to explain the situation by locating the responsibility primarily with the individual. The sociologist would seek the cause at another level, not the individual level. The sociologist would examine a group of married persons who live at the home of in-laws. They would determine whether, on the average, the group of married couples living with in-laws differed from the group of married couples living by themselves. The researchers might find that, generally speaking, the characteristic of the group of married persons living with in-laws was that they felt personally violated because they had no privacy, whereas the group living alone generally felt a sense of privacy. If these findings were supported, the conflict between the parents and the new couple would not be explained by the personalities of the individuals, but by the characteristic arrangement of the group. The conclusion would be that the arrangement itself predisposes people to fighting due to a perceived lack of privacy.

Another example is the high United States divorce rate. It is the result of conflict between incompatible personalities, or might we find a better answer in the framework of current American society? Today it is more acceptable for women to work outside the home and to be financially independent than in the past. This arrangement weakens the ties of dependency between husband and wife and, therefore, people may divorce more often because they are less reliant on each other. Remember, the characteristic of the group, not a characteristic of the individual, explains or determines the behavior.

One final example is the child who falls asleep every day in class. The teacher initially blames the child; the child is too *dumb* to understand what is going on. The sociologist would, however, look outside the individual to explain the child's behavior. The sociologist might look at the arrangement of the class so that the size of the class becomes important in the analysis. The sociologist knows that, in general, *dumb* children in classrooms of fifteen or twenty students fall asleep less than *dumb* children in classrooms of thirty-five to forty students. It is a characteristic of the classroom that may be at fault rather than the child's personality. Thus an outside condition may impose itself on the child to bring about a particular behavior.

Structure

Social *structure* refers to the patterned expectations for interaction in a social system.[4] These patterned expectations direct the interactions of persons in all human societies although the exact character of the relations among them varies from one society to another. These expectations are referred to as *statuses* and *roles*. This is the case whether we are referring to expectations for individuals (micro level) or for whole societies (macro level). A status or position in the system (for example, a farmer) with its role (behavioral expectations that correspond to the status of a farmer), form the anatomy or social structure of the body social. The various shared agreements (statuses and roles) that characterize society as a group, including its component groups, pertain to different aspects of cooperation for survival. For example, we have agreements (in the form of statuses and roles) about how to reproduce, how to nurture our young, how to get food and shelter, how to find a purpose in life, how to protect ourselves from harm. The notion of social structure is expressed in the thought of Herbert Spencer (Carneiro, 1967):

> Society is more than just an association between members, but like living bodies, is an aggregate in which the parts are differentiated into different structures and functions towards the maintenance of the whole unit. The mutual dependence of the parts, living by and for another, form an aggregate constituted on the same general principle as is an individual organism. For example, in a living organism,

the heart has a unique structure and function in the system, and its unique qualities make the existence of a lung possible. That is, a different structure is necessary to carry out the oxygen exchange function required for the organism to stay alive.

Constraints

One other attribute of a social phenomenon is the property of *constraint*. Formal or informal expectations about how to act impose themselves on individuals as boundaries, thus directing and channeling their propensities. Constraints not only act on an individual as impositions from the outside, but also become part of the individual's consciousness; society's expectations become the individual's preferences (an aspect of personality). What we think is ours first belongs to society. For example, while dogs and cats mate with their own offspring, human beings' propensities tend to be shaped by society's rules. A characteristic of how some if not all societies exert their influence on individual behavior is in their prohibition of *incest*. A characteristic regulation by society concerns who should mate with whom. The discomfort one experiences at the thought of copulating with one's brother or sister, mother or father, is not caused by a genetic predisposition to feel that way. We make agreements with others that sexual practices should be regulated to enhance survival in some way. The agreed-upon sentiment is transmitted from one generation to the next. We come to want and not want certain behaviors, not because we have a gene that structures our behavior, but because society teaches us what we want.

To this point, we have seen that what one does and is as a human being has meaning only in light of or in association with what *others* in the same society do. We have seen that social phenomena act as major determinants of our behavior through virtue of their properties (exercising constraints, existing in their own right, having a structure, and constituting a system). Social phenomena can be classified into more general principles that specify how others influence us. Now let's explore in more detail the *six principles* that explain how *social phenomena* (other people) affect our conduct. Subsequent chapters detail these principles and how they are used as analytical tools to understand what *education* is about.

Sociology as the Study of the Social Realm

Six major categories or types of social phenomena appear universally (and operate simultaneously) to maintain order in all human societies. These social forces can be thought of as principles for making rules for living with other people. The six principles might also be thought of as five variations of the principle of *organization* (rules guiding the arrangement of individuals into groups to accomplish a task). When human arrangements result in the transmission of the rules of society so that they become embodied in the individual as personality, we refer to the principle of *socialization*. When the arrangement specifies a pecking order as to who will get what of society's desirable things (wealth, power, and prestige) and under what conditions, we observe the principle of *stratification*. When the internalization of rules is asymetrical, humans arrange themselves in ways that bring conformity to the rules according to the principle of *social control*. The principle of *social change* operates as human arrangements that result in changes in the rules. The principle of *institutions* operates as human arrangements at the societal level that regulate major human needs (clusters of rules are directed toward a major task in the larger system; kinship rules for example, guarantee that society's members will care for their young). The following brief introduction to these principles outlines how the following chapters refer to these principles to account for human behavior in the context of education.

Six Principles of Constraint

Institutions

One principle of constraint is institutions. At the individual level, the principle operates as the predisposition to make shared rules that result in provision of general human needs. When these rules become collective, they are the *externalized form of individual subjective consciousness*; ultimately the rules take on objective existence as a body or system of rules called *society*. Society's rules must be interpreted as part of a whole interrelated structure. Within the total social system (society) are subsets of the system (*subsystems*) designed to (1) produce new members and to teach them the values shared by those who live in their world (the family); (2) mobilize scarce resources to distribute goods and services that people want (the economy); (3) protect members from external threat such as invasion or internal threat such as crime (the military or police); (4) prepare people for occupational statuses and roles (education); and (5) motivate people to keep with the system's expectations for behavior by giving life meaning and ultimate purpose in the face of the unknown (religion). Like organs of a living organism, each subsystem or institution maintains the whole system by getting persons to act in stable patterns of behavior. The principle of institutions therefore presumes the operation of all the other principles as they are directed to accomplish the maintenance of the *subsystem*.

Education, for example, the institution that constrains human behavior to accomplish the transmission of a society's knowledge and skills to each generation, primarily illustrates the operation of the principle of socialization. Through socialization, individuals acquire their preferences. The values of intelligence and curiosity are instilled, and norms, such as mandatory school attendance, are reinforced through the statuses of teacher and students in group contexts such as classrooms and peer groups.

In this book, special attention is given to education as an institution and to the controversies surrounding the function of education in selecting, training, and allocating persons to various occupational roles in society. Although *selection* and *allocation* are clearly the major roles of education, what is unclear is the nature of institutions in general as *coercive* or *functional* processes. For us to answer whether the principle of institutions operates as behavioral prescriptions to meet the recurrent demands of social living or whether it operates to benefit some groups of individuals more than others, we will:

- Define the principle of institutions and discuss education as one of several selected societal institutions;
- Apply the principle of institutions to school issues such as socialization and selection–allocation (finding the right persons for the right jobs);
- Examine theory and research on how education as an institution operates by considering variations in educational systems around the world, and the interdependence between education and other institutions in society—the influence of the home on the school, the separation of church and state, school financing, and governmental regulation;
- Scrutinize whether socialization, social control, and stratification variously contribute to education and institutions as more coercive than functional in their influence on our behavior.

Socialization

Socialization is a second type of constraint that influences our behavior regardless of our will. Socialization refers to human arrangements which facilitate learning the rules of the system we are in. It is the rule for learning the rules. The transmission and reception of the conventions of the group include rules for institutions, organization, stratification, social control, and social change. The group's rules become part of the inner needs (personalities) of its individuals.

Recall that without rules we would not know what to do to get what we need; without rules human action and interaction would bog down. For example, I frequently order out Chinese food from a nearby restaurant. When I open my apartment door to take the food, the delivery person bows repeatedly. The problem is that I do not understand the meaning of this bowing behavior. I do not know whether to bow back, to pay for the food, to pay a tip, or to invite the person into my home: the expected ways for this person to behave are different from those for myself. Similarly, if I walked into the classroom the first day of school wearing scuba gear instead of my suit, students would not know how to respond to me; they would be confused because the patterned or recurrent expectation is defied. Think about the rules of the system that have become our preferences and distastes through socialization. Most of us don't eat dog meat; most women shave their legs and wear brassieres. We don't share our underwear or our toothbrushes, we don't burp or flatulate in another person's face, we don't take food from our neighbor's refrigerator, and so on.

More specifically, the rules for cooperation as values, norms, statuses, and roles characterize the group at the societal level (macro level) and become represented in individual behavior at the micro level (as personality via language, cognition, and emotion).

Controversy over how the principle of socialization affects our behavior in the context of education concerns *what should be taught* (curriculum) and *by whom, when,* and *under what conditions* (pedagogy). To address these issues of socialization, we must consider a number of theoretical and empirical investigations. For example, is socialization (becoming human through the internalization of values, norms, statuses and roles) a *functional, interactive,* or *coercive* process?

In the exploration of the influence of socialization in education, we need to rectify the results of studies on a variety of *form* and *content* questions:

- When should children start school?
- Do children show the same rate of cognitive development if someone other than the mother is a primary caregiver?
- Do children from homes without a father do as well in school as children from homes where the father is present?
- Do children living in *reconstructed* families—those that include stepparents and children from previous marriage(s)—do as well in school as children living with both their own parents?
- Does having a mother who works affect student performance?
- What are the consequences of teaching students to be obedient versus independent?
- What is the role of the television as an educator?
- Is the school responsible for teaching children about sex?
- Should prayer be part of the school curriculum?
- How are children educated by their peers?

Stratification

A third principle of constraint refers to the rules for acquiring the desirable things in life (wealth, power, and prestige) and the ranking of individuals according to these characteristics. Contention over how stratification operates in the educational context focuses on the topic of equality of opportunity—educational and occupational attainment according to gender, race, ethnicity, and age. Our theoretical interests will be about whether students are rewarded for their achievements or for having a particular characteristic unrelated to merit. Our empirical concerns include questions such as:

- What is the role of education in stratification?
- What is the nature of gender differences in educational experiences and opportunities?
- Are boys inherently more able to do mathematics?
- Does schooling help poor children to have better life chances than their parents?
- Are we fair in measuring student ability and achievement?
- Do desegregation, integration, and busing equalize opportunity for students?
- Is there a difference in performance between children who attend urban as opposed to suburban schools?
- Does compensatory education work?

- Does equality mean every child having a computer at home and in school?
- Are private schools *better* than public schools?
- What is the association between race and intelligence?
- Does grouping students according to their ability improve their performance?
- What are the consequences of vocational and liberal arts tracking in high school?
- What constitutes equal opportunity in the education of the gifted versus the mentally or emotionally handicapped?
- What is the purpose and outcome of bilingual education?
- Is the quality of education in an open admissions college the same as in other colleges?
- How are Scholastic Aptitude Test scores used for college admission?
- How do financial aid, tuition tax credits, and vouchers for college equalize opportunity for students?
- What are the causes and consequences of college minority and developmental education programs?
- Does affirmative action work?
- When is a student too old to enroll in college?
- What are the opportunities for women who return to school?
- Are women and minorities underrepresented in science and engineering fields?
- What is the relationship between college type and occupational selection?

Organization

The principle of organization refers to formal and informal arrangements for accomplishing a task. This social force can be observed most readily, in the context of education, by viewing the school as a formal organization. Traditional theory on formal organization is employed to explain the school as a *bureaucracy.* We describe schools in terms of the characteristics of bureaucracies and their consequences. Then we consider the following questions in discussing whether the school, as an organization, fits the bureaucratic model and how this theory is inadequate for accounting for much of what happens in schools:

- What are the functional division of labor, rules of procedure, hierarchy of authority, and staff roles as offices as they pertain to school roles (the chancellor, the community school board, the district superintendent, principals, teachers, students and service personnel)?
- As a bureaucracy, is the school efficient?
- Is teaching a profession?
- Do teacher credentials affect the quality of instruction?

- What are the outcomes of decentralized versus centralized school control?

The second organizational feature of schools is their informal arrangements that make the school an institution to serve in the maintenance of the system. The dynamics of the principle of organization can be more fully understood by discussion of the school's hidden curriculum—what individuals really have to know to survive (Ballantine, 1989). There is contention over whether the informally organized aspects of schools operate to replicate the social class position of students or whether it fosters equality of opportunity. The principle of informal organization, as it pertains to education, is investigated by examining the theoretical and empirical work concerning the *hidden curriculum*:

- School climate;
- School values;
- Power dynamics;
- Student strategies;
- Classroom climate.

Social Control and Deviance

The principle of social control and deviance refers to the regular ways we organize to prevent rule-breaking. As another sociological principle, it provides us with insights on how and why people are influenced by others in the context of the activity we call *education*. The principle of social control and deviance is illuminated particularly by issues of student discipline. The disagreement over how the principle of social control and deviance operates is about whether it serves the institution of education and the social system in general by insuring the inculcation of values (for example, obedience) that help individuals to fit into society in acceptable ways, or whether social control and deviance are mechanisms whereby individuals are controlled and sorted in ways that perpetuate differences of social class. Theories and empirical work that aid in documenting and explaining the operation of social control and deviance in the educational context of schools include:

- The open classroom;
- Authoritarian discipline;
- Teenage suicide;
- Drugs in schools;
- Teenage pregnancy;
- Testing;[5]
- Dropping out.

Social Change

The principle of social change refers to how we organize to change the rules of society. This principle is manifest in education in issues over school reform. We will consider how various educational movements have contributed to our understanding of social change. An important aspect of social change is collective social action in the form of social movements (in which large numbers of people join to resist or support change). Social movements can be classified into three types—utopian, regressive, and reform. To explain social change (social movements), sociologists have posited macrolevel theories, sociocultural evolution theory, functionalist theory, and conflict theory. No theory seems able to account for all social change; nevertheless we examine empirical work to understand how the principle of social change stabilizes and integrates society and how it creates coercion, tension, and change. Our discussion addresses studies in these areas:

- Mandatory schooling;
- Vocational or liberal arts in higher education;
- Back-to-basics;
- Progressive education;
- The pursuit of excellence;
- What every American child should know;
- Quality or quantity in higher education;
- Public and private sector collaboration in schooling;
- Modernity and identity.

Summary

This chapter introduced the concept *social* as a major determinant of our behavior. Social influences on our behavior usually escape our everyday awareness, but are the subject matter for scientific study by sociologists. The social causes of our behavior affect us regardless of our will and are necessary for human survival because human beings do not have instinctual regulation of their actions. Instead, humans have an enhanced adaptive capacity through *culture* to make seemingly arbitrary rules for cooperation; they make agreements on how to meet basic human needs, and then obey the rules. These agreements are *social facts* which, together, compose *social structure* and ultimately constitute the general body or *system* of rules we call *society*. Society's agreements are external to and exist beyond the lives of individuals and each society has a set of distinctive, interconnected beliefs about how to go about living. The most provocative insight of the sociologist is the idea that the individual is inseparable from society. The very society that we create both empowers us and constrains us at the same time. Knowledge about the social realm helps us to understand what it is to be human in the same way that knowing something about sea water tells us about sea life. It would be difficult to explain the existence and operation of the gill or fin of a fish without acknowledging the water environment that exists independently of the fish (*sui generis*). Overall, the social realm consists of social phenomena that exert their influence on our behavior as six principles of constraint—*institutions, socialization, stratification, organization, social control,* and *social change.* These principles have been introduced as tools for the sociological analysis of education, and reciprocally, theory and empirical literature promise to enhance our knowledge of the nature of each sociological principle.

Vocabulary

association
constraint
cooperation
institution
organization
social change
social control
social facts
socialization
social (phenomenon)

social structure
social realm
social system
society
sociological awareness
sociological principle
sociology
stratification
sui generis

Questions

1. What is sociological awareness? Illustrate a possible test for sociological awareness.

2. Describe a social phenomenon; what are its properties?

3. Identify the six principles of social phenomena that determine our behavior.

4. Present a sociological analysis of why a child might demonstrate poor academic performance in school.

5. Discuss how various everday school-related issues can be explained by the principles of sociology.

References and Suggested Readings

Babbie, E. *Sociology: An Introduction*, 2nd Ed. Belmont, CA: Wadsworth, 1980.

Ballantine, J. *The Sociology of Education: A Systematic Analysis*, 2nd Ed. Englewood Cliffs, NJ: Prentice-Hall, 1989.

Berdyaev, N. "Third Meditation: The Ego, Solitude and Society; Part I, Solitude and Sociability." In N. Berdyaev, ed., *Solitude and Society*. London: Centenary Press, 1938.

Berger, P. *Invitation to Sociology: A Humanistic Perspective*. New York: Doubleday, 1963.

Blau, P. "Structural Constraints of Status Complements." In L. Coser, ed., *The Idea of Social Structure*. New York: Harcourt Brace Jovanovich, 1975, pp. 117–38.

Bourdieu, P. and J. Passeron. *Reproduction In Education, Society and Culture*. London: Sage, 1977.

Carneiro, R., ed. *The Evolution of Society: Selections from Herbert Spencer's Principles of Sociology*. Chicago: University of Chicago Press, 1967.

Durkheim, E. *The Rules of Sociological Method*. Glencoe, IL: Free Press, 1958.

———. *Suicide*. New York Free Press, 1951.

Fredericks, M. and S. Miller. "Paradoxes, Dilemmas, and Teaching Sociology." *Teaching Sociology*, 18(3):347–55.

Illich, I. *Deschooling Society*. New York: Harper and Row, 1971.

Kaplan, A. *The Conduct of Inquiry*. San Francisco, CA: Chandler, 1964.

Lenski, G. and J. Lenski. *Human Societies: An Introduction to Macrosociology*, 5th Ed. New York: McGraw-Hill, 1987.

Merton, R. *Social Theory and Social Structure*. New York: Free Press, 1968.

Mulkey, L. "The Relation of Principles to Theoretical Logic in Sociology: A Re-Examination of a Field of Study." Working paper available from author, 1992.

———. "Consequences of Too Many Sociologies for Teaching Sociology of Education." *Teaching Sociology*, (1990) 18(3):356–61.

The Sociological Spirit: Critical Essays in a Critical Science. Belmont, CA: Wadsworth, 1988.

Turner, J. *The Structure of Sociological Theory*. Homewood, IL: Dorsey, 1974.

Notes

[1] Freedom has a broader meaning that is introduced in the last chapter. It refers to Peter Berger's (1963) idea that only by stepping out of the taken-for-granted routines of society is it possible for us to confront the human condition without comforting mystifications. *Freedom* presupposes a certain liberation of consciousness that cannot be realized if we continue to assume that the everyday world of society is the only world that exists. Freedom is the development of an awareness of self as indestructible and impervious to material (natural) and social determinants.

[2] There is much debate over what constitutes the subject matter of sociology (refer to the Preface and to Mulkey [1992] for additional technical detail). The domain of sociology presented here is based on several presuppositions: (1) an *integrated paradigm* of the many sociologies that explain the lawlike principles of sociology; (2) an integrated paradigm that views social scientific thought as one type of awareness of reality (consciousness) on a comprehensive *continuum of human subjective and objective consciousness*; (3) a first property of consciousness on the continuum as *prereflective* (this is a *subjective* orientation—the "I" that precedes the "I" in Descartes's, "I think, therefore I am." Rather, it is "I am, therefore, I think" [Berdyaev, 1938].); (4) a second property of consciousness as *social scientific* (it is characterized mostly as an *objective* property, manifested when *society* creates the *social self*. That is, *society* is the objectified and collective individual consciousness and the result of the individual's rule-following and rule-making orientation—the *principles of sociology*. It is a set of aggregate behavioral prescriptives that reflect the individual's inherent tendency toward cooperation. The essential forms appear as prescriptions for socialization, organization, institutions, stratification, social control and deviance, and social change.

Persons are *objects* in that, through the process of socialization [internalization, as when the rules become part of the individual's personal and stable prefererences or personality] they equate themselves with the *statuses* and *roles* society bestows upon them. There is a range of individual freedom, subjectivity, voluntary action, so to speak, when individuals become self-objectified or competent in ways society or others prescribe, but this is not true freedom because individuals simply exchange one social role for another and remain identified or equated with one or the other: *liberal* rather than *racist, pilot* as opposed to *neurosurgeon.*); (5) a third and final property on the continuum as *transcendent* (this property is a restoration of the prereflective "I." The social self, a fundamental prerequisite consciousness for cooperation, is placed in a different perspective so that *social roles* become the opportunity for expression of the *true self;* the self as a prereflective property of consciousness radiates through all social forms of expression rather than equates itself with these social forms.); and (6) a distinction in orientation to order and action—in contrast to social scientific consciousness as an instrumental, rational, self-preserving orientation to order and action, transcendent consciousness adopts a self-giving orientation to order and action (the individual develops an awareness of itself as a Self brought to society for its manifestation, as opposed to a self solely dependent on society for the construction of itself as a social self).

[3]Note again that while human social behavior is more adaptive than bee social behavior, the aribtrariness made possible by culture does not seem to be an adequate definition of individual freedom, of what gives the individuals ultimate say in who they are and what they do. Chapter 11 provides a glimpse of individual freedom when it discusses that there is a part of being human that is not socialized into social identity; this residual state of unsocialized self is eventually realized in a person's awareness; that is, self exists before society defines a social self. There is no need to depend on society for identity because it is available before it is expressed socially.

[4]The concept of *structural constraints* has been of central significance in Merton's theoretical analyses and the fundamental question he regularly poses, in Durkheimian fashion, is how external social constraints influence observable patterns of conduct. He answers this question by analyzing the *structures of role relations* among persons that exert external and often unanticipated influences on their orientations and behavior (Blau, "Structural Constraints of Status Complements," pp. 117–118).

[5]Achievement and ability testing are also discussed in Chapter 7 to illustrate another sociological principle—stratification.

How Do We Know?

Casual And Scientific Inquiry

The photograph of the group of children shown above is the same one that appeared at the beginning of Chapter 1; we examined this group of children by thinking about it *sociologically*, by thinking about how being an individual human means being the product of other people (the group). The rules of the group determine the behavior of its individual members, what they are wearing, the spacing between them, who is sitting in contrast to who is standing, how much they talk or smile, and whether they will be a member of that group according to age, race, and gender. Now we will think about the same group of children by giving attention to a second feature of thinking sociologically. Sociology's contribution is in *what* it observes as well as in its *method* for finding out how other people influence us. For example, most of us are convinced that we understand or recognize the nature of things, how one thing affects (causes) another, for instance, how eating too much chocolate is related to getting pimples, getting cavities in our teeth, and getting fat. We are convinced we know either through direct experience, or from what someone else tells us. The problem is, sometimes we think we *know*, but often we do not. Earl Babbie (1988) asks you to imagine a conversation with a friend in which you assert the value of going to college. Your friend disagrees: "College is a waste of time. You should get a head start in the job market instead. Most of today's millionaires never went to college, and there are plenty of college graduates driving taxi cabs or out of work altogether." That's what you hear people say, but does it stand up to logical and empirical testing? Logically, sociologists would immediately recognize that the question of interest concerns the social principle of *stratification* (rules for acquiring the desirable things in life) and perhaps use Functionalist Theory to explain how the stratification rules work. According to this theory, people who have the training (merit) to fill valued occupational slots in the society will get paid more than persons without the learned competence for the jobs. A college education would therefore seem to give a person access to high-paying occupations not open to people with less education. How does the claim hold up to empirical verification? The median incomes of families headed by individuals of different educational levels, as reported by the United States Bureau of the Census (1985), are $20,800 for high school graduates and $34,709 for people with four or more years of college. No scientific evidence supports the assertion that education is a futile financial investment, even though some individuals are exceptions to the rule. The point is that in order for us to really understand how we are affected by the social realm, we have to *find out* scientifically.

Outline

*T*he previous chapter emphasized that sociology is able to tell us things we haven't known before. Sociologists study the *social realm* (aspects of reality) and show us how, more than we realize, being an individual human being means being predominantly the product of other people. Sociologists have identified six principles of how agreements we make for surviving together (shared expectations about how to behave) constrain our lives—the principles of institutions, socialization, stratification, organization, social control, and social change. Sociology is therefore important to us because of *what* it observes, but also because of *how* it observes. It is a special kind of knowing because it helps us to get around the obstacles we typically encounter when we rely on our *everyday knowing*. The principles of sociology, applied to education in later chapters, are exemplified through scientific knowing. This chapter distinguishes everyday knowing from scientific knowing (Babbie, 1989).

The Limits of Everyday Knowing

Knowing is a necessary part of our daily functioning. As humans, we get around in the world because we are aware of what to expect in a given situation—how one circumstance is related to another. When we get into an elevator, we anticipate that it will go up or down. When we put our foot on the brake pedal in our automobile, we expect the car to stop. We say we *know* this because, for instance, we have observed the regularity with which pushing the "up" button on the elevator panel results in the elevator's moving upward. What we call *common sense*, however, can mislead us. Most are convinced, for example, that the rich commit fewer crimes than the poor, or that those who do well in college will do well in their occupations, or that people over sixty are not interested in sex. Scientific observation has found all of these statements to be false. In the process of *everyday knowing* we limit our awareness because we:

- Are inaccurate;
- Overgeneralize;
- Observe selectively;
- Are illogical;
- Get personally involved in what we observe;
- Close the door to further inquiry.

Unconscious versus Conscious Observation

When scientists say that our everyday knowing is based on inaccurate observation, they mean that the process of noticing things that go on around us is very much *unconscious*. We attend to some things and disregard others simply because we cannot see everything at once. We also do not remember some of things we see, and if we do remember, we are not precise in what we recall. For example, if you are sitting in one of your classes today, do you think tomorrow you would be able to recall what the person sitting to your right was wearing? Your recollection would be much better, however, if you are asked ahead of time to observe *deliberately* what that person was wearing.

Selective versus Representative Observation

We frequently draw conclusions based on observations of a few things. For example, let's say you are having a telephone conversation with a good friend who tells you that her boyfriend is a real *chauvinist pig* because he doesn't think she should major in geology because only men should be geologists. You tell her that your boyfriend is the same way because he doesn't want you to major in engineering. You both conclude that all men are alike; no men think women should become geologists or engineers. This kind of conclusion drawing is called *overgeneralization*.

When what is observed in a few cases is applied to all cases, it is also a form of *selective observation*. In other words, if we met some females who had favorable attitudes toward men becoming nurses, we probably wouldn't know about them because we would see all women in one selective way. In the future, we would focus on those situations that correspond with the pattern we believe to be true and ignore those that don't. Racial and ethnic prejudices, referred to as *stereotypes*, depend on this type of selective observation.

Science prevents overgeneralization and selective observation because it specifies in advance the number and kind of observations to be made as a basis for drawing a conclusion. For example, science would require that a *sample* of cases for observation is drawn from the population of persons we wish to generalize about. If we want to make claims about male attitudes toward women scientists, for all men in New York, then we would be expected to have a sample of men to observe who are typical of all men in New York.

Through *conceptualization* and *operationalization*, science requires that, after surveying the thousand or so subjects in our study, we base our conclusions on an analysis of all the respondents' replies to the same questions. Science also prevents overgeneralization by *replication*. This means that a study is repeated to see if the same results are obtained each time. The study may also be repeated under varied conditions. Are male attitudes toward women scientists the same for men from Texas as for men from New York? Are they true for older as well as younger men? Another obstacle to knowing, similar to selective observation, occurs when we observe something other than what we expected. Maybe we are vacationing in Oregon. While dining in a restaurant we meet a couple who are both geologists for the National Geological Survey. We find out that the husband had encouraged his spouse to major in geology when they met in college. Our everyday resolution to the problem of encountering a case that doesn't fit our expectations is to *explain away* the contradiction. This man knew he had to travel a lot if he became a geologist and the only way he could have his wife around would be for her to do the same thing. Or maybe he couldn't get the girl of his dreams, so he had to settle for an *odd* female. Science would ask that we examine all the evidence (everyone in our sample) before we draw any conclusions.

Illogical Reasoning versus Logical and Empirical Observation

Another pitfall of everyday knowing is that it is sometimes based on illogical reasoning. Logic insists that one thing consistently follows another. Perhaps we have observed repeatedly that a bullet leaves a gun after the trigger is pulled, but not before, or that children are younger than their parents. A predictable association exists between situations that have been established through empirical (based on the senses) observation. Some people make claims of knowing that are grounded neither in logic nor empiricism. There is no reason to believe that one thing is associated with another. For example, *superstition* is one form of illogical reasoning. No evidence supports the idea that seven years of bad luck follow if one breaks a mirror.

Emotionally Involved versus Emotionally Neutral Observation

Another obstacle to knowing is letting our emotions get in the way of finding out. For example, let's say that a chemist stands to make several million dollars on a new low-calorie aritificial sweetener. She might refuse to conduct research on the consequences of using the sweetener or she might be inclined to withhold the results of a study she conducts if she finds that one of the side effects of prolonged use of the sweetener is brain disease and cognitive impairment. For knowledge to be advanced, scientists must withhold emotion so that they are able to make their findings known to the scientific community. Science does not resolve controversies of value; for example, it cannot determine whether school children *should* be corporally punished, but it can disseminate knowledge of the behavior of children who are physically punished in comparison with those who are not. Emotional involvement also occurs with the choice of what is to be studied. A well-known case of how scientists let their personal prejudices creep into their scientific work is documented in the work of Stephen Gould (1981), *The Mismeasure of Man*. Gould discusses how Cyril Burt and his colleagues used data on cranial capacity as evidence of racial differences in intelligence. Persons with lower intelligence were reported to have smaller brains and skull sizes compared with more intelligent persons whose skulls and brains were larger. Gould discusses how the eagerness of Burt to find evidence to bolster his already existing racial prejudices affected his interpretation, or misinterpretation, of the findings of his study.

Closed versus Open-Ended Observation

Science is open-ended and its conclusions are always open to further questioning. Two other obstacles to knowing are believing we know everything we need to know and believing some things are not for us to know. Babbie (1992) refers to these attitudes as *premature closure of inquiry* and *mystification*. In both situations, we bring inquiry to a stop. For example, in Galileo's time it was common "knowledge" that the earth was flat and contrary suggestions went against religious teachings. When religious ideas not grounded in empirical evidence contradict science, closure of inquiry is premature (Barber, 1952) (that is, we already know everything we need to know). For years, intelligence testing seemed to yield unbiased results about the inherent cognitive abilities of individuals; however, intelligence tests have been shown to be culturally biased and do not measure a universal inherent capability in humans. *Mystification* is illustrated when people have the attitude that "Those things are only for God to know." In the case of molecular biology, for example, some persons believe that God does not want us to explore altering and fabricating the genetic makeup of human beings; this attitude has consequences for continued investigations in genetic engineering. When we believe that something is unknowable, then we will not continue to inquire about it.

Knowing Scientifically

The Traditional Model of Science: Theory and Research

Science gets around obstacles to *finding out* or *knowing* because of the following standards for attitudes and techniques:

- Logical (Theory)
- Empirical (Research)
  - conceptualizing;
  - measuring social concepts;
  - what or whom is observed (sampled);
  - modes of observation (experiments, surveys, field research, evaluation, secondary analysis).

The best way to understand how our everyday knowing differs from scientific knowing is to go through the process of scientifically observing a social phenomenon—how we are influenced by others via the six principles of social constraint. First we need to discuss the nature of theory and research.

Theory and Research

In the traditional model of science, we find out about the world through logical and empirical investigation. Another way of saying the same thing is that science produces knowledge on the basis of logical and empirical evidence. The logical part of science is referred to as *theory*. A theory is simply a logical statement of the relationship between two things. The empirical part of science is usually referred to as research. Research is a procedure that allows us to observe with the senses, to decide if the relationship stated in the theory is, in fact, true.

Two types of theoretical or logical thinking are *inductive* and *deductive*. When we think from specific instances to general principles, we use inductive reasoning. For example, when I first moved to my Manhattan apartment and would leave for work, about 8:30 A.M., I observed that many children between the ages of about five and eleven years walked alone or were escorted by an adult to Public School 41. During the past ten years, this same behavior continued except during July and August. Based on my observation, I could infer a relationship between being a child and attending public school. From repeated observations, I inferred that if one is between five and eleven years old, one must go to school. Now that I am pretty sure that young children go to school, I derive a theory based on repeated observation of the relationship between being a child and going to school. I can *generalize* the relationship to all children, so that if my mother, who lives in California, calls me and says her new neighbor has two children, one ten and the other seven, I don't need to fly to the west coast to find whether they go to public school. I can now *deduce* that if young children go to public school, then it is likely that my mother's young neighbors go to public school.

This second type of logical reasoning, *deduction*, involves *applying* a theory. It can also involve *testing* a theory. For example, I might deduce from my theory (if one is a child, one must go to school) and generalize the relationship to children on the west coast. However, I might not be sure whether it would be true for children in other countries, and I would have to test the general principle for, say, Australia. If my Aunt Ruby, who lives in Australia, says her neighbor has children between ages seven to ten, I could fly to Australia to verify whether the children go to public school. We look to see if the theory that young children go to public school is true for every new child we encounter in other parts of the world. This factual or empirical verification of theory in a new case is what we refer to as the *research* aspect of science—*theory* is a statement about the facts, whereas *research* observes the facts.

What if we find that in certain parts of Australia children do not go to public school? Then we would have to revise our theory to account for the facts. We might find that only in very industrialized areas of the world do children go to public school.

Science is not just a matter of mentally storing statements of how two things are related. It bases thought on information gathered by the senses. We must see or hear what we experience. Science is more than just *thinking* about the way things are in the world. Science checks to see whether what we think can be verified by the facts, by the sense experiences we have. Another word that we will use to refer to fact is *empirical* evidence. For example, let's say that it seems logical to us that people who have a college education are likely to marry persons who also have a college education. We now must go out into the world and observe whether people who are married have equal amounts of education.

Common sense is logical in the same manner that science is logical; scientists have no patent on logic. For example, based on our repeated observations of the room brightening when we move the light switch to the "on" position, we apply what we know to future situations. We predict what will happen on the basis of past observations. The logic of science differs from common sense mainly in degree: it draws more carefully and precisely from existing principles and theories about how things are related in the world. Our everyday verification of the facts, as we discussed earlier, is threatened by various obstacles to knowing. We call the precise empirical verification of whether two things are related (a theoretical statement) *research*.

An Illustration of Science

We said that in the science of the social realm, we want to observe the regularity with which people (groups) influence us. The best way to further distinguish everyday knowing from scientific knowing is to go through the process of each type of inquiry. We said that sociologists are fascinated by how our behavior can be understood by seeing it as determined by the expectations of those with whom we associate. Those with whom we associate make up the group, and the group is arranged according to agreed-upon rules that exist as expectations or rules independent of any one individual in the group. An expectation which characterizes the group, "American women," is that women shave their legs and armpits, but not their heads. Therefore, if you are an American woman, you probably do these things. Sociologists, through the six principles of constraint, have discovered the major types of group influence. But to learn about how a group influences its members' behavior, we must observe how shared expectations of particular types of groups affect its members. For example, we might ask how the characteristic rules of one-parent families affect the school performance of children from those families; or we could ask whether living in or being a member of a particular country causes people to be more likely to commit suicide. The following example of finding out *scientifically* illustrates how we circumvent the obstacles to knowing that we encounter in *everyday knowing*.

1. The first step in the research process is *curiosity*. What is it that really interests us? What do we want to find out? Maybe we want to know whether going to school really makes a difference in what we learn. Common sense might tell us that going to school is a joke and that for most people learning could take place regardless of whether one goes to school. Or popular opinion might be that everyone learns to read and write at school, not at home. Can we prove that participating in school makes a difference in what children learn?

2. The second step of the process is to inventory what others have found about the relationship between going to school and learning. At this phase of the research process, it is important to conduct a *review of the literature* to find out how other scientists have studied the problem and what theories they have drawn upon. From the library, we obtain articles from professional journals that describe the pertinent research on the topic. We notice that the research of Samuel Bowles and Herbert Gintis (1976) draws upon *conflict* theory to explain what happens to kids in school. The purpose of schooling is for students to learn the ways of those ruling the society. *Functionalist* theory, on the role of the school, claims that schools teach students the knowledge, skills, and attitudes necessary for survival in the society and for carrying out adult occupational roles (for example, how to calculate how much money you have after using your computer

banking card to withdraw money, or how to read a seismograph so that you can predict earthquakes). Christopher Jencks et al. (1972) and James Coleman et al. (1966) tested these ideas and concluded that schools perpetuate the disadvantages that students bring to school. One could also begin by reasoning theoretically, as did George Homans (1971), using *exchange* theory to explain levels of education. This is a *broad range theory* because it applies to all of human social life, not just Americans. He began by thinking that all human behavior is determined by the individual's perception of rewards versus costs. Persons are more likely to perform an activity when they believe the reward for performing that activity is greater than for performing other activities. A greater number of persons in industrial societies are prepared to perform activities (jobs) that involve literacy; and therefore, a greater proportion of persons in industrial societies will perceive the acquisition of literacy as rewarding and will attempt to acquire literacy. A conclusion based on Homan's theory is that by going to school, children will become literate.

3. The third step is to derive from our theory the *idea*, the testable and verifiable *hypothesis*, about the relationship between schooling and learning. For example, if Homan's theory is true, what do we expect to happen? We formulate concepts that will allow us to test our hypothesis. We have logically reasoned (theory); now we must test our ideas using empirical evidence. We expect that one thing (x) will affect another thing (y). An easy way to think about hypotheses is to use the notation: $x \longrightarrow y$. Take note, for sociologists, x refers to a social force, how, in general, membership in a group (in this case, school) causes our behavior, y, to differ from the behavior of those who are not in our group.

4. The fourth step is where scientific observation becomes very deliberate and conscious. To be sure that their observation is accurate, and so others can test the same phenomenon in the future, scientists specify clearly what they attempt to observe and how. They make a conscious effort to observe. These aspects of the research process are called *conceptualization* and *operationalization*. For example, let's follow Barbara Heyns (1978) as she goes through the research process, from her hypothesis through the point of conceptualization and operationalization. To find support for Homan's theory, Heyns would have to prove that schools are effective in helping children to learn. To find out if schooling works, Heyns hypothesized that learning for kids who have been going to school will be different than learning for kids who are not in school. How could she test this idea if children are in school most of the year? She was able to resolve the problem by comparing the learning that occurs during the school year with that occurring during the summer vacation. Her *concepts* for study were schooling (x) and learning (y). Schooling was *operationalized* as being in school for the fifth and sixth grade years versus not being in school for the summer between fifth and sixth grades. Learning was measured by scores on verbal achievement tests administered at the beginning and ending of each school year.

5. The fifth step is to decide on the *sample*: who will be observed? Heyns sampled 2,978 students enrolled in public schools in Atlanta, Georgia. Sampling is a technique that counteracts the overgeneralization that results when we observe casually. Random or probability sampling ensures that no one person has a better chance of being selected for study than any other person. In this way, one of every type of student in public school in Atlanta had a chance of being chosen and what Heyns observed in the sample is likely to be observed of all the children in Atlanta public schools. She did not claim for everyone what was true for only a few persons who are not typical of all public school students in Atlanta. In this manner, Heyns made sure she didn't pick persons for her study who had characteristics that would confirm what she already believed to be true about students.

6. The sixth step entails choosing a *mode of observation*, deciding how to collect the information, for example, whether through survey, experiment, field research, or secondary analysis. Heyns employed two modes of observation. She used a survey (questionnaire) given to school officials, which allowed her to collect data on students who were enrolled in school for the periods of her interest and to document the test scores for these students. She also carried out an experiment to get information that allowed her to isolate the effects of x (also known as the *independent* or *causal variable*, or the *treatment* [in this example, x is *going or not going to school*]). She compared outcomes for students who were similar to other students except that one group of students was in school and the other group was not.

7. The seventh step tests our hypothesis using *statistical techniques* to analyze the data. Heyns performed an analysis using a mathematical technique to detect whether every change in x (going to school or not going to school) was accompanied by an expected change in y (higher or lower test scores). Essentially, the computer program permitted Heyns to employ various statistical techniques to summarize an otherwise unmanageable mass of information. She was able to identify each of over two thousand children, and for each student to measure whether a change in school attendance corresponded to a change in test performance (the statistical correspondence is true most of the time, with perhaps five chances out of one hundred of being unreliable). Heyns found that when children are in school, they learn more than when they are out of school.

8. The eighth step is to *report the results* of the analysis that tested whether a change in our hypothesized cause brought about the change we anticipated, whether the hypothesis was confirmed or rejected, and how this relates to our theory.

Heyns found that school is not a joke after all. In fact, in general, children learned less during the summer vacation than they did in an equivalent time period during the school year. Their verbal achievement test scores increased on a monthly basis during the school year more rapidly than during the summer vacation. Furthermore, Heyns found that children from higher-income families learned about as much during vacation as during the school year while children from lower-income families actually lost ground during the summer. Their scores were lower in the fall than they were in the spring before summer vacation.

Heyns found conclusively that school affects students' learning and that, contrary to theories that the school perpetuates disadvantage by maintaining the differences children bring to school, schools greatly improve the situations of poor children. The rates of learning during the school year were relatively the same for higher- and lower-income children and for black and white children. However, the well-to-do students learned more than the poorer children during summer vacation. Schools therefore minimize the disadvantages that some children have because of their family background by helping them to keep up with their more privileged peers. Why did the more advantaged children learn more during the summer? Heyns found that, when measured by the number of books read (by the time spent reading, or by the regularity of library usage), reading during the summer systematically increased the vocabulary test scores of children. For every four books read during the summer, an additional correct answer on verbal achievement tests resulted. The results of the Heyns study suggest the application and further testing of theory. The application would be that schools could help poor children learn more if the school year were extended than if it excludes the summer months. Or, as a test of theory, differences in scholastic achievment could be measured for students who attend all year versus those who do not attend during the summer (if school policy gives children the choice).

Other researchers have gone through the research process to address the questions of whether schools make a difference in what students learn. For example, an extension of Heyns's analysis to high school students was done by Karl Alexander, Gary Natriello, and Aaron Pallas (1985), who compared test scores for students who remained in school versus those who dropped out. They also found that contrary to the theory that claims schools reproduce disadvantage, dropping out had the greatest negative effects on students from the most disadvantaged backgrounds.

By leaving the question open to further study, we are able to continue finding out about how we are likely to be affected by the social forces around us, the groups of which we are members.

Scientific reports or observations appear as articles published in professional journals. They have a precise stylistic format and are not considered for publication unless the report meets with the approval of other scientists. The process of scrutinizing a scientist's observation or research for technical and stylistic adequacy is called *peer review*. Published research means that the observation has not been of the everyday variety, but is scientific in that it has taken care to avoid the obstacles to knowing that we have discussed.

Summary

Sociologists are concerned with both what they know and also how they know. The subject matter of sociology is social behavior, or the way others influence our behavior. Sociologists observe these phenomena scientifically rather than casually. They can be confident in what they know because their observations are logical and empirical. The logical part of science is called theory and the empirical part is called research. The research process consists of beliefs and techniques that help the scientist circumvent obstacles to knowing. With conceptualization, operationalization, sampling, and a mode of observation, the researcher avoids inaccurate observation, overgeneralization, selective observation, illogical reasoning, ego involvement, premature closure, and mystification of the unknown. When we discuss the principles of sociology applied to education in later chapters, all of the claims made will be based on scientific observation.

Vocabulary

closing door to inquiry	mode of observation
conceptualization	observing selectively
conscious observation	operationalization
deductive logic	overgeneralization
empirical	personal involvement in
everyday knowing	observation
hypothesis	research
illogical	sample
inaccuracy in observation	scientific inquiry statistical analysis
inductive logic	theory
logical	

Questions

1. What is meant by the statement, "Sociology is important to us, first because of *what* it observes, and second, because of *how* it observes"?

2. How is scientific knowing distinguished from everyday knowing?

3. Illustrate the following:

   - Inaccurate versus conscious observation;

   - Selective versus representative observation;

   - Illogical reasoning versus logical and empirical observation;

   - Emotionally involved versus emotionally neutral observation;

   - Closing versus open-ended observation.

4. Explain how theory is related to research.

5. How, recalling the discussion about using deductive and inductive models of science, might you analyze the association between gender and educational attainment?

6. Discuss the role of statistics in the research process.

References and Suggested Readings

Alexander, K., G. Natriello, and A. Pallas. "For Whom the School Bell Tolls: The Impact of Dropping Out on Cognitive Performance." *American Sociological Review*, (1985) 50:409–25.

Babbie, E. *The Practice of Social Research*, 6th Ed. Belmont, CA: Wadsworth, 1992.

_____. *The Sociological Spirit: Critical Essays in a Critical Science*. Belmont, CA: Wadsworth, 1988.

Barber, B. *Science and the Social Order*. New York: Free Press, 1952.

Bowles, S. and H. Gintis. *Schooling in Capitalist America: Education and the Contradictions of Economic Life*. New York: Basic Books, 1976.

Coleman, J., E. Campbell et al. *Equality of Educational* Opportunity. Washington, DC: United States Department of Education, 1966.

Gould, S. *The Mismeasure of Man*. New York: W. W. Norton, 1981.

Heyns, B. *Summer Learning and the Effects of Schooling*. New York: Academic Press. 1978.

Homans, G. "Reply to Blain." *Sociological Inquiry*, (1971) 41:23.

Jencks, C., M. Smith, H. Acland, M. Bane, D. Cohen, H. Gintis, B. Heyns, and S. Michelson. *Inequality: A Reassessment of the Effects of Family and Schooling in America*. New York: Basic Books, 1972.

U.S. Bureau of the Census. *Statistical Abstract of the United States*. Washington, DC: United States Government Printing Office, 1985, p. 443.

One Sociology, But Many Sociologies

Theories Explaining Principles of the Social Realm

Although sociologists have identified what we are calling the general principles of constraint, many theories vie for prominence as systematic explanations for these observed laws. For example, we will attempt to explain why the children in the photograph shown above are in school, rather than employed, by using a theory of stratification. We know that people are ranked in all societies, but how do we explain why persons are ranked so that some people have more of the *desirable* things in life than others? The photo shows American children in 1980. American children in the early part of the twentieth century were not in school but were working as coal miners. One theory, the *functionalist* theory, explains the status of different age groups in terms of society's needs: when child labor served a societal need, it flourished; now that child workers are no longer needed, children are expected to be in school. In the same way, the elderly lose many roles because their economic contribution is no longer socially necessary. *Conflict* theorists reject the functionalist explanation and argue that the various age categories are really social strata. Each stratum is ranked in a hierarchy of power, prestige, and wealth, and members of one stratum versus members of another stratum are in constant competition for scarce resources. Each stratum defends its own interests. In a postindustrial society, with no shortage of labor, mandatory schooling keeps the very young out of the work force, and mandatory retirement ensures that the old give up their jobs.

Outline

The first two chapters of this book represent an attempt to catch the rabbit because the most important ingredient in rabbit stew is the rabbit. That is, we won't be able to interpret what goes on in *education* unless we have the main ingredients of the stew. But now that we have the *perspective* (a social one) and the *method* (a scientific one) clear in our minds, we will add a few more ingredients, perhaps less significant but necessary nonetheless.

One Sociology, but Many Sociologies: Social Principles and Their Explanations

Sociologists have identified what we are calling the general principles of constraint—institutions, socialization, stratification, organization, social control and deviance, and social change—which operate universally in human societies. These principles represent the major types of *behavioral directives that regularize human acitivity and ensure the survival of the individual, who must live with other individuals.*[1] They constitute the *social realm* that is open for scientific study—*sociology*. Sociologists are devoted to finding out how and why these principles came about. The explanations of the nature and effect of these social forces are known as *sociological theory*. The many theories or systematic explanations put forth to explain the observed laws of the social realm can be referred to as the *many sociologies* (Mulkey, 1990).

Theories Explaining the Principles

Theories About Institutions

The principle of institutions refers to the *patterned sets of interactions to meet basic human needs* (education, religion, family, government). That is, all societies contain clearly defined expectations about how to transmit to each new generation the valued ways of doing things; how to answer questions of ultimate meaning (those that posit the existence of the supernatural), how to produce and distribute goods and services, how to maintain order by rewarding compliance to and punishing deviation from the rules.

One theoretical explanation of institutions is *structural–functionalism*. Structural–functionalist analysts view human agreements about how to think, feel, and act in the world as part of a whole system of agreements called a social system. All sociology is concerned with how we are influenced by others; institutions influence us through expectations that ensure the overall well-being of the whole system and thereby of each of its members. Obligations that people have to their families, friends, strangers, and country are specified through patterned expectations in the form of *statuses, roles,* and *norms*. The social system is analogous to a human organism comprising its interrelated organs, each of which performs a particular function for the whole system, which benefits each of its members. Researchers try to explain what various structures accomplish for the larger system. As physiologists ask, "What does the heart do to maintain the functioning of the system and how is it related to the lung and the brain?," so sociologists ask, "What does *education* do to maintain the functioning of the system and how is it related to the family and religion?" More specifically, examples of questions from the structural–functionalist perspective might be: What is the role of the school in society? What is its contribution to the maintenance of human life? What are the social agreements that maintain schooling?

Notice that in the structural–functionalist framework we see the fundamental question of sociology addressed—how are individuals constrained by others? The sociological insight is always that characteristically the group's rules determine behavior, not the individual's. Functionalist theorists are interested in what functions or effects a given institution has in contributing to the stability and maintenance of the social system. Consider, for example, the functions of the family and education. Family expectations regulate how to care for the young. Schooling represents expectations about how the young should prepare for adult occupational roles. Research from the structural–functionalist perspective would examine the structure and function of the social constraint. What are the rules and what are they doing for the group and society as a whole system? Sociologists therefore describe the nature and consequences of particular expectations on behavior. For example, in American society, children are expected to live with either their mother or their father or both; this expectation has outcomes for children. Those children who live in families with one parent are less likely to do well in school than children from two-parent families (both biological parents) because they have been emotionally traumatized by the disruption of their parents' marriage.

Functionalists argue that although institutional structures like schooling and family work together to maintain the homeostasis of the system, structural arrangements also can be dysfunctional. For example, the system may be designed to prepare the young for adult responsibilities through schooling, but if certain agreements about how to structure the family and how to be schooled are not compatible and children fail to perform the designated and anticipated functions, then these agreements are dysfunctional for the system (Merton, 1968).

Conflict theorists explain institutions and the scope of human initiative as expectations among people about how to conduct human relations that represent the interests of those in power in the society. Agreements emerge as the result of conflict or confrontation between individuals or groups over scarce resources or incompatible goals. Because humans act in self-interest, when given the opportunity to choose under conditions of scarcity, they will favor themselves over others. Agreements that bring gains to those in power bring losses to those not in power. Conflict theorists would do research on institutional agreements by asking whose interests are served by a particular school expectation. For example, Bowles and Gintis (1976) argue that the educational system, with its integrative function, must in some way legitimate preexisting economic disparities. They claim education legitimates economic inequality by providing a seemingly meritocratic mechanism for allocating individuals to unequal economic positions. The educational system fosters and reinforces the idea that economic success depends basically on the possession of technical and cognitive skills (which it makes available in an equitable manner on the basis of merit). They argue that beneath the facade of meritocracy is an educational system aimed at reproducing economic relations only partially explicable in terms of skill competence. The educational meritocracy is a symbolic meritocracy used to reinforce the belief that economic success is dependent upon possession of skills obtained in an unbiased manner. A functionalist would look at how expectations for academic credentials guarantee that people have the knowledge and skills to assume certain jobs needed in the occupational structure, whereas the conflict theorist would test whether credentials ensure that persons get jobs according to their skills or according to the status associated with the credential (Collins, 1979).

Theories About Socialization

A third principle of how we are constrained by others, open for explanation by various theories, is *socialization*. Socialization refers to those agreements about how persons *become* fully human via the development of personality. Society becomes embodied in the individual as *personality*, a local map, so to speak, of the conventions (values, norms, statuses, roles) of the society. We come to believe that what we have learned is natural. The most profound issues in socialization concern who we learn we are, and more importantly, what we have not learned.

Symbolic–interaction theorists study constraint at the capillary level—at the very point at which the society and the individual intermingle. Constraints affect us at this level in two ways. One is learning society's rules through *language*; the other is through becoming a *self*. The symbolic–interaction theory says that we are influenced by others in such a way that we cannot be human without others. It interprets how individuals are affected by others by focusing on symbols, the mechanisms that permit and regulate human behavior. Humans do not know how to respond to other people and other things directly. A symbol represents the meaning of something else. For example, burning a one hundred dollar bill would elicit a different response than burning today's newspaper, even though they are both made of paper. People respond to things according to the meanings they have given to them. The symbolic–interaction perspective looks at how the broad societal values are reflected in the subtleties of daily life. For example, the American value of the right of the individual is reflected in tacit agreements about cutting in front of people waiting in line or belching in someone's face. No inherent meaning is attached to any of these behaviors except how we choose to view them. We are more likely to help a stranger by sharing our coat than by sharing our toothbrush or underwear. The meanings inherent in the tone of our voice, the look of an eye, and the words we speak, must be learned so that they mean the same thing for you as for me. *You pig!* denotes something different than it connotes. The connotation contains the meaning, or the message, about how we should feel about, believe in, or act toward something.

The symbolic interactionist thus explains how people become aware of themselves as individuals according to how well they construct, transmit, and negotiate the meaning of things through symbols. The first concern of the symbolic interactionist, therefore, is how, through language, we acquire a mental map of how to get around in the world. In a sense, we belong first to others. A two year old child does not walk around naming the world. Instead, the child is presented with the meanings people have already assigned to the world. Without this map, human action and interaction bog down; on the individual level, it's like meeting a person who speaks a language you cannot understand. When we share meaning, we are part of others and they are part of us. We act in the world according to our view of it and that view of how *things should be* constrains our actions.

Language may be viewed as the determinant of thought; language shapes thought by providing socially acquired concepts or categories into which people mentally sort their perceptual stimuli. Our perceptual capabilities are altered by the acquisition of language. Hence, we adopt the view of the world that is constructed and represented by our language. We selectively screen sensory data in terms of the way we are programmed by our language; thus speakers of different languages inhabit different sensory worlds.

Differences between the grammars of the Navajo and English languages, for example, crystallize and perpetuate divergences in the thinking of the speakers of those languages. The symbols (words) employed linguistically by a people reflect their chief cultural concerns. Are perceptual capabilities altered by the acquisition of language? Is a person, regardless of his or her language community, able to distinguish among the varieties of rice that receive special labels in the Philippine Hanunoo community, even if the person cannot give the Hanunoo names? The same is true for the varieties of snow recognized by Eskimos or the fine points about rain itemized by Navajos. Language seems to be the container of already established thought. Therefore, thought takes place independently of language; language functions simply as a mode for conveying thought. Thus, for example, before formal cultural training and before acquiring language, infants might evidence a high degree of organization of the color world. One interpretation of how speech shapes thought emphasizes the role of learning factors; the other emphasizes that thought shapes speech and is the outcome of prewired hereditary factors. What we think affects what we say, and what we learn through verbal communication affects our thought.

Both views of how language and thought interact emphasize how people come to want what they are taught to want. In both cases, one's experiences shape how one thinks, and reciprocally, experience is determined by how one thinks (which is determined by language that directs one's attention). People come to be in the world, to act and to think and to feel, in relation to an existence they can afford. Caviar and imported (out-of-season) fruit are staples in the lives of those who can afford them. Children who grow up in urban ghettos develop an attitude of despair when they become aware that, to do well in school, they must overcome limiting conditions in their homes and neighborhoods; many become increasingly discouraged and eventually conclude that aspiring to success is hopeless. The economic conditions of parents are experienced by children, and perhaps recorded in their thought, and encoded in language. Perhaps the language of poverty restricts a child's thought and perception. Eventually, our perceptions of the world are limited to those with which we are most familiar, and have made our own. For example, when Captain Nemo, of the *Nautilus* in Jules

Verne's *Twenty Thousand Leagues Under the Sea,* announces to his dinner guests that they are eating crème sauce made of milk from the giant sperm whale, a salad of sea snake and barnacles, and a pudding sauté made of unborn octopus, they quickly lose their appetites.

A second concern of symbolic interactionists is with the formation of the *self.* The self is the awareness a person has of his or her competence at relating to things and persons in the environment. The child comes to see a self according to how she or he sees others see her or him. This means that a person is not, first and always, an individual, a static entity. A person is a process. The young child incorporates society's expectations and successfully learns to respond to the symbols and meanings of the system; the child develops a sense of competence and a sense of being both subject and object in the world. The self is the general awareness that a person has of his or her competence at relating to things and people in a successful way that enhances that person's survival.

Many theories derived from the symbolic–interaction perspective are useful for an understanding of what goes on in the sphere of education. The works of Alfred Schutz (1967), George Mead (1934), and Charles Cooley (1902) are exemplary. In Chapter 4 we will look particularly at Mead's ideas and how they have shown that the principles of sociology are useful for interpreting *educational* phenomena.

The structural–functionalist perspective of socialization emphasizes moral integration—a general consensus about what the young should learn for their survival. In a complex society, the state regulates socialization into uniform beliefs and represents public control of a set of universal precepts or rules for living. Public control of schooling, for example, functions to integrate society by prohibiting control of education by any special group. The functionalist view of socialization explains why state agencies continue to issue policies about what every American should know and how they should come to know it.

A conflict interpretation of why people value what they do and why they believe, think, and act the way they do is related to the conditions determining the production of goods and services. The ideas of those ruling the society express the dominant material relationships. The ruling group in a society controls the productive forces and the ways of thought; they legitimize what is acceptable and right and provide expectations about how people should act in the world.

Theories About Stratification

The principle of *stratification* refers to *expectations about getting the desirable things in life (wealth, power, prestige): who gets what and under what conditions.* It also refers to *the ranking of persons into categories according to how much of the desirable things in life they accrue.* To explain society's distribution of the desirables, functionalists use the principle of stratification to explain the designated rights and responsibilities of different age groups, for example, by suggesting that the trends are to benefit everyone in the society. Because everyone will eventually die, a society must, if it is to outlive its individual members, arrange an orderly transition from the aged to those who are younger. Society phases out those individuals whose future contributions are not likely to continue. Agreements evolve to provide the guidelines for the process: the standard practice to retire at about sixty-five, or to begin mandatory schooling at about six. When the old forfeit their roles to younger members of society, the whole society functions more smoothly as a result. When child labor was socially useful, it was encouraged; now that child workers are no longer needed, children are expected to be in school. Similarly, the aged now lose many roles because their economic contributions are no longer socially necessary. The purpose of *compulsory education* is to teach the young the skills necessary to contribute to an industrialized economy. So rather than let the young, the middle-aged, and the old compete for social and economic statuses in the job market, society allocates the various statuses more efficiently, according to age.

Conflict theorists would argue, in the case of stratification by age, that the various age categories are really *social strata*. As such, they are ranked in a hierarchy of power, prestige, and wealth, and are in constant competition for scarce social resources. Any given stratum has its own interests to defend. The young, for example, are likely to think that cheaper and better college education is a top priority, the middle-aged are more likely to be concerned about increases in income taxes and the aged have a vested interest in better Social Security benefits. But society has limited financial resources to distribute among its age strata, so what one stratum gains, another stratum may lose. Conflict theorists reject the functionalist explanation of why the status of both the elderly and the young has changed in the contemporary world. They point out that in a preindustrial society, the elderly and the young are expected to work because there is a labor shortage. But in industrialized societies, the problem is not a shortage of labor, but a surplus; these economies have a chronic problem of unemployment and underemployment. In response to this difficulty, industrialized societies arbitrarily exclude two categories of the population, the young and the old, from the competition for jobs. A new social invention, compulsory schooling, keeps the very young out of the work force, and another new invention, compulsory retirement, ensures that the old give up their jobs. Earlier in this century, in fact, much of the pressure to abolish child labor and to introduce mandatory retirement came from organized labor, which aimed to reduce the pool of the unemployed in order to improve workers' salaries.

Theory About Organization

Remember, what is important to the sociologist about organization is that it is fundamentally a universal constraint. Thinking of organization as constraint refers to how the rules of a group result in the arrangement of its members to accomplish a common goal or purpose. Depending on the nature of the task, a group is characterized by *formal* and *informal* rules for interacting. For example, as discussed in the previous chapter, in order for scientific knowledge to be produced, a property of the group of scientists is that members must withhold emotion when making observations; they must make general claims only when a sufficient number of cases have been observed; they must make observations based on the senses rather than on faith or supersititon. Organization, as a principle of constraint, is a universal phenomenon like light, and our understanding of it requires theoretical explanation—testable ideas of how it affects us. In the same way that physicists seek evidence to test wave and particle theories of light, so sociologists put forth explanations of how organization determines the behavior of individuals. We must keep sight of the central theme that others affect us, and organization is one major way in which we are constained to act. The most recognized theory of organization relevant to education has been Max Weber's (1968) conflict theory of bureaucracy. Bureaucratic rules are necessary when the public values a rational and technical lifestyle. Authority is a legitimate form of domination (the probability that certain commands will be obeyed by a group of people). Domination can alternately have an illegitimate form. Although bureaucracy is a form of legal authority, it can serve either the interests of an elite or the interests of the group at large. Weber's theory of organizations is, therefore, a conflict theroy because it deals with a conflict over whose interests are served (Ritzer, 1988). Four features characterize this type of organization: a division of labor, a hierarchy of authority. staff roles as offices, and formal procedures.

Theories explaining informal (implicit, tacit) organizational arrangements for accomplishing the goals made explicit by formal arrangements are less powerful in their ability to account for school behavior. Because the empirical evidence on schools could support either conflict or functional explanations, a more general theoretical position is in order: simply, informal organization accompanies and, in fact, makes possible the attainment of the aims of formal organization. Perhaps it is useful to think of informal organization as the margin of flexibility afforded for breaking the formal rules; otherwise, given their rigidity, the formal rules would not be viable. Informal organization operates both to serve the interests of the dominant group and to structure behavior that is functional for the system. More generally (and specifically in the case of the school as an informal organization), the characteristically diffuse, emotional nature of informal organization tempers and makes tolerable the demands made by the formal organization with its characteristically segmented, non-emotional properties.

Theories About Social Control and Deviance

It is quite amazing to think about how the *world stays together* given that we perceive ourselves as unique individuals with *minds of our own*. In fact, we are able to feel like individuals only through our shared agreements with others about how to live as an individual among others. We have individual identity in relation to our function in the whole system. Deviance refers to those behaviors that do not conform to the rules of society (values and norms). Deviance, for the sociologist, also means violation of expected ways to behave when they are considered inappropriate by a large number of people. No act is inherently deviant; what is deviant in one society may not be in another. Social control refers to the penalties for breaking the rules. Every society has mechanisms to reinforce the rules and behaviors that are deemed more deviant than others. As sociologists, we are interested not so much in why some people deviate, but why so many people keep the rules!

Two main theories have been prominent in explaining the sociological principle of social control and deviance. The first is the *symbolic–interaction* perspective, which has generated two explanations of deviance—*cultural transmission* theory and *labeling* theory. Functional theory has been the basis for the development of structural strain and control theories.

Cultural transmission theory explains deviance as behavior that is learned in the same way as conformity. People will go along with the rules if their socialization rewards obedience to the norms, or they will disobey if their socialization emphasizes disrespect for the rules for behavior. The transmission of respect versus disrespect is determined by the intensity of contacts with others, the age at which the contacts take place, and the ratio of contacts with deviants to contacts with conformists. Family members and friends have a great influence over individuals; childhood influences are stronger than those influences occurring later in life; and the more one interacts with deviants rather than conformists, the greater the likelihood of becoming deviant. Behavior which the wider society or culture prescribes may be regarded as deviant by the subculture. For a female child born in the ghetto, becoming a mother at age fourteen may be regarded as conformity to the expectations of the street culture, but deviant to the main society. This perspective, however, does not account for why some people do not become deviant despite their association with deviants, nor does it address why some people become deviant without any association with deviants. *Labeling* theory attempts to explain why certain individuals and acts are considered deviant. It emphasizes the relative nature of deviance and how the label of an act or person as deviant is more significant than the act or actor. Labeling theorists discuss deviance as the process by which people define others as deviant. They posit two stages in the process: primary deviance, a state of temporary nonconformity, and secondary deviance, the ongoing nonconformity of a person who accepts the label of deviant. For example, the primary deviant may be a person who steals an apple from the Korean fruit market, but does not regard herself or himself as deviant and is not regarded as deviant by others. If the deviant act, however, is discovered and becomes public, the offender is confronted by evidence that is used to degrade the person and to assign that person the label of *deviant*. Other people then begin to respond to the person as one who behaves in a nonconformist manner all the time. Eventually, the person perceives herself or himself as deviant and other people accept the label, restricting the person's options and reinforcing her or his deviance. A psychiatrist, as an authority for example, is an agent of social control, one who interprets the rules of society and decides who is deviating from them. Although there is no inherent meaning in an act that makes it deviant, labeling theory tends to distract us from the fact that some behaviors seriously interfere with social order more than others.

The structural–functionalist perspective of deviance is another approach to explaining how social forces influence our behavior. *Structural strain* theory explains deviance as a result of pressures that society exerts on people. When an imbalance exists between socially approved goals and the lack of availability of socially approved means of achieving those goals, people will deviate rather than conform to society's rules for behavior. For example, most Americans believe that they are successful if they can be wealthy. This theory locates the source of deviance in society rather than in its members. *Control* theory explains deviance as a result of the absence of social control. Control theorists are more concerned with why people conform than with why they deviate, and argue that deviance, not conformity, is the norm. The world stays together because society is able to control persons' behavior—the absence of controls would be indicated by lack of conformity.

Theories About Social Change

The last principle of constraint is social change. Social change simply refers to alterations in the regular rules for living (social structure). Sociologists have identified that, ironically, what does not change is that agreements for living always change. Sociologists are particularly concerned with the sources of changes in the rules and about which aspects of social change are due to our seemingly arbitrary choosing and which are recurrent patterns to be found in all societies. Some theories of social change illustrate the profound insight of the sociologist in that they account for changes in *personality* by attributing the source of change to society. The large-scale societal-level influences of the group on personality are found, for example, in the work of Inkeles (1983) on how modernity or changes involving the modernization of society affect changes in the *average personality* of members of that society.

The lawlike nature of social change that has been observed by sociologists is explained by a set of three theories that attempts to understand how and why change takes the forms that it does: sociocultural evolution theory, functionalist theory, and conflict theory.

Sociocultural evolution theory points out that societies grow more complex through time. The major source of change is in the society's mechanism of subsistence. As the society changes from agricultural to industrial to postindustrial, each structure of subsistence leads to a more affluent lifestyle for larger populations.

Structural–functionalist theory emphasizes stability, integration, and shared values. When society grows more complex, differentiation takes place. Schools, for example, emerge to take on the functions that were previously undifferentiated. The school and other institutions are integrated to work harmoniously.

The conflict theory of social change views tensions between competing interest groups over values and scarce resources as the cause of change in the rules for living. Tensions between such interests as teachers and students generate change.

Overall, our understanding of human behavior is enhanced through the sociologist's ability to develop and apply theories of how social forces operate in the context of education.

Summary

This chapter has discussed the traditional explanations of why and how we form institutions, stratify, socialize, organize, and employ social control, and why we change social structure. Several theories have been set forth to explain the universal principles for conducting human activity such as functionalist, conflict, and symbolic interaction. Before we use the basic principles and related theories to interpret education, in Chapter 4 we will trace how, to date, selected major sociological theories have evolved and have been used to describe and explain educational phenomena. Chapter 5 begins our discussion of sociological constraints and their application to education.

Vocabulary

bureaucracy	sociocultural evolutionary theory
conflict theory	structural–functionalist theory
control theory	structural strain theory
cultural transmission theory	symbolic–interaction theory
labeling theory	

Question

1. What is the relationship between principles of sociology and theories of sociology?

References and Suggested Readings

Berdyaev, N. *Slavery and Freedom*. New York: Charles Scribner's Sons, 1944.

Berger, P. *The Sacred Canopy* . New York: Doubleday, 1967.

Bowles, S. and H. Gintis. *Schooling in Capitalist America*. New York: Basic Books, 1976.

Collins, R. *The Credential Society: An Historical Sociology of Education*. New York: Academic Press, 1979.

Cooley, C. *Human Nature and the Social Order*. New York: Scribner's, 1902.

Inkeles, A. *Exploring Individual Modernity*. New York: Columbia University Press, 1983.

Mead, G. *Mind, Self, and Society: From the Standpoint of a Social Behaviorist*. Chicago: University of Chicago Press, 1934.

Merton, R. *Social Theory and Social Structure*. New York: Free Press, 1968.

Mulkey, L. "Consequences of Too Many Sociologies for Teaching Sociology of Education." *Teaching Sociology*, (July 1990) 18(13):356–61.

Parsons, T. "Prolegomena to a Theory of Social Institutions." *American Sociological Review*, (1990) 55:313–45.

Ritzer, G. *Sociological Theory*. New York: Knopf, 1988.

Schutz, A. *The Phenomenology of the Social World*. Evanston, IL: Northwestern University Press, (1932) 1967.

Weber, M. *Economy and Society*. Totowa, NJ: Bedminster Press, (1921) 1968.

Note

[1]Assume here that in the human being the urge toward preservation is manifested not as specific directives on how to respond to persons and things, but as the *principles of sociology*—the individual predisposition (*orientations*, as Parsons [1990] explains) to make and follow group agreements that ultimately result in the protection of the individual members of the group. The principles, a predisposition at the individual level, are manifested at the collective level as essential forms or rules for behavior (Berdyaev, 1944; Berger, 1967; Parsons, 1990). Society first exists in the individual as the precondition to act socially.

CHAPTER
4

Many Sociologies and Many Sociologies of Education

History of the Sociological Study of Education

The purpose of this chapter is to discuss the emergence of the subfield of the sociology of education by identifying how theoretical explanations of sociological principles have been tested and applied using educational issues. Sociologists would probably agree that the behavior of the children in the photograph above is in many ways a response to what we are calling the general principles of constraint, which operate universally in human societies. They would not agree, however, as to which of the many theories or systematic explanations for the observed laws of institutions, socialization, stratification, organization, social control and deviance, and social change best accounts for how social forces determine the children's behavior. More attention in later chapters will be given to selected theories when we discuss each constraint and its application to education.

Outline

Classical writings disclose the assumptions on which a field of thought (scholarly discipline) was founded; they enable us to gauge the distance that a field has traveled since its inception, and they pose questions for current study (Sieber and Wilder, 1977). This chapter presents some of the historical developments that led to the delineation of the subfield, the sociology of education. The sociology of education as a substantive domain of inquiry emerged from and reflects the theoretical foundations and principles of its parent discipline, sociology. Our discussion will show the relevance of various theorists' formulations of how the principles of constraint operate to inform our understanding of education.

The previous chapter identifies the six principles of social constraint and provides an overview of the major theoretical explanations of how they work. This chapter links the six principles and their theoretical explanations with the classical theorists who formulated the ideas. By documenting the historical development of the theoretical explanations of social forces and their relevance to education, we document the emergence and evolution of the sociology of education as a substantive domain of inquiry.

Sociologists spend most of their time investigating how human behavior, in all of its forms, illustrates a response to the principles of sociology.[1] In this chapter we chart the developments of the various explanations of how social forces (constraints) influence us and how these theories have been applied in interpreting education and tested for educational phenomena. Although the theoretical and empirical investigations were motivated by various factors such as prevailing historical issues, they all inform our understanding of the more general operation of social principles. The historical and chronological events surrounding the emergence of the subfield have been documented by others.[2] Later chapters will present in more detail the theoretical and empirical literature as well as the educational issues which illustrate the influence of the more general principles of the social realm on our behavior. We will, so to speak, look at the zebra and horse to find the more general principles pertaining to mammals.

Many Sociologies and Many Sociologies of Education: Principles, Theories, and Education

If we understand the contributing ideas of the so-called founding fathers of the discipline of sociology, we can see how the sociology of education has developed. Each of the social theorists discussed in the following pages attempts to explain social constraints and has created a foundation of ideas upon which others have built. While many theorists have built this foundation, those theorists whose work has been the most useful for interpreting education have been selected as a focus of attention.

Structural–Functionalist Interpretations of Social Constraints in Education

Two theoretical developments in the history of sociological ideas formed the foundation for a sociological understanding of education as an institution, a mechanism of socialization, an organization, a vehicle of stratification, an illustration of social control and deviance, and an instrument of social change. These theories, *structural–functionalist* and *conflict*, have dominated as explanations of the principles of social behavior.

Structural–functionalism (also known as *consensus* theory) originated with the work of Auguste Comte, Herbert Spencer, Emile Durkheim, Talcott Parsons, and Robert K. Merton.

Auguste Comte (1798–1857), a French philosopher, is considered by some sociologists to be the founder of sociology. He argued for a sociology, a science of society. He was curious about the forces that keep human life stable.

Herbert Spencer (1820–1903), like Comte, was interested in those social forces that promote order among individuals. He advocated that human societies be scientifically studied in the same way that the physiologist studies the human organism. The parts of a living organism are interdependent and contribute to the overall well-being of the whole organism. Education, the economy, religion, and the polity are analogous to the organs of the body, which work together to maintain the whole system. In his claims that the social system evolves from a simple form to a complex form, Spencer drew upon the insights of Charles Darwin.

Emile Durkheim (1858–1917), a French sociologist, also conceived of society as a system of shared beliefs and values. He asked, "What do shared beliefs do for the system? What are their function or consequences?" He believed that the shared rules for living, such as education and religion, exist as social facts, in their own right, and direct the lives of individuals. Education is, then, only the means by which society prepares, within the children, the essential conditions of its very existence. Its object is to arouse and to develop in the child a certain number of physical, intellectual, and moral states that are required for participation in society (Durkheim, 1956). Society can survive only if a sufficient degree of homogeneity exists among its members; education perpetuates and reinforces this homogeneity by fixing in the child, from the beginning, the essential similarities that collective life demands.

The American sociologist *Talcott Parsons* (1902–1979) built on Durkheim's work. He argued that society consists of interdependent parts, each of which helps to maintain the stability of the entire social system. In the same way that the human body tries to maintain homeostasis, society, as a whole, tries to maintain a constant balance or equilibrium. When Durkheim established the foundations of a functionalist approach around the beginning of the century, the functionalist perspective focused on social order rather than on conflict. In the late 1950s and into the 1960s, major social conflicts occurring in the United States questioned Parsons's theory. In response to the criticisms of the relevance of functionalist theory, Parsons (1961, 1966) argued that as a society grows more complex, it differentiates and integrates. Simple societies contain few institutions, and any one of them may have several functions. The family, for example, is responsible for reproduction and education. Differentiation occurs when the society grows more complex. Other institutions, such as schools, emerge to take on the functions or responsibilities that were previously undifferentiated. The new institutions are joined together through integration. For example, new norms develop to resolve conflict and to enhance the relationship between the school and the family. Society changes in the direction of greater complexity, but maintains its balance and stability by integration of its parts or institutions. Parsons (1961, 1966) saw social change as a result of strains to the system that disturb its equilibrium. The imbalance stimulates adjustments that return the system to equilibrium and the new equilibrium contains different social arrangements.

Parsons explained classrooms in terms of their functions for the school, the school in terms of its functions for the educational system, and the latter in terms of its functions for society. His grand theory begins with an explanation of individual behavior. All action is goal oriented and in pursuit of our goals we take into account the purposes of other people. Our behaviors, or actions, are determined by five *pattern variables: affectivity* and *affective neutrality, specificity* and *diffuseness, universalism* and *particularism, self-orientation* and *collectivity orientation, achievement* and *ascription.* Each social system, thought Parsons, can be analyzed according to *functional prerequisites: requirements of adaptation* (allocation of resources), *integration* (commitment of members to the system), *goal attainment* (consensus of goals), and *pattern maintenance* (repair of damage to the parts of the system).

Parsons's work, extended through the work of *R.K. Merton* (1968) when he distinguished between the manifest function of an act (that intended by the actor) and the latent function (the unintended or unrecognized consequences of action) has also affected developments in our understanding of education. For example, the manifest function of education is to stimulate curiosity, but its latent function is to kill any curiosity and stimulate obedience and conformity. The utility of functionalist analysis, with its emphasis on the system, is that it depicts the function of education in fostering in the child a certain number of physical, intellectual, and moral states that are necessary for the child's survival in society. Functionalist analysis contributes to our understanding of selection and allocation. The limitation of functionalist theory is that explaining the function does not explain the cause. Why do certain demands of the society become recognized in schools while others do not?

The work of Robert Dreeben (1968), also from a functionalist perspective, described how the educational system transmits culture by perpetuating the accepted or mainstream ideas. Jerome Karabel and A. H. Halsey (1977) have also been recognized as proponents of the functionalist perspective. Because functionalists identify the functions of an item within a society and examine the interconnections between the constituents of the society and its relationship to other societies, the perspective is very compatible with quantitative analyses and large-scale multivariate analyses. For this reason, most of the developments in the sociology of education, while seemingly methodological and moderately atheoretical, lend support to the functionalist interpretation of the social forces operating in education. The research has often been a response to historical factors such as funding opportunities rather than to good theory (Hallinan, 1985). Empirical research in two traditions, (1) *educational productivity* (school effects) and *status attainment* and (2) sophisticated statistical applications (modeling techniques and the use of large cross-sectional and longitudinal data sets), have characterized the dominant body of work in the field (see the work of Blau and Scott, 1962; Coleman, 1966; and Sewell and Hauser, 1975).

Conflict Interpretations of Social Constraints in Education

Karl Marx (1818–1883) was less concerned with education than Durkheim (Robinson, 1981). He was from a middle-class family in western Germany. Most of his life was spent in England as a political refugee. He studied at the University of Berlin, where he was influenced by G. W. F. Hegel's philosophy, particularly Hegel's idealist view that people's knowledge about the world derives from their ideas about the world, and although these ideas change and develop, people create their reality (Robinson, 1981). Contrary to Hegel, Marx claimed that it is not the people's consciousness that determines their being but, on the contrary, their social being that determines their consciousness. For Marx, the relationships of the workplace permeate the whole of life so that people become what they are in labor. The nature of people therefore depends upon the conditions determining their work. The ideas that rule society at any given time are nothing more than the ideal expression of the dominant material relationships in that society (Marx and Engels, 1970). The dominant group controls not only the productive forces within a society, but also the ways of thought. It legitimizes what is right and acceptable, and it provides the framework from which thought emanates. Because of differences in material conditions, two classes emerge, the rich and the poor: the dialectic between these two classes results in revolution, the redistribution of resources, and the eventual reshaping of ideas.

Theoretical developments that further contributed to the formation of the subfield concerned conflict explanations of the principles of sociology. The work of Karl Marx, as it applies to an analysis of education, was followed by that of Ralf Dahrendorf (1959), Martin Carnoy (1972), and Samuel Bowles and Herbert Gintis (1976). The work of Max Weber was followed by that of Randall Collins (1975) and Paul DiMaggio (1979). The work of Willard Waller is also on conflict (1932). These theorists addressed questions that had not been raised by functionalists. They believed that inequality of resources in society is the source of conflict and that schools are ultimately linked to the kinds of economic opportunities individuals have. In this perspective, the system of class status appears more inflexible than egalitarian and schools are linked closely to the structure of inequality.

In this line of thought, other theorists (frequently called *reproduction* theorists) do not view the school as promoting democracy, social mobility and equality. Rather, they see the school as a mechanism that reproduces the values of the dominant social group (Carnoy, 1972; Persell, 1977; Boudon, 1974). As an *insti-*

tution, the school *socializes* students into the formal language of the mainstream culture (Bernstein, 1977; Bourdieu and Passeron, 1977) and *organizes* or sorts students into professional versus vocational roles. The work of Henry Giroux (1983) also shows how schools provide students from different social strata with the knowledge and skills they need to occupy their respective places in the labor force. Schools, for Giroux, reproduce the culture of the dominant social group in society. Reproduction theorists who see the school's purpose as maintaining and reproducing society's class structure have developed models at the macro level (societal context) and at the micro level (classroom context) for conducting large-scale quantitative analyses similar to the functionalists. Interestingly, the same empirical evidence can be used to lend credibility to either theoretical framework. The work of these theorists is discussed later in more detail, as they inform our understanding of each sociological principle.

 Critical theorists and reproduction theorists interpret the purposes of schooling similarly. Both groups believe that schooling serves the interests of the dominant group in society. Critical theorists, however, emphasize the power of individuals to structure their own destiny and to ameliorate the oppressive nature of the institutions in which they live. Critical theorists have been concerned most with the practice of teaching and its role in transforming society. Critical theory in education has its historical roots in the work of the Italian Marxist Antonio Gramsci (1971), and the work of Brazilian educator Paulo Freire (1970). Critical theorists research ways to understand how the dominant ideology of society is translated into practice in schools and the ways in which the impact of the ideology is obscured. The work of Michael Apple (1978) and Henry Giroux (1983) typifies this line of thought. Their work has been stimulated by the inadequacy of both reproduction and interpretive theories to encompass and explain the relationship between schooling and society. Apple and Giroux argue that reproduction theory examines only the structural concerns of schools and at interpretive theories are limited to microlevel examinations of classroom interactions. Critical theory integrates macrostructural and microinteractional approaches in the study of schooling.

 The work of *Max Weber* (1864–1920) is also linked to the camp of conflict theory. He contributed an *interpretive* understanding of social action. Like Marx, he saw that individuals who are in the same economic position belong to the same class group, but unlike Marx, he did not see the means of production as the fundamental determinant of subjective human action. Weber's development of the concept of the *status group* was an elaboration on the link between class structure and the conscious sharing of prestige within a society in the form of lifestyles. According to this concept, people of the same status group share subjective meaning. In a famous work called *The Protestant Ethic and the Spirit of Capitalism* he illustrates how religious ideas can be foundational and antecedent to economic condition (Weber, 1958). From his theory of subjective action (interpretive) he developed an analysis of class and status. He was concerned with the societal forms of authority within which the individual act is located. He examined what he called traditional, charismatic, and legal-rational forms of authority, and this latter form of legitimation gave rise to his thinking on the bureaucracy. Weber's concept of *bureaucratic organization* has yielded to the sociology of education an understanding of the school as a formal organization. More contemporary theorists such as Georg Simmel (1955), Randall Collins (1975), and Alfred Schutz (1967) build on Weber's notion of *interpretive* understanding.

The work of *Alfred Schutz* (1899–1959) extends Weber's ideas. Schutz argues that Weber developed a sociology of meaning without discussing how meaning itself arises, is sustained, and changes. Schutz emphasizes how the world is represented subjectively in the mind of individuals; he makes a clear distinction between personal subjectivity and the objectivity of society. In his microlevel analysis of Weber, Schutz draws heavily on the philosophy of Edmund Husserl and Henri Bergson and, in the process, prepares the groundwork of a *phenomenological* sociology later elaborated by Peter Berger and Thomas Luckman (1967) (Robinson, 1981).[3] Within an interpretive paradigm, the central concern is with *phenomenology*—the study of how people construct meanings in their interactions with one another. Reality is something not given, but constructed within (the moment) of social interaction. The interpretist emphasis moved sociology of education from the study of macrostructural concerns to micro level analysis of interactions of actors in schools and classrooms. For example, the concept of what constitutes a "good reader" is developed through the interaction between teachers and students in classroom practice (Bennett and LeCompte, 1990). A more recent extension of Schutz's ideas is found in the work of Harold Garfinkel and is known as ethnomethodology (1967). Ethnomethodology refers to the process through which people negotiate the routines of everyday life, especially in conversation. Conversation or talk, as an interpretive procedure (Cicourel, 1964) is the topic for ethnomethodological enquiry. This type of analysis focuses on the ground rules of everyday life as negotiated by individuals.[4] The exploration of the ground rules of everyday life has contributed to the development of the sociology of education (McDermott, 1976). Studies of the classroom in which children must interpret teacher talk, for example, provide a fine-grained understanding of how social life is *done*.

Symbolic–Interaction Interpretations of Social Constraints in Education

Interpretive theory has not only developed into the work represented by the phenomenologists and ethnomethodologists but also into another field of inquiry known as symbolic interaction. Although interpretive theorists (phenomenologists and symbolic interactionists, for example) study social meanings at the micro level through qualitative and descriptive research methods, they tend to exclude macrolevel linkages to social constraints. Symbolic interactionism (Blumer, 1969) is the study of the meanings people construct in their interactions with one another through time. Symbolic interaction has become most associated with the work of *George Herbert Mead* (1863–1931). Mead saw the individual as both the active creator of the world and also the product of the world. He believed that human beings act toward things on the basis of the meanings that the things have for them. These meanings are a product of social interaction in human society; they are modified and handled through an interpretive process that is used by each person in relation to the things she or he encounters. We act according to our view of how the world is constructed and to an extent are constrained by that world view. Still another major theoretical development in sociology, which further contributed to the formation of the subfield of the sociology of education and concerns a symbolic–interactionist explanation of the principles of sociology, is the work of Howard Becker (1961) on deviance and Erving Goffman (1959) on total institutions. This line of thought focuses on the individual actor in the wider structural setting of action, without particular reference to the historical and political context.

Summary

Chapter 4 has shown how the fundamental principles of sociology have been explained by the founding theorists and used to interpret what we commonly refer to as *education*. Theoretical and empirical work on the fundamental principles of social constraint led to the development of sociology of education as a subfield of sociology. Comte, Spencer, Durkheim, Parsons, and Merton are identified as consensus theorists or structural–functionalists. This tradition of thought explains education as an institution, a group in which all principles are constraints aimed at reproducing in each generation the conventions of the system. For example, stratification for the functionalists accounts for education as a meritocratic basis for rewarding wealth, power, and prestige. Marx and Weber have made the greatest contributions to our understanding of how social forces operate in education from a conflict perspective. The focus of their work is on coercion and on how competition for scarce resources leads to the development of dominant and subordinate groups, with the dominant group imposing its values on the less powerful group. Last, the work of Weber eventually resulted in a distinctive interpretive approach reflected in the work of Mead and the school of symbolic interaction. This chapter has discussed the emergence of a sociology of education as a response to traditional explanations of how we form institutions, socialize, organize, stratify, employ social control, and why we change social structure.

Vocabulary

conflict theory	symbolic interaction
functionalist theory	

Question

1. What are some developments in explanations of the social principles as they apply to education?

References and Suggested Readings

Apple, M. "The New Sociology of Education: Analyzing Cultural and Economic Reproduction." *Harvard Educational Review*, (1978) 48:495–503.

Ballatine, J. *The Sociology of Education: A Systematic Explanation.* Englewood Cliffs, NJ: Prentice-Hall, 1989.

Becker, H., B. Geer, E. Hughes, and A. Strauss. *Boys in White: Student Culture in Medical School.* Chicago: University of Chicago Press, 1961.

Bennett, K. and M. LeCompte. *How Schools Work: A Sociological Analysis of Education.* New York: Longman, 1990.

Berger, P. and T. Luckmann. *The Social Construction of Reality: A Treatise in the Sociology of Knowledge.* New York: Anchor Books, 1967.

Bernstein, B. *Class, Codes and Control. Vol. III: Towards a Theory of Educational Transmission.* London: Routledge & Kegan Paul, 1977.

Blau, P. and W. Scott. *Formal Organizations: A Comparative Approach.* San Francisco: Chandler, 1962.

Blumer, H. *Symbolic Interactionism: Perspectives and Method.* Englewood Cliffs, NJ: Prentice-Hall, 1969.

Boudon, R. *Education, Opportunity, and Social Inequality: Changing Prospects in Western Society.* New York: John Wiley, 1974.

Bourdieu, P. and J. Passeron. *Reproduction in Education, Society and Culture.* London: Sage, 1977.

Bowles, S. and H. Gintis. *Schooling in Capitalist America: Educational Reform and the Contradictions of Economic Life.* New York: Basic Books, 1976.

Brim, O. *Sociology and the Field of Education.* New York: Russell Sage Foundation, 1958.

Carnoy, M., ed., *Schooling in a Corporate Society: The Political Economy of Education in America.* New York: McKay, 1972.

Carnoy, M. and H. Levin. *Schooling and Work in the Democratic State.* Stanford, CA: Stanford University Press, 1985.

Cicourel, A. *Method and Measurement in Sociology.* New York: Free Press, 1964.

Coleman, J. *Equality of Educational Opportunity.* Washington, DC: United States Government Printing Office, 1966.

Collins, R. "Functional and Conflict Theories of Educational Stratification." In J. Karabel & A.H. Halsey (eds.), *Power and Ideology in Education*, pp. 118–36. Cambridge: Oxford University Press, 1977.

———. *Conflict Sociology: Toward An Explanatory Science.* New York: Academic Press, 1975.

Dahrendorf, R. *Class and Conflict in Industrial Society.* Stanford, CA: Stanford University Press, 1959.

DiMaggio, P. "Review Essay On Pierre Bourdieu." *American Journal of Sociology*, (1979) 84(6):1460–74.

Dreeben, R. *On What Is Learned in School.* Reading, MA: Addison–Wesley, 1968.

Durkheim, E. *Moral Education: A Study in the Theory and Application of the Sociology of Education.* Glencoe, IL: Free Press, 1961.

———. *The Division of Labor in Society.* New York: Free Press, 1956.

_____. *Education and Society.* New York: Free Press, 1956.

Freire, P. *Pedagogy of the Oppressed.* New York: Continuum, 1970.

Garfinkel, H. *Studies in Ethnomethodology.* Englewood Cliffs, NJ: Prentice-Hall, 1967.

Giroux, H. "Theories of Reproduction and Resistance in the New Sociology of Education." *Harvard Educational Review,* (1983) 53:257–93.

Goffman, E. *The Presentation of Self in Everyday Life.* Garden City, NY: Doubleday, 1959.

Gramsci, A. *Selections from the Prison Notebooks.* New York: International, 1971.

Gross, N. "Some Contributions of Sociology to the Field of Education." *Harvard Educational Review,* (1959) 29:87.

Hallinan, M. "Sociology of Education: The State of the Art." In Jeanne Ballantine, ed., *Schools and Society: A Reader in Education and Society,* Palo Alto, CA: Mayfield, 1985.

Hargreaves, A., and P. Woods. *Classrooms and Staffrooms: The Sociology of Teachers and Teaching.* Milton Keynes, England: Open University Press, 1984.

Karabel, J. and A. Halsey, eds., *Power and Ideology in Education.* New York: Oxford University Press, 1977.

Marx, K. *Economy, Class, and Social Revolution.* New York: Scribner, 1971.

Marx, K. and F. Engels. *The German Ideology.* London: Lawrence & Wishart, 1970.

McDermott, R. *Kids Make Sense: An Ethnographic Account of the Instructional Management of Success and Failure in a First Grade Classroom.* Unpublished doctoral dissertation, Stanford University, CA, 1976.

Merton, R. *Social Theory and Social Structure.* New York: Free Press, 1968.

Parelius, R. and A. Parelius. *The Sociology of Education.* Englewood Cliffs, NJ: Prentice-Hall, 1987.

Parsons, T. *Evolutionary and Comparative Perspectives.* Englewood Cliffs, NJ: Prentice-Hall, 1966.

_____. "Some Considerations on the Theory of Social Change." *Rural Sociology,* (1961) 26:219–39.

_____. "The School Class as a Social System: Some of its Functions in American Society." *Harvard Educational Review,* (1959) 29:297–319.

_____. *The Social System.* Glencoe, IL: The Free Press, 1951

Persell, C. *Education and Inequality: The Roots and Results of Stratification in America's Schools.* New York: Free Press, 1977.

Robinson, P. *Perspectives on the Sociology of Education: An Introduction.* Boston: Routledge & Legan Paul, 1981.

Schutz, A. *The Phenomenology of the Social World.* Evanston, IL: Northwestern University Press, 1967.

Sewell, W. and R. Hauser. *Occupation and Earnings: Achievement in the Early Career.* New York: Academic Press, 1975.

Sieber, S. and D. Wilder. *The School in Society.* New York: Free Press, 1977.

Simmel, G. *Confict.* Glencoe, IL: Free Press, 1955.

Waller, W. *The Sociology of Teaching.* New York: John Wiley, 1932.

Weber, M. *From Max Weber: Essays in Sociology.* In H. Gerth and C. Mills, Eds. New York: Oxford University Press, 1958.

———. *The Protestant Ethic and the Spirit of Capitalism.* New York: Scribner's, 1958.

Notes

[1]For a detailed discussion of issues related to the origins of the social directives of human behavior, refer to Chapter 1 notes; also see articles by Charles Camic, "An Historical Prologue;" Talcot Parsons, "Prolegomena to a Theory of Social Institutions;" James Coleman, "Commentary: Social Institutions and Social Theory;" and Jeffrey Alexander, "Commentary: Structure, Value, Action," *American Sociological Review*, 55:313–45.

[2]For other state of the art reviews of the literature, see Ballantine, 1989; Hallinan, 1981; Parelius and Parelius, 1987; and Robinson, 1981. Despite Durkheim's work at the turn of the century, the emergence of sociology of education as a substantive area of inquiry is of fairly recent origin. Education itself, as a substantive area of inquiry, is also of fairly recent origin. In the beginning of the twentieth century, sociologists and educators (for example, William James, John Dewey, and Lester Ward) collaborated to work in a field referred to as Educational Sociology. The incentives for an educational sociology were founded on the belief that the study of education from a sociological perspective could bring about needed changes in society. The emphasis on the applied aspects of the field led to tensions between sociologists and educators. Sociologists began to view educational sociology as an applied field (see Donald A. Hansen, "The Uncomfortable Relation of Sociology and Education," In Donald A. Hansen and Joel Gerstl, eds., *On Education: Sociological Perspectives*, New York: John Wiley and Sons, 1967) and stressed the need for theoretically grounded empirical research. In the forties, little systematic research was conducted (Brim, 1958). Eventually, what had been the *Journal of Educational Sociology* became the journal of the *Sociology of Education* and the sections in the American Sociological Association were also renamed. Although sociologists of education emphasize the practical application of sociology to formal schooling (Gross, 1959), issues in education such as mandatory school-starting age, curriculum and pedagogy, equality of opportunity, school desegregation, and the school as a bureaucracy all inform sociological theory.

[3]Note here that the history of the sociological study of education is somewhat subject to the ways in which sociologists organize theory. *Metatheorists* study the logic of the integration of theory (Ritzer, 1983). Kathleen Bennett and Margaret LeCompte, for example, discuss interpretive theory under the rubric of *social transformation* theory. (See Bennett and LeCompte, *How Schools Work: A Sociological Analysis of Education.* New York: Longman, 1990.) Sociological theories in this camp are those of *transformation* rather than *transmission* of culture.

[4]William Goode, in *Principles of Sociology* (New York: McGraw Hill, 1977), explains that sociologists who are ethnomethodologists do not assume motives and norms are definite things within the individual that they can study as one might study a rock. Rather, people who interact with the individual "construct" these things. See, for example, "Motives," in Peter McHugh, Stanley Raffel, Daniel O. Foss, and Alan Blum, *On the Beginning of Social Inquiry* (London: Routledge, 1974). People do construct others' motives and then respond to what they think others feel

PART

II

Describing and Explaining Education from a Sociological Perspective

Part II of this book applies the principles of sociology to education. Once we learn the rules which govern the mighty waves of the Atlantic or a steep mountain face in the Alps, we can surf and climb them. Theoretical and empirical investigations are used to highlight where and how social forces structure the interactions of individuals to produce the phenomenon we refer to as *education.*

Part I of this book has introduced to you the mental (cognitive) tools that will be useful for understanding what we commonly refer to as education. The first mental skill important for our enhanced understanding is to focus on one aspect of *reality*—in our case, the social aspect. The social aspect refers to how our behavior is continually determined by other people in one way or another.

We then referred to six major types of social forces or major principles of how others influence our behavior and how sociologists have explained these principles (through the many theories or sociologies). The principles serve as a unifying theme for organizing our knowledge. The principles identify the major social constraints or influences on our behavior. Now that we are aware of those principles, the following chapters in Part II will describe each of them in detail and will illustrate its occurrence in the context of education. Next, theories will be presented to help in our understanding of how each particular social constraint determines our behavior in the arena of education. Lastly, the research studies which have been conducted to test how each principle operates will be used for drawing inferences for the theories presented.

We emphasized that sociologists have observed that each social force operates universally in all human societies, but just how the laws or principles of constraint operate is unclear to us. For example, in the physical sciences, the principles of light are not fully understood. Different explanations have been put forth about how light travels. Some researchers have reasoned that light travels as waves and others claim that light travels as particles. Theories are open for further empirical testing even though the laws, not fully known to us, continue to operate.

In Part II, each principle will be applied to education using the same logic that knowledge of the laws of the mountains, or of the ocean waves, or of human anatomy, gives to the skilled mountain climber, surfer, and surgeon. Theories which try to explain how each principle influences our behavior can be used as a handbook to guide educators in their practice. For example, knowledge of those conditions apart from the individual, the properties of the groups of which individuals are members, influences the behaviors of those individuals. Theory on the principle of organization tells us how various arrangements of the classroom facilitate instruction. Theory on the principle of stratification tells us how gender and racial or ethnic groups having characteristic incomes and levels of education affect the educational aspirations and achievements of offspring from these groups. Theory on the principle of social control tells us how students who are characterized as low-ability foster the labeling of children as incompetent, which further perpetuates their incompetence. Theoretical knowledge, therefore, guides practice by suggesting when and what kind of interventions either mediate the effects of or change the group conditions.

Practical applications, reciprocally, generate and verify the credibility of theory. For example, we could develop a theory of organization based on our observation of classrooms. Some children organized within their classroom by ability may show a better academic performance than if they were organized on some other basis. Teachers can employ new techniques based on scientific research to be more effective in the classroom. Sociology is a surprise because sometimes those very teaching strategies that you borrowed from a favorite teacher might be shown, in fact, to be ineffective.

Lastly, in Part II, the second mental skill (presented in Part I) that makes sociology what it is—the awareness that we are to observe social forces scientifically—will be practiced by the inclusion of theoretical and empirical investigations relevant to each sociological principle. We therefore meet the standard or requirement that to be sociological we must exercise logical reasoning (how one thing is related to another or regularly follows another chronologically) in figuring out how one or many social forces cause us to act as we do in educational settings.

Part II (Describing and Explaining Education from a Sociological Perspective) of this book applies sociology to education. Chapters 5 through 10 are each devoted to a discussion of one of the six principles of the social realm and where the principle is manifested in the context of education. The chapters present theories that sociologists have put forth as their best hypotheses about how the laws of the social realm work and offer empirical investigations on various issues that illustrate each principle. Chapter 5 (**Institutions: Patterned Interactions to Meet Basic Human Needs** examines issues relevant to education as an institution. Chapter 6 (**Socialization: Becoming Human by Learning Society's Conventions**) discusses curriculum and pedagogy as major issues of socialization in education. Chapter 7 (**Stratification: Rules for Acquiring the Desirable Things in Life**) is concerned with equality of opportunity—educational and occupational attainment according to gender, race, ethnicity, and age—as the main issue of stratification in education. Chapter 8 (**Organization: The Arrangement of Individuals into Large and Small Groups**) details the nature of organization and treats formal organization issues concerning the school as a bureaucracy and informal organization in the case of the *hidden curriculum*. Chapter 9 (**Social Control and Deviance: Actions Taken to Get People to Conform to Society's Conventions**) examines theory and research as they pertain to classroom discipline as an issue of social control and deviance in the context of education. Chapter 10 (**Social Change: Change in the Rules for Living Together**) investigates the nature of social change and identifies the operation of this principle in education in the form of educational social movements. Chapter 11 (**Enduring Questions: How Does Education Influence Your Life? Can You Influence Education?**) is the phoenix emerging; it addresses the ultimate issue in any sociological analysis—how much is the individual responsible for his or her actions and how much is society responsible?

5

Institutions

*Patterned Interactions to Meet
Basic Human Needs*

You might think of the children in the photograph above as students obeying their teacher, but the children are actually obedient to another teacher—society—with its expectations for formal learning. In some human societies, survival has depended more on the ability of its young male members to learn to kill a caribou with a single poison arrow than on passing an examination such as the California Achievement Test or the Degree of Reading Power Test, or eventually the Scholastic Aptitude Test. What does it mean when we say the children in the preceding photograph are educated? What is education?

Outline

W hat does it mean to be educated? To answer this question, first we must assume that the human, for its survival, is a social being; it must take into account other people to preserve itself. Although we cannot make precise predictions about how persons will behave according to sheer biological inheritance, this endowment is a precondition. In other words, it is difficult to show there are social patterns determined by specific biological correlates. Most fundamentally, our biological heritage requires that social patterns satisfy biological needs. For example, if our social patterns did not make provision for food, we would die; if they did not provide for care and rearing of infants, the species would become extinct. However, the kinds of social patterns designed to meet these biological imperatives vary greatly, except at what appears to be a basic level of *determinateness*. The biological structure ensures that some kinds of social solutions are more likely to recur than others. The human genetic template makes us sensitive to social stimuli such that biological factors make social life necessary as well as possible. As has been emphasized, the biological foundations necessary to be social are the principles of sociology, a predisposition to act socially (that is, to make and to follow prescriptions for behavior) in six primary ways.

At the individual level, then, the *principle of institutions* is the predisposition to make shared rules that result in provision for child-rearing, distribution of scarce resources, and so on. When these rules become collective, they are the externalized form of subjective consciousness; ultimately the rules take on objective existence as society. Society is first to dictate how we should behave, and in this way we are rule-following before we are rule-making.[1] Another way to think about the principle of institutions is that it is an elaboration of the principle of socialization and the principle of organization. When we see values and norms result in the arrangement of individuals into groups to accomplish goals and basic life needs, we are observing the principle of institutions.

The Principle of Institutions

An *institution* is a social force (the composite of all the other social forces or principles) that influences us to behave in predictable ways by establishing expectations concerning general human needs. Within the total social system (society) are subsets of the system (subsystems) designed to

- Produce new members and to teach them the values shared by those who live in their world (the family);
- Mobilize scarce resources in order to distribute goods and services that people want (the economy);
- Protect from external threat such as invasion or internal threat such as crime (the military or police);
- Prepare persons for occupational statuses and roles (education);
- Motivate people to conform to the system's expectations of behavior by giving life meaning and ultimate purpose in the face of the unknown (religion).

Like organs of a living organism, each subsystem or institution maintains the whole system by encouraging people to act in stable patterns of behavior.[2]

As noted in Chapter 1, any given social phenomenon has a systemic property, meaning that society's rules (social structure) must be interpreted as part of a whole, interrelated structure. The illustration was the individual violinist whose musical part is a reflection of the whole symphony. In the same manner, persons follow behavioral prescriptions that tell them how to act when they are in certain positions, and all the positions work together to ensure the homeostatic operation of the whole system (society).

The principles, therefore, are fundamental operations through which society is constructed and the principles of socialization, stratification, organization, social control and deviance, and social change direct the actions of individuals. The principle of institutions is qualified or distinguished from the others because it is an orientation to rule-making and rule-following at another level. In later chapters, each principle is applied to illustrate its operation primarily *within* the system of education in the United States. But to understand how the principles of sociology operate together in a particular configuration, as the principle of institutions, we must make an observation at two higher levels. In the same way, one would observe human cells at both the *microscopic* level and the higher *macroscopic* level as the aggregate of cells, an organ, where the cells form a specific configuration to accomplish a task necessary for the overall maintenance of the system.

Using our cell-organ-system analogy, we can see that what goes on in American schools (the cellular level) reflects what goes on *between* schooling and family and religion and government (the other organs), all of which in some way reflect and serve the societal system. Also, we will observe the principle of institutions as it operates *interinstitutionally* (education in relation to other institutions in the society) and *between* institutions (across societies). Each society can also be interpreted as an even broader macrodeterminant, a global system. Ultimately, however, while global prescriptions for behavior exist as a reality separate and beyond the life of any one person, their influence is invoked when people respond to the rules as they are perceived in their "heads." In this manner social interaction is both a macro determinant of behavior and, simultaneously, enacted in a moment-to-moment construction of interaction.

Only in this chapter do we discuss how the principles that work together at one level are reflected at a lower level. The following chapters treat each principle within education at a lower level but do not necessarily illustrate the connection to the higher order principle of institutions. To illustrate this point of the interdependence of the macro and micro levels of social phenomena, let's try to understand why schools function as they do. Education prescriptions interrelate and are compatible with the structure and function of other institutions in the system so that a society with a capitalist economy has a religious institution that endorses free enterprise, a polity that upholds capitalism, and an educational institution that encourages competition. A society with a socialist economy will have institutions that interrelate with that system.

In looking at variations in educational systems from a functionalist stance, we must ask which functions or effects a given institution has in maintaining the social system. The regulation of human behavior into predictable patterns is necessary for society's survival. Any behavioral patterns that have a negative effect imbalance the system and are thereby dysfunctional. Equilibrium is restored by correction of these elements. The major function of education, from this perspective, is as a solution to the recurrent demands of social living—socialization, selection and allocation. Conflict theorists, on the other hand, are more interested in interpreting which groups of individuals benefit from the institutional arrangements. The principle of institutions is illustrated by the fact that all nations have some form of formal education. These two approaches address different aspects of the principle of institutions. We will examine their relative explanatory power in the following discussion of variations in education as an institution around the world.

Applying the Principle to School Issues: Socialization and Selection–Allocation

A sociological analysis always entails the application of the principles of sociology to human action, the biological predispositions to making rules for living cooperatively. These principles work together simultaneously to bring about coordinated human activity (even though, for analysis, we apply them separately in the chapters which follow). *Education*, the institution that constrains human behavior to accomplish the transmission of a society's knowledge and skills to each generation, primarily illustrates the operation of the *principle of socialization*. Through socialization, individuals acquire their preferences. The values of intelligence and curiosity are instilled, and norms, such as mandatory school attendance, are reinforced through the statuses of teacher and students. The *principle of organization* explains the arrangement of students into group contexts such as classrooms and peer groups to facilitate learning. Moreover, students are *selectively* prepared for the occupational roles that society *allocates* for its maintenance.

Theory and Research on Education as an Institution

Macrosociological Analyses of Educational Systems

Several theoretical perspectives aim to account for how the principle of institutions operates in the case of education.[3] Conflict and functionalist (consensus) theories can be viewed as an integrating paradigm, a typology for other theories. Conflict interpretations of educational systems focus on the role of education as a means to perpetuate the status of the elite and functionalist interpretations of educational systems emphasize the provision of opportunity for individuals to succeed by acquiring the skills needed for the system's economic development.

Human capital theory explains the role of educational systems as necessary for the preparation of those skills, knowledge, and values that are fundamental to economic modernization. In this view, the system is meritocratic, meaning that achievement is based on ability (as opposed to ascriptive characteristics such as race and gender). People get where they do because they have worked hard for it. Gary Becker (1980) sets forth a human capital interpretation of how the principle of institutions operates in the case of educational systems. He sees education as a capital good that can increase the individual's value in the labor market. Research supporting this explanation of the operation of some educational systems indicates that few systems operate as ideal meritocracies (Krauze and Slomczynski, 1986).

In some ways, human capital theory can be seen as a functionalist interpretation of how the principle of institutions works in the case of educational systems. This is evident also in modernization theory (Inkeles and Smith, 1974), which states that formal education operates toward *functional integration* of persons into the system in accordance with the kinds of skill and literacy demands of that system. When a society values economic development, the kind of persons required to sustain the system and individuals in it is the *modern* person. What Daniel Bell (1973) calls a *postindustrial society*, Edmund King (1979) refers to as the *communication society* (a technological age), in which much of the labor force performs information functions. In subsistence agricultural societies, the transition to becoming modern requires the motivation and cooperation of all institutions in the society to develop the human capital required to conduct the activities of an economically developed or modern society.

The evidence, however, does not fully support this explanation of the association between education and economic development (modernization). Individuals from developing countries who receive a higher education become the elite in that system, but the availability of jobs for which they are trained is not necessarily functional for the system. The system or country is not prepared to accommodate these persons, or more accurately, their skills (status and role). Education does not affect the advanced productivity of the underdeveloped country (Brookover and Erickson, 1975). Data from other countries such as Ghana, Argentina, and Nigeria show that advanced training did not facilitate economic development (Foster, 1966). Therefore, the assumption that a country investing in education is contributing to its economic development is not necessarily true. Data also show that Third World countries, in contrast to industrial nations, are becoming increasingly deficient in school quality and per-pupil expenditure. The wealth of the country is the major determinant of this situation (Fuller, 1986).

Still other evidence suggests that in an economically advancing system, education plays more a part in perpetuating dominance than in meritocratically structuring its opportunites. Urban schools in developing nations are like Western schools, and these schools serve the elite (Mingat, 1986). In Nepal for example, the link between economic development and formal educational systems is not consensual (democratic). Almost all of Nepal's fifteen million population engage in subsistence agriculture; about 40 percent of the men and 9 percent of the women have attended primary school. Formal schooling is available only to an elite few and this pattern reproduces itself (Shrestha, 1986).

Last, some evidence suggests that patterns of domination are interspersed with an integrated consensus operation (agreement by the people) of the principle of institutions. Across societies in the global system is a growing standardization of the elementary school curriculum (Benavot, 1988).

Some research shows an association between education and economic development. The number of children in school in a given country is related to that country's level of economic development (Ballantine, 1989). Although global statistics show more than 500 million primary and secondary students in the world, the proportions vary according to economic indicators (ranging from 10 percent of children who should be in school in poor Asian countries to nearly 100 percent of children who attend school in Western countries) (Cowen, 1980).

Even stronger evidence of the relatedness of education and economic development is introduced by Francisco Ramirez and John Boli (1987), who argue that economic competition between nations has caused the incentive for nations to organize state-governed educational systems. Paul DiMaggio and Walter Powell (1983) interpret this as institutional isomorphism; their observation of the increased occurrence of national developments in education patterned after the European system suggests that education functions in an integrative way to advance national interests. The global similarity of educational systems is manifested in compulsory education policy, increased state funding and control, and mass education—equal educational opportunity for all with corresponding increases in enrollments. The similarities in educational systems may be due to the pressure of international competition and conflict, but they may also be due to the functional integration of the global system.[4]

Aligned with the view that the principle of institutions operates as a combination of patterns of domination interspersed with patterns of integration and consensus, *dependency* theory interprets education as a negative force in economic development. These theorists believe that educational institutions operate in a society in the context of that society's role in the global economy; formal education plays a relatively minor part in affecting economic development (Benavot, 1987). These scholars posit a global capitalist economic system characterized by inequalities both between *and* within nations. Third World nations are seen as constituting a peripheral component of the global system that continues to supply raw materials and cheap labor to the industrial centers. The system is dominated by Western school-educated elites who oversee profits through core nations and multinational corporations. These international *bourgeoisie* intensify inequality through reinforced dependency of Third World underdeveloped nations and inhibit their economic development.

Robert Arnove (1980) posits a version of dependency theory to explain how the principle of institutions operates in education around the world. He sees the peripheral, underdeveloped third-world countries as exploited because even though they get needed resources, they remain dominated by the developed countries. In other words, "domination" is not by consent of the people. For example, Arnove argues that a global curriculum is established by powerful organizations such as the World Bank and Unesco. Also, Arnove shows how American corporations benefit when higher education faculty in third-world countries become scholars through the support of American foundations and how the production of knowledge is monopolized by those industrialized countries with a small percent of the world's population.

William Morgan and J. Armer (1988) further explain the operation of the principle of institutions in their study of a world educational system. They ask whether Western education is providing the universalistic human-capital skills and credentials required in the modern-sector labor market. By studying education in Nigeria, Morgan and Armer conclude that it is still too early to predict the extent to which the Nigerian system is moving toward Western education standards as opposed to Islamic standards. Islamic knowledge, for example, makes provision for "cultural capital" (in Bourdieu's sense of the term) that creates opportunities in the modern labor market. The social structure of northern Nigeria may be more conducive to the Islamic model because the society is communal as opposed to that of advanced Western industrial societies. Based on this study, the acceptance of a world system is not inevitable and may be strongly influenced by local and regional needs.

Immanual Wallerstein (1964) proposes a *world systems perspective* of educational systems. He says a global ideology of progress (growth is good) is the underlying assumption of development of educational systems. This perspective challenges the claim that education is a positive force in economic development. The argument is aligned with dependency scholars' views and suggests that the global capitalist economy is a system characterized by structural inequalities both between and within nations.

Another perspective that explains how the principle of institutions operates in the case of education (with some similarity to dependency theory) is *reproduction* theory (Carnoy, 1982). Education is viewed as an institution that replicates the class structure of peripheral nations and colonial patterns of domination keep countries in oppressed and dependent conditions. The position of national elites is strengthened, and although economic growth occurs, the profits are distributed outside the country and the populace experiences little benefit.

Marxists (for example, Apple, 1979, 1982) contend that the cultural dominance of the capitalist class results in society's inundation with the symbolic forms of the capitalist social order—the values and language are specified by the elite. Education rewards students from various backgrounds differently so that middle-class students will fit into higher-status positions; the less advantaged students, marked by their speech and manners, will be fitted into blue-collar work. Evidence for this is inconclusive (Olneck and Bills, 1980). Conflict theorists such as Samuel Bowles and Herbert Gintis (1976) and Burris (1983) see schools as agencies that reproduce the existing social relations of production. They argue that the purpose of education in a capitalist society is not to select and train the brightest, but to perpetuate differences and legitimate them with so-called objective certificates of educational achievement. Randall Collins (1971, 1979) says that most occupations (except perhaps specialized professions like medicine and engineering) require few of the skills that schools teach and that the skills and knowledge necessary for job performance are obtained on the job. Employers, however, rely on educational credentials in hiring and promotion, not because of the technical skills they supposedly represent, but because the assumption is that the employee has been socialized into the values and norms of the dominant culture.

Clark Kerr (1979) theorizes that the principle of institutions, as it operates in education, takes on characteristic *production-oriented forms.* These forms more or less reflect how, and the degree to which, an elite is served in the system. The *pure pyramid* is linked with manpower planning, a universal base of literacy, and is topped by progressively smaller components of training for clerks and technicians, advanced technicians, scientists, scholars, and professionals. For example, in Russia, 90 percent of students are in technical colleges and the remaining 10 percent are in universities. The *truncated pyramid,* as seen in Japan, shows emphasis in primary and secondary schools on higher education. The *half pyramid,* for example, the educational systems of France and India, emphasizes training for the public civil service rather than for private industry and commerce. The *pyramid rising* alongside an older elite system, seen in England, occurs when the best universities (Oxford and Cambridge) enrolled students from the private boarding schools rather than from the public grammar schools. The *rounded-top, advanced-stage pyramid* indicates the existence of increasingly more occcupations that require increasingly more training.

These theories attempt to account for the influence of the principle of institutions in educational systems by arguing its role in the system as fostering economic development versus its role in the system (and in the global economy) to reproduce the status of elites. Available evidence helps determine the explanatory strength of these theories, and we see that educational systems *both* reproduce social class as well as provide students with opportunities for mobilizing on their merits.

Education's Interdependence with Other Institutions

Another approach to understanding how the principle of institutions operates in the case of education as an institution is to examine its *interdependence* with other institutions in the society. Other important institutions include the family, religion, and political economies.

Family and School Relations

The relationship between the family and the school has been interpreted in a wide variety of explanations. Some evidence suggests that the biggest predictor of school success (achievement) is the home—the early influence is crucial (Coleman et al, 1966). Supporting evidence of the importance of the family shows that children's educational aspirations and attainment benefit when parents are involved as definers of behavior, models of behavior, and as *partners* with teachers and with homework (Cohen, 1987; Baker and Stevenson, 1986; Epstein, 1987, 1988).

Other evidence indicates that in societies where the living standards are poor, the school compensates for poverty in the home (Passow, 1976). The relationship between the family and the school, according to Jeanne Ballantine (1989) changes when a society becomes modernized. For example, in some developing countries, formal education is not a viable option. Paulo Freire (1973) argues that educationally elite landowners dominate rural uneducated peasants in a cycle of poverty in which the poor do not think critically about their situation.

The interdependence between the family and education has been interpreted by Ralph Turner (1960) as the mechanism for upward mobility such that the family socioeconomic status affects the child's chances for education and eventual place in the educational system. In other words, the school reproduces the social class structure that the child brings to school. A *sponsored* form of mobility is characterized by elites selecting elites, thereby perpetuating their status roles. *Contest* mobility takes the individual's abilities into consideration; American schools, in contrast to British schools, are in this way more meritocratic.

Education and Religion

The institution of religion in a society legitimizes the existing social order; in other words, God says this is how things should be done (Berger, 1967). The degree to which religious ideas are used to legitimize practices characteristic of the other institutions varies. For example, in the United States, the relation of religion to education is expressed in the *separation of Church and State*. The First Amendment of the United States Constitution prohibits interference of religion in school concerns, and in this way fosters the freedom to worship. The teaching of evolution and the practice of saying prayers in school have been points of contention; group recitation of the Lord's Prayer, for example, has been ruled unconstitutional (Ballantine, 1989). Controversy has also come about over public funding for private religious schools. In Iran, fundamentalist Muslim schools support the status quo and reflect the leadership of Muslim religious leaders; in Northern Ireland, the Catholic parochial schools and the state schools, attended mostly by Protestants, protect and perpetuate a distinction between segments of the society. In Israel, Hebrew language and religious training provide unifying themes in an otherwise heterogeneous society.

Education and the Political Economy

Functionalists interpret the growth of schools as a response to the *economic* needs for an educated labor force: schools prepare people for occupations and occupations anticipate formal socialization into these roles. Conflict theorists also see schools as preparing people for the economic and occupational needs of the society, but they view the process as an attempt to stratify opportunity on a non-meritocratic basis that perpetuates an elite. Education in the United States is financed by local, state, and federal funds. The relative contribution of local funding is decreasing. Property taxes are the source of these monies and, of course, taxes vary between districts. Suburbs provide more tax money for better schools. About 43 percent of total school revenue derives from local funding sources, and state support is increasing its contribution (Adden and Augenblick, 1980). State funding of education has increased to 50 percent of the total funding (monies obtained from sales tax and personal income tax). More than forty states have state-wide sales taxes, which make up more than 30 percent of state revenues. Tax rates depend on the state. State monies come to local districts through four main methods: flat grants, foundation plans, power-equalizing plans, and weighted student plans (Orstein and Levine, 1985). The issue of using property taxes to help finance schools has led to many conflicts. The argument is about the fact that wealthier districts end up having better quality schools. The United States Supreme Court held that education is not a fundamental interest or right and rejected the case against property tax support (Brodinsky, 1979). Federal funding for education is affected by the nation's economic status. Federal compensatory programs are reduced when recession occurs. Urban schools suffer the most from these cutbacks. Proposals to enhance the funding of education have included private-sector support, lotteries, tuition tax credits, and vouchers. Much contention has arisen over vouchers, critics maintaining that families selecting a school of their choice would result in segregation of schools, a breakdown in the concept of mass public education.

The *political* institution also has a profound effect on education through its ideological stance and policy-making capacity. The governance of education both worldwide and in the United States concerns structural politics: Should children be provided with a comprehensive education or *tracked* into separate academic and vocational curricula? Should the administrative authority be centralized or decentralized? Also at issue are human capital politics that concern efforts to educate a certain proportion of the population (Garnier and Hage, 1991)[5]; cultural capital politics are conflicts over definitions of legitimate knowledge (the distribution of symbolic authority in the form of textbooks and curricula); and displacement politics are educational disputes that become avenues for other noneducational conflicts (Apple and Weis, 1986).

Passing and enforcing legislation related to school functioning are shown by the federal ruling in the 1954 *Brown* v. *Board of Education* case or the 1964 Civil Rights Act. Public Law 94–142, the Education for All Handicapped Children Act (1975), requires schools to mainstream handicapped children. This decision is a reflection of the degree to which the principle of institutions operates on the basis of consensus to represent the interests of the majority.

Legislative activities at the state level of reform have concerned a wide variety of issues, including: *administration* (training for school board members, changes in certification for administrators, competency testing and evaluation programs for administrators, staff development programs); *school districts* (curricular accountability, programs to lower class size, district reorganization); *early childhood* (prekindergarten programs, mandatory kindergarten, early intervention programs, smaller classes for early elementary years); *finance* (tax increases for reforms, funding innovations, teacher salary increases, merit pay); *teachers* (instructional time, teacher shortage, certification, preservice, competency testing, merit pay, staff development); *students* (programs for at-risk youth, curriculum change, competency testing, academic recognition, placement, home instruction); *postsecondary* (admission requirements, quality of undergraduate education efforts); and *general reform* (adult literacy, computers, governance changes, changes in length of school day and year, parental involvement, programs for special populations, guidance counseling) (Pipho, 1986). These regulations receive varied response in the community (Ballantine, 1989).

Ballantine remarks that the polity changes in response to pressures from private interest groups; for example, many persons agree that the basic curriculum, originally designed to socialize children to a standard of the dominant group, needs to be revised to accommodate intercultural programs supporting the diversity of groups in the American system.

According to Bill Williamson (1979), education reflects the position of the dominant group in a society, and the form and content of education across societies varies in relation to its political and ideological characteristics. For example, he presents a fourfold typology of societies: developed socialist (then USSR, East Germany, Hungary), underdeveloped socialist (China, Cuba, Tanzania), advanced capitalistic, (United States, West Germany, Britain), and dependent (Brazil, Nigeria, Ghana).

The principle of institutions is shown by the interdependence between institutions, the home, religious groups, the economy, and the legal system. The school replicates the inequalities children bring to school and sometimes mediates the negative effects of the home. In some societies, religion is separate from the state; in others, religious teaching is part of formal schooling. Federal, state, and local funding of education creates an unequal distribution of quality of education, sometimes at odds with the aim of providing equal opportunity. Government influences on educational policies come mostly through the restriction of funding; the court has made some decisions that have attempted to enhance the life chances of groups that might otherwise be treated unfairly.

The question is, how does the principle of institutions, and the theories explaining its operation in the context of education, illuminate the nature of the macrosociological determinants of our behavior? Specifically, what are the consequences of consensus and conflict in the operation of educational systems for the freedom of the individual in society?

Clearly educational systems as institutions are macrodeterminants (through the processes of selection and allocation) of the actions and interactions of society's members. Elements of both conflict and consensus appear in education but in varying proportions. Although conflict and consensus are both regulated by self-interest, conflict-based educational systems, in which education serves the interests of an elite few, in contrast to consensus-based systems, in which education represents the consensus of the group, tend to constrain individual actors in their opportunities to *choose* what they should *know* and *do*. Just how much does deliberate human action find a place in the context of educational decision-making?

Perhaps we hamper our understanding of the consequences of conflict and consensus in education when we do not consider more carefully the conceptualization of their dynamics. William Goode (1975), for example, contends that Marxist theory does not entirely ignore human decisions because it declares that history depends on the deliberate acts of people. Nevertheless, what people decide is rational action is also determined by economic necessity. (Chapters 10 and 11 discuss in further detail the issues of social determinism and individual freedom.)

Sociologists are in the habit of examining the nature of social forces as either conflict or functionlaist. Earl Babbie (1988) makes some comments that allow a broader conceptualization of conflict. Basically, he says, although it is possible to see all social life as a struggle for domination, just as we can see it as a process of structuring of social statuses, conflict also can be seen as the most fundamental aspect of social life. At the individual level, social conflict is simply *resistance* to whatever exists. More simply, conflict means being *different*, as a subtle form of the same thing, or to be *at variance* with something. Being different is basic to distinguishing ourselves from others and *the individual exists* by his or her resistance to everyone else; except for this conflict, there would be no separation.

In interpreting the evidence, using the traditional conceptualizations of conflict and consensus, we are not able to talk about what happens very well. Alternatively, we must consider other notions of conflict and consensus and in doing so we are able to better understand the nature of the operation of the principle of institutions. Perhaps a useful conceptual approach is one proposed by George Ritzer (1988). He as well as other social theorists acknowledge efforts by sociologists to reconcile structural–functionalist and conflict theories. The work of Lewis Coser (1956) and Joseph Himes (1966), for example, integrate the theories by giving attention to the functions of social conflict and with the equilibrating effect of conflict. For example, a teachers' union will conflict with the administration in its view of faculty salaries, but the resolution of the conflict is based on consensus about what is fair rather than on force. An enhanced understanding of the dynamics of conflict and consensus also depends on what Ritzer recommends as parallel work discussing the disequilibrating effects of order. Certain kinds of order or too much order can lead to disequilibrium in the social system; for example, totalitarian rulers, despite their emphasis on order, can destroy the stability of society.

The view of conflict as part of consensus as articulated by Coser and Himes is applied to education in the work of John Meyer (1980). Meyer would, at a general or macro level, view educational systems as constraining and powerful determinants of individual action, but he would interpet the trend toward global mass formal educational systems as evidence of order through consent. Individuals are coerced in their actions, at one level, but derive a sense of being individual and participatory subjects at another. Power becomes legitimized through consensus authority. For example, Meyer contends that education's macroinstitutional effects have been underestimated; education selects and allocates, but more importantly, legitimates. He proposes legitimation theory as a way of conceptualizing the relative contribution of conflict and consensus in the operation of educational institutions. Allocation theory is a limited special case of a more general institutional theory—legitimation theory—which treats education as both constructing or altering roles in society and authoritatively allocating personnel to these roles. He says that modern educational systems involve large-scale public classification systems that define new roles and statuses for both elites and members. Not only new types of persons but also new competencies are created and such legitimizing effects of education transcend the effects education may have on the individuals being processed by the schools. The legitimizing effects, Meyer notes, transform the behavior of people in society quite independent of their own educational experience. Mass education, he argues, is indicative of the societal effects of education and in societies with more mass education, both masses and elites should be found to perceive more common interests and ideas in the population and less conflict and diversity. Elites planning new regimes in such societies should be found to employ more strategies of control through mobilization rather than through traditional authoritarianism. He also contends that conventional allocation theory, while considering the institutional properties of educational systems, focuses mainly on the outcomes for the individuals being processed and that it tends to assume that education has no effect on the distribution of political, economic, and social positions in society.

Summary

This chapter has examined education sociologically by applying one of the major analytical conceptual tools of the field, the principle of institutions. Most fundamentally, education is an institution, the collective representation of the human predisposition to follow group rules by making provisions that sustain the well-being of the group and each member. In this case, education as an institution is viewed as expectations that guide the development of individuals to fit into the society, especially into occupational roles. Insight into the nature of the principle of institutions is gleaned by observing it from several perspectives as it operates as part of a global system of societies. In this light, the principle is seen as interdependent with education across societies in its function in a global system. Further understanding of the characteristic operation of the principle of institutions is obtained by viewing education within American society (in relation to other institutions) and globally (in relation to other educational systems). From this investigation, it appears that the principle of institutions operates to tell us what it means to be *educated*. Evidence supports those who argue that the institution, education, represents collective agreements to prepare persons in relation to the economic development aims of the system—elements of both coercion and consensus are attributes of the principle's operation. What is clear from our sociological understanding of education as an institution is the predominance of the patterned and *functionally* integrative nature of behavioral prescriptions toward global, societal, and individual levels of cooperation.

Vocabulary

conflict theory	Marxist theory
dependency theory	modernization theory
functionalist theory	principle of institutions
human capital theory	production-oriented forms
interinstitutional interdependence	reproduction theory
macrosociological	world systems perspective

Question

1. What kind of behaviors go on in schools that can be explained by the principle and theories of institutions?

References and Suggested Readings

Adden, A. and J. Augenblick. *School Finance Reform in the States: 1980.* Education Finance Center, Education Commission of the States, pp. 22–32.

Apple, M. *Education and Power: Reproduction and Contradiction in Education.* Boston: Routledge & Kegan Paul, 1982.

_____. *Ideology and Curriculum.* Boston: Routledge & Kegan Paul, 1979.

Apple, M. and L. Weis. "Seeing Education Relationally: The Stratification of Culture and People in the Sociology of School Knowledge." *Journal of Education,* (1986) Vol. 168, pp. 19–20.

Arnove, R. "Comparative Education and World-Systems Analysis." *Comparative Education Review,* (1980) 24:49.

Babbie, E. *The Sociological Spirit: Critical Essays in a Critical Science.* Belmont, CA: Wadsworth, 1988.

Baker, D. and D. Stevenson. "Mothers' Strategies for Children's School Achievement: Managing the Transition to High School." *Sociology of Education,* (1986) 59:156–66.

Ballantine, J. *The Sociology of Education: A Systematic Analysis.* Englewood Cliffs, NJ: Prentice-Hall, 1989.

Becker, G. *Human Capital: A Theoretical and Empirical Analysis with Special Reference to Education,* rev. ed. Chicago: University of Chicago Press, 1980.

Bell, D. *The Coming of the Post-Industrial Society: A Venture in Social Forecasting.* New York: Basic Books, 1973.

Benavot, A. "Education and Economic Growth in the Modern World System, 1913–1985." Paper presented at American Sociological Association annual meetings, Chicago, 1987.

Benavot, A., D. Kamens, S. Wong, Y. Cha, and J. Meyer. "World Culture and the Curricular Content of National Educational Systems, 1920–85." Paper presented at American Sociological Association; Atlanta, GA: August, 1988.

Bennett, K. and M. LeCompte. *How Schools Work: A Sociological Analysis of Education.* New York: Longman, 1990.

Berger, P. *The Sacred Canopy: Elements of a Sociological Theory of Religion.* Garden City, NY: Doubleday, 1967.

Bowles, S. and H. Gintis. *Schooling and Capitalist America.* New York: Basic Books, 1976.

Brodinsky, B. "Something Happened: Education in the Seventies." *Phi Delta Kappan,* (1979) 6:241.

Brookover, W. and E. Erickson. *Sociology of Education.* Homewood, IL: Dorsey Press, pp. 73–5, 1975.

Burris, V. "The Social and Political Consequences of Over-education." *American Sociological Review,* (1983) 48:454–67.

Carnoy, M. "Education for Alternative Development." *Comparative Education Review*, (1982) 26:160–77.

Cohen, J. "Parents as Educational Models and Definers." *Journal of Marriage and the Family*, (1987) 49:339–51.

Coleman, J. et al. *Equality of Educational Opportunity*. Washington, DC: United States Department of Education, 1966.

Collins, R. *The Credential Society*. New York: Academic Press, 1979.

———. "Functional and Conflict Theories of Educational Stratification." *American Sociological Review*, (1971) 36:1001–18.

Coser, L. *The Functions of Social Conflict*. New York: Free Press, 1956.

Cowen, R. "Comparative Education in Europe: A Note." *Comparative Education Review*, (1980) 24:98–108.

DiMaggio, P. and W. Powell. "The Iron Cage Revisited: Institutional Isomorphism and Collective Rationality in Organizational Fields." *American Sociological Review*, (1983) 4:147–60.

Epstein, J. "Toward a Theory of Family-School Connections: Teacher Practices and Parent Involvement Across the School Years." In Hurrelmann, K. and F. Kaufman, eds., *The Limits and Potential of School Intervention*. New York: De Gruyter/Aldine–Aldine, 1987.

Foster, P. "The Vocational School Fallacy in Development Planning." In Anderson, C. and M. Bowman, eds., *Educational and Economic Development*. Chicago: CASS, 1966.

Freire, P. *Education for Critical Consciousness*. New York: Herder & Herder, 1973.

Fuller, B. "Is Primary School Quality Eroding the Third World?" *Comparative Education Review*, (1986) 30(4):491–508.

Garnier, M. and J. Hage. "Class, Gender, and School Expansion in France: A Four-Systems Comparison." *Sociology of Education*, (1991) 64:229–50.

Goode, W. "Homan's and Merton's Structural Approach." In Peter Blau, ed. *Approaches to the Study of Social Structure*. New York: Free Press, 1975, pp. 66–75.

Himes, J. "The Functions of Racial Conflict." *Social Forces*, (1966) 45:1–10.

Inkeles, A. and D. Smith. *Becoming Modern: Individual Change in Six Developing Countries*. Cambridge, MA: Harvard University Press, 1974.

Kerr, C. "Five Strategies for Education and Their Major Variants." *Comparative Education Review*, (1979) 23:171–82.

King, E. *Other Schools and Ours: Comparative Studies for Today*, 5th ed. London: Holt, Rinehart & Winston, 1979.

Krauze, T. and K. Slomczynski. "How Far to Meritocracy? Empirical Tests of a Controversial Thesis." *Social Forces*, 63:623–42.

Meyer, J. "The Effects of Education as an Institution." *American Journal of Sociology*, (1980) 83:1

Mingat, A. and J. Tan. "Who Profits from the Public Funding of Education: A Comparison of World Regions." *Comparative Education Review*, (1986) 30:260–70.

Morgan, W. and J.M. Armor. "Islamic and Western Educational Accommodation in a West African Society: A Cohort-Comparison Analysis." *American Sociological Review*, (1988) 53(4):634–39.

Olneck, M. and D. Bills. "What Makes Sammy Run? An Empirical Assessment of the Bowles-Gintis Correspondence Theory." *American Journal of Education*, (1980) 89:27–61.

Orstein, A. and D. Levine. *Foundations of Education*, 3rd Ed. Boston: Houghton Mifflin, 1985.

Passow, A., et al. *The National Case Study: An Empirical Comparative Study of Twenty-One Educational Systems.* New York: Wiley, 1976.

Pipho, C. "States Move Reform Closer to Reality." *Phi Delta Kappan*, December 1986, pp. K1–K8.

Ramirez, F. "Institutions and Interests: A Critical Comment on Walters, McCammon, and James." *Sociology of Education*, (1990) 63:142–44.

Ramirez, F. and J. Boli. "The Political Construction of Mass Schooling: European Origins and Worldwide Institutionalization." *Sociology of Education*, (1987) 60:2–17.

Ritzer, G. *Sociological Theory*, 2nd Ed. New York: Knopf, 1988.

Shavit, Y. and V. Kraus. "Educational Transitions in Israel: A Test of the Industrialization and Credentialism Hypotheses." *Sociology of Education*, (1990) 63:133–41.

Shrestha, G. et al. "Determinants of Educational Participation in Rural Nepal." *Comparative Education Review*, (1986) 30:508–22.

Turner, R. "Personality in Society: Social Psychology's Contribution to Sociology." *Social Psychology Quarterly*, (1988) 51(1)1–10.

———. "Sponsored and Contest Mobility." *American Sociological Review*, (1960) 25:855–67.

Wallerstein, I. *The Modern World System.* New York: Academic Press, 1974.

Williamson, B. *Education, Social Structure and Development.* London: Macmillan, 1979, pp. 36–46.

Notes

[1]Ralph Turner, in his article "Personality in Society: Social Psychology's Contribution to Sociology" (*Social Psychology Quarterly*, (1988) 51(1)1–10), refers to this priority of effects when he apologizes for the one-sided neglect of individuals' effects on society; an understanding of socialization should help us contribute to sociology in assessing the effect of individuals on the structure and processes of society.

[2]Sociologists often study other institutions, such as sports and science, not discussed here.

[3]Theories explain the nature of principles, particularly as to their stratification characteristics. Therefore the principle of stratification operates alongside (in conjunction with) all other principles and is shown by discussion of the theoretical interpretation of the nature of other principles.

[4]For a careful case study presentation of four educational systems—British, Russian, Chinese, and Ghanaian—their similarities and differences, historical background, national goals for the educational system, structural features of education, number of years of schooling and curriculum, and equality of opportunity, see Ballantine (1989).

[5]Maurice A. Garnier and Jerald Hage (from "Class, Gender, and School Expansion in France: A Four-Systems Comparison," *Sociology of Education*, 1991) investigated material incentives and institutionalized values as the basis of educational expansion in four secondary school systems in France from 1881 to 1975. They found class more important than gender in determining expansion because state policies emphasized or valued class more than gender in determining "supply." State educational policy reinforces class differences because they affect the educational decisions of males and females who attend either mass or elite systems.

CHAPTER
6

Socialization

*Becoming Human by Learning
Society's Conventions*

John Denver wrote a folk song that contains the lyric, *He learned to be a man that way*. What does the photograph above convey about how we learn to be in the world? Imagine the boys and girls in the photo above are indistinguishably alike except for anatomical differences. They think alike, act alike, and feel alike. Both sexes are equally demure, aggressive, affectionate, generous, honest, nurturant, rational, instrumental, and self-controlled. Both feel equally comfortable wearing nail polish, earrings, and playing with dolls. They both like school. Is it possible to be human without other people? Socialization concerns less what we are as humans than what we leave out in the process of becoming human and who decides.

Outline

W e know that coded into the biological make-up of the salmon is a template for its destiny: to swim for miles upstream to the spawning grounds, to lay its eggs, and then to die from exhaustion. In Hakkado, Japan, the Red Crown crane mates for life according to what its genes dictate. African weaver ants (*Oecophylla longinoda*) have distinctive places in the caste system of their colony; for example, the minor workers attend eggs and small larvae, the task to which they are specialized (Oster and Wilson, 1978). But how do we explain why a young American-Asian undergraduate sits down on the front lawn of his parents' house and kills himself by cutting open his abdomen after being denied admission to medical school? For humans, the parameters of destiny are predictable in a different way; humans have the freedom to develop creative ways for cooperation, and in turn, are determined by their own instructions.[1] Humans are predestined by their genetic structure not simply to follow the rules encoded in their genes, but to make rules for living and then follow them. The human urge toward self-preservation is manifested as a predisposition or orientation to develop and conform to group rules as a mechanism to ensure the survival of each individual member of the group. Our template universally ordains participation in the activity of *socialization* (the learning of the values, knowlege, and skills of the group into which one is born [that is, one's family and society]) so that we learn not merely what other people believe, but we come to *prefer* what they believe.

The Principle of Socialization

To repeat, *socialization* is perhaps the most profound of the principles of sociology because for most living organisms, as far as we know, the world inside determines how they respond to the world outside. But for human beings, the world outside comes inside. That is, the values of the group, *society*, become the preference of the individual. In all human societies, much time is spent in getting the group's values to become part of the inner needs (personalities) of individuals. That is why some people can't wait to have an evening meal of dog meat, while the thought of a dog-meat dinner for others would make them nauseated. It is not through the genes, but what one is taught to want, that one comes to want. Individuals are not their own persons because they have an *essential sociality*; they are *constrained* in their behavior in a number of ways by the rules of the group of which they are members. That is, the individual's urge toward self-preservation is manifested in the tendency to engage in rule-making and rule-following behavior. Group rules take on a life of their own (*society*) and thereby ensure the life of each member of the group when the shared prescriptions on how to interact become translated into the individual's preferences. Humans, through consensus or shared beliefs, systematically, in patterned forms, either make rules or follow them or both. The universality of the essential sociality of the human organism is expressed as six rule-making and conforming activities, the *principles of sociology*—lawlike operations of the more generic properties of social phenomena (the social realm).[2]

Socialization is the major social principle because it is a process whereby the human being actually becomes human via his or her essential sociality.[3] Humans cannot exist apart from the group (society, others). The law-like process of becoming a social being through the principle of socialization, entails three dynamics: *externalization, objectivation,* and *internalization.* These dynamics represent the dialectical relationship between the individual and the group such that the human is a product of society, yet no social reality exists apart from the human. Society (the group) is thus a dialectic phenomenon in that it is a human product that continuously acts back upon its producer (Berger, 1967). *Externalization* is the outpouring of the physical and mental activity of a person. In this way, society is a human product. *Objectivation* is the attainment by the products of physical and mental activity of a reality that confronts its original producers as a facticity (condition of fact) other to and external to themselves. Society becomes a reality *sui generis. Internalization* is the reappropriation by persons of this same reality, transforming it once again from structures of the objective world into structures of the subjective consciousness. The human is, at this point, a product of society.[4]

Becoming Human through Externalization

Externalization concerns understanding human behavior by knowing that the human being cannot be understood as somehow resting within itself in some closed sphere of interiority, and then setting out to express itself in the world (Berger, 1967). In other words, the biological constitution of *Homo sapiens* occupies a unique place in the animal kingdom. This peculiarity, Peter Berger states, manifests itself such that, contrasted to other higher mammals which are born as essentially completed organisms, humans are unfinished at birth. The process of finishing human development, which has already taken place in the fetal stage in other higher mammals, occurs in humans during the first year after birth. The essential sociality, or social nature of humans, is the biological predisposition to becoming human by developing a *personality. Personality,* in this sense, is a mechanism that creates and records in the individual the rules of the group of which one is a member. This *world-building* activity is a direct consequence of the human biological constitution and manifests itself as the human's ongoing efforts to establish a relationship with the world because he or she has no built-in relationship to it. The same process of humans producing their own instructions for how to relate to people and things in their environment allows for humans to produce—to create—themselves. This package of instructions produced by humans as shared rules for living constitutes what we refer to as *society.*

Sociologists use the metaphor *structure* when they analyze human societies. A society has social structure much like a building, for example, consists of floors, walls, a roof, an entrance, and other parts that fit together in a patterned way; each part of the building is related to other parts in a systematic fashion, all playing a part in allowing the building to stand. In a social system, the structure refers to the specified interrelationships between its component parts.

The components of social structure are *values* and *norms* in the form of *statuses* and *roles.* These instructions can be deduced in a specific manner from the inherent nature of humars to basic values orientations to act socially (to live cooperatively through rule-making and rule-following). Individuals are representations of society as the musician is representative of the symphony. Society is the score for coordinated, cooperative living (participation) and is represented in the *ego* or *personality* of the individual through such vehicles as language, cognition, memory, and emotion. Personality is the apparatus that permits the replication of society in each individual. Thus society and all its forms are human meanings (consciousness) externalized in human activity. For this reason the sociologist should not treat society solely, reductively, or independently of the human enterprise that originally produced it.

Becoming Human through Objectivation

To speak of externalization is to imply that the results is a reality perceived as separate from the producer. Society derives from humans, but also comes to confront them as a condition of fact (*sui generis*) outside of themselves—this is *objectivation*. The humanly produced world becomes something "out there." In this way, it becomes capable of resisting the desires of its producer. Society is rooted in individual, subjective consciousness, but once formed, it cannot be reabsorbed into consciousness at will. The humanly produced world has attained the character of objective reality. For example, humans take on a language that shapes their thinking and experience of the world. This objectivity of society is a shared, coercive fact; it encompasses collectively produced and collectively recognized meanings (shared intersubjectivity). Society, as a social phenomenon, cannot be located by introspection; the individual must go outside himself or herself to understand it, to locate it. Society as an object exists in its own right, and it is confronted as an object by individuals. Its objective attributes comprise its structure. This system of shared behavioral directions are in the form of statuses and roles. Values and norms are the building blocks of statuses and roles, or the positions deemed important (good) and how people should behave in these positions.

Becoming Human through Internalization

When social structure in the form of statuses and roles (specific expressions of values and norms) is internalized in the individual's subjective consciousness, the various elements of the objectivated world are sensed as internal or as part of one's nature. Each new generation learns the behavioral prescriptions, and a highly successful socialization results in a high degree of objective and subjective symmetry.

It must be emphasized that the individual's urge toward self-preservation is manifested in the essential sociality or tendency of the person to engage in collective rule-making and rule-following. The principle of socialization refers to the universal inclination to, and the process of, sociality by means of the threefold process designed to order the experience of human beings. This reciprocal or dialectical activity is that we produce the society that produces us. Because humans are biologically denied ordering mechanisms, they are compelled to impose their own order upon experience. The presupposition is referred to as *essential sociality* (it and the collective character of this ordering activity are expressed as the *principles of sociology*). This predisposition is in the biological constitution of *Homo sapiens*. To examine more fully how being human is possible only through the influence of others, let's consider in more detail some of the individual mechanisms required by the activities of externalization, objectivation, and internalization.

Language, Cognition, and Emotion

Our capacity for *language*, to assign meaning to things in the form of symbols (something that represents something else), gives the individual the capacity for survival in the group. Symbols give us the ability to represent feelings, others, and things to ourselves and to other people. Words represent whatever we choose them to represent. If we agree on what they mean, we can share our experience about how to relate to people and things. Words are used in a system of sentences known as language, which allows us to further elaborate meanings about what aspects of the perceived world are important and how to relate to them. Information on how to respond in a given situation is stored in our brains rather than in our genes. For example, a fish will die out of water, but humans can act like fish by devising scuba gear. Humans are not bound by their biology; they can create many options for getting around in the world. They are the most *adaptive* creatures. It is through the use of language that humans are flexible in how they respond to their environment. In fact, humans respond not to the world per se, but to the meanings they give to it. Birds salvage the lives of their offspring at the expense of their own, but they do this according to genetic dictates. Humans are the only creatures that can transcend biological dictates. Other organisms are governed by the instinctual or biological rule of self-preservation; humans can, through language, define dying as meaningful and give up life for the sake of others.

However, while language can expand what humans can do, it also directs our attention to certain aspects of experience to the neglect of others. Language reflects what is societally important to a group of people. For example, the word *policeman* reflects an experience (behavioral repertoire, role) that for decades was typically relegated to males to the exclusion of females.

Cognition includes a number of abilities such as perceiving, remembering, reasoning, calculating, and believing. These abilities develop in stages (Piaget, 1950, 1954). Numerous other theorists explain the dynamics of social learning.[5]

Emotion, or the affective domain, parallels the development of cognition through a process of learning (Hochschild, 1979; Kagan, 1984; Kemper, 1987). The variety of feelings emerges in a sequence, with each new emotion being built on the one preceding. The content of emotions—when to feel what and how it will be expressed—is arbitrary. In the first stage of life, the emotions consist of reflexive responses such as pleasure, disgust, distress, surprise, curiosity, joy, anger, fear, and sadness. By two years of age, the child can be tender and affectionate.

By five, the child senses others as separate and can perceive how others judge them. Confidence, insecurity, pride, humility, jealousy, envy, sympathy, and empathy develop. The capacity for abstract thought permits the generalization of feeling to whole categories of people such as the wealthy or the homeless.

Values and Norms

Children must learn both the right actions and the right emotions when they acquire any social-role behavior (for example, how to behave in school), for they learn it as a whole unit. These aspects of social learning are not merely something children must do in order to survive; they are needed for society to survive. Therefore, what children learn is related to the larger social structure in the form of values and norms, statuses and roles. How do we know how people will act in a given situation? If humans do not all have the same biological instructions that tell them to stop at a red light, how can we predict whether people will stop at a red light? Behavioral expectations become encoded in language and are shared by a group of people. We then assume that others in our group are following the same guidelines for behavior that we are. The rules for living that we refer to as society take two fundamental forms, *values* and *norms*. Values are ideas about what is *good, right,* and *just*, which usually refer to how we evaluate people, objects, and events as to their worth, merit, beauty, and morality. The "right of the individual" is a prominent value in the United States, but it means nothing until we (society as embodied in the United States Constitution and Bill of Rights) define it behaviorally. It is a general idea that has no meaning until we specify the *norms*, or behavioral definition that reflects the value. In the United States the right of the individual means not cutting in front of people when in line at the bank; it means not standing too close to the person with whom you are talking; it means not flatulating in public, or not taking the life of another person, or parents not having sexual relations with their children. *Values* and *norms* are the basic building blocks of social structure in that they are the components of the more specific components, *statuses* and *roles*. The right of the individual is a societal value that becomes expressed through statuses and roles.

Statuses, Roles, and the Formation of Self

The mapping of a person's behavior through social rules takes the more general forms of values and norms. and more specifically, takes the form of statuses and roles. (Recall from Chapter 1 that these rules are interrelated and comprise the structure of a system or society.). *Status* refers to a position that a person holds in the group (society) and *role* refers to the set of norms (behavioral expectations) specific to the status. The *self* is an awareness about one's competence in the roles; it is an abstraction that we have about our characteristics and capacities. Each of us has the sense of being a distinct unit or locus of experience. How we esteem ourselves depends upon how we measure up to societal standards and group norms once these standards are incorporated into our personal expectations for ourselves.

More specifically, we know how to act toward others, what to expect from them (and they from us), by locating their position or status. Student, professor, sister, brother, parent, or neighbor are statuses valued by society for the maintenance of itself and its individual members. The position or status which we hold has a corresponding role or set of behavioral expectations which define the status. We retain these behavioral expectations or roles in our our minds so that we are prepared to act in appropriate ways depending upon what status we are occupying. Roles allow us to channel our propensities and experiences. We order our experiences by fitting the world into these mental categories. For example, a male gynecologist is expected to withhold any sexual feelings for his patients. Seeing a male student's name on the roster, a teacher would be surprised to look up and find that the student wears red lipstick and long, polished nails. A new status can be gained or a current one lost, or at least perceived as lost. For example, a woman can derive her sense of competence from caring for her family. However, if she loses her husband through divorce and her children when they leave home, even though she remains a mother in society's eyes, she may essentially lose her sense of human competence or sense of self-worth. Sometimes we expect to occupy a certain status and when we fail to do so, the sense of self is threatened. For example, many women who have not had children by the time they reach the last phases of the child-bearing years report feeling incomplete and not fully women. The son whose father wants him to be a lawyer but whose grades will not permit his entrance into law school, or the daughter with a big nose and big breasts whose parents want her to be a model also feel a diminished sense of self-worth.

Roles restrict behavior. Take, for example, sex roles: women are expected to be nurturing, emotional, delicate, whereas men are expected to be instrumental, insensitive, and fearless. Our sense of self is developed through this limited grid of permissible behaviors. Society legitimizes certain kinds of feelings and behaviors and the conditions under which they should be felt; these standards shape our basic, amorphous human predisposition into socially acceptable attributes. For example, a male surgeon does not suppress emotion while doing surgery, but simply has not been taught to feel emotion in the operating room (no association exists). The late eighteenth century philosopher Jean-Jacques Rousseau writes in *Emile* that women are quite content to embroider while men are only content with formal and sophisticated knowledge.

Social scientists agree that without other people, becoming a fully functioning human being is virtually impossible. We are not born human, but rather become human through our relations with other people. We need a set of rules to direct what is essentially an amorphous biological predisposition to become human. Even more provocative is the fact that we do not make the rules; they already exist as shared agreements by those who are in the world before us. We call these rules *social structure* because they are a characteristic and interrelated part of the whole group (society); they result in patterned and predictable human behaviors that are integrated functionally into the system. Society, therefore, is not the aggregate of individuals, but rather society, in a sense, imprints itself on individuals. Personality, or the perception of a self, is the individual representation (Durkheim, 1956) of society. Furthermore, the sense of being a self develops from our competence at being the way society prescribes. As Vivian Gornick puts it in an introduction to Erving Goffman's *Gender Advertisements* (1976), we come to perceive as natural what is really unnatural. In this process of becoming human, we should ask not what we are as much as what we are not. Society refers, then, to a set of rules for experiencing the world—thinking, feeling, and acting—that we share with other members of our group. You are, right now, able to make sense of the words you read because we agree on their meaning. When I say the word nose-picking, it triggers a mental picture and an emotional response. The behavior, nose-picking, and how we should feel about it are part of our culture. How we feel comfortable being in the world seems as "natural" (the only reality we know) to us as water is to fish; it is impossible to be aware because we cannot separate ourselves from it long enough to examine it. Until the world becomes a "strange" place to us through sociological insight, it is an "ordinary" place. For example, kissing, a natural form of expressing affection for Americans, is experienced as unnatural for persons of other cultures. As another example, American males typically view themselves as having uncontrollable sexual urges that they cannot regulate, leaving all the control over the sexual encounter to the female. Thus, our predecessors make society, which in turn makes many statuses and roles available to us, and we become human selves who make society. This is the principle of socialization.

Major Issues of Socialization in Education: Curriculum and Pedagogy

The principle of socialization operates in all human societies as the transmission of the knowledge, skills, and beliefs required for survival and becoming a human being. This becoming, or learning, we sometimes refer to as *education*. Emile Durkheim says it well:

> Education is the influence exercised by adult generations on those that are not yet ready for social life. Its object is to arouse and to develop in the child a certain number of physical, intellectual and moral states which are demanded of him by both the political society as a whole and the special milieu for which he is specifically destined . . .
> (Durkheim, 1956.)

The principle of socialization operates universally in all human societies, but the nature of its operation, as it is articulated in theoretical and empirical work, is not fully understood. Disagreements about how socialization takes place can be investigated in the context of schooling: *what is taught (content), when,* and *how (form)*. Is society merely reproduced in each new generation; does society change its knowledge prescriptions?

Logical (theoretical) ideas about how the principle of socialization works have been tested by an assortment of research studies. We can infer from these observations some sociological explanations and we can deduce the conditions under which socialization takes place. The following sections sometime present theory as a broad generalization that lacks specific prediction; sometimes theory is applied to empirical findings only in a post hoc manner; and sometimes specific cases rather than comprehensive reviews of the literature on a topic are presented. Regardless, the intent here is to encourage a more integrated sociological understanding of school behavior. Explanations of socialization range from those that see the individual as mostly the passive product of society to those that see individuals as active participants in structuring their wants and dislikes.

Investigations of Curriculum and Pedagogy

What Gets Taught, and How

The utility of the principle of socialization and theories explaining it for understanding school behavior is in its application to issues of the school curriculum. From a sociological angle, we are interested in the school curriculum as it concerns the construction in the child of a self-identity (by anticipation of the statuses and roles provided by the society) and the fostering of his or her competence in these prescribed behavioral situations.

The formal transmission of knowledge (schooling) deemed important for survival in the group, in any society, promotes the standardization and homogenization of the children's socialization process and knowledge base. It does so by guiding the development of children's identities, which is accomplished not only by the school's formal curriculum but also via an informal curriculum (the *hidden curriculum*), for example, peer groups and the media. Curriculum issues concern what gets taught, and under what conditions the teaching takes place to ensure optimal learning, with special attention given to whose interests are served in these processes.

Active and Passive Explanations

To account, then, for the school's behavior as an agency of socialization, we must explain how socialization operates in the case of the school curriculum. The available theoretical interpretations of how the principle of socialization operates in schools concerning what gets taught and the factors affecting optimal learning can be dichotomized into passive and active theories of socialization (Robinson, 1981).

The passive theories are those of functionalism as espoused by Durkheim, Parsons, Merton, Dreeben, and others. The active theories include:

- Conflict theory as set forth by Marx, 1955; Simmel, 1955; Coser, 1956; Dahrendorf, 1959;

- Reproduction theory as presented by Carnoy, 1972; Persell, 1977; Bowles and Gintis, 1976; Boudon, 1974; Bernstein, 1977; Bourdieu and Passeron, 1977; Karabel and Halsey, 1977, Anyon, 1988; Apple, 1988;

- Interpretive theory as articulated by Mead, 1961; Schutz, 1967; Blumer, 1969; Cicourel, 1964, Garfinkel, 1967; Berger and Luckmann, 1967;
- The critical (Frankfurt) school of thought as proclaimed by Gramsci, Freiri, Giroux, and Apple.[6]

Functionalism offers one explanation of how socialization operates. Central to functionalism is the view that consensus about what counts as knowledge is required for keeping the system balanced; when conflict over what is valued occurs, adjustments are made toward regaining consensus. It presents a benign, unquestioning view of the social system and accepts existing structures as appropriate. Functionalists see the school as a means of reinforcing the mainstream social order. An educational system is a structure that carries out the function of transmitting knowledge to each new generation. The primary manifest function of schooling is to prepare the child for the adult world (Parsons, 1959). It does so in the context of contemporary education in the United States by fostering student acquisition of basic skills in reading, mathematics, the natural and social sciences, and analytical skills. A second function of the school is selection and allocation, or the preparation of students for later work roles. In addition, the attitudes and behavior that schools foster via the hidden curriculum include cooperation, conformity to authority, punctuality, gender appropriate attitudes, neatness, task orientation, care of property, and allegiance to the team (Bennett and LeCompte, 1990).

A competing theoretical perspective, *conflict* theory, finds the functionalist approach inadequate to explain the dynamics of the school. Conflict theory, an active theory, emphasizes that inequality of property or resource distribution is the major source of conflict in society and is reflected in schools. These theorists, especially those aligned with reproduction theory, view schools as socializing institutions that reproduce both the values and ideologies of the dominant social groups (Carnoy, 1972; Persell, 1977; Bowles and Gintis, 1976; Boudon, 1974; Carnoy and Levin, 1985). The work of Max Weber (1958) is also in the conflict tradition because it focuses on the conflicting interests of groups and their influence on educational systems. Weber would interpret the principle of socialization as it operates in schools as a struggle for domination between status groups which vary in property ownership, prestige, wealth, and power. Schooling is seen as contributing to the production of a disciplined labor force for political and other arenas of control (social institutions) and exploitation by the elite. In contemporary society, the dominant status group mobilizes the authority of rational-expert leadership. Schools serve to maintain and reproduce the class structure within the society through preparation for stratified roles in the work force, through rewards for use of dominant language and cultural capital, and through state regulation over most aspects of school life. In this view they differ very little from the functionalists; they vary, however, in that rather than accept the status quo as normal and natural, they are discontent with the inequalities that reproduction perpetuates.

These explanations of the principle of socialization are useful for analyzing curricular issues in schools, namely, which curriculum, and how it is transmitted.

Empirical evidence on *what* consitutes the curriculum and *why* is available concerning many school issues; among these are textbook content, publishing, and adoption–censorship, drug and sex education, creationism versus evolution, and liberal arts versus practical college programs. Concerns over *how* or under what conditions knowledge should be transmitted to be effective are reflected in numerous, wide-ranging studies on

- When knowledge should be transmitted to be effective;
- The media and peers as agents of socialization;
- School effects, such as private versus public schooling;
- One-parent families and families with working mothers;
- Cooperative learning, ability grouping, and vocational tracking;
- The parent-teacher connection.

Some of these topics are treated in the chapter on stratification (Chapter 7) because these behavioral prescriptions have outcomes for the ranking of individuals according to wealth, power, and prestige. As discussed in this text, the topics are amenable to investigations of the principle of socialization, a specialized case of the principle of organization, in which human arrangements for interaction with others transmit the values and norms of the system.

Research Support for Active and Passive Explanations

What Gets Taught

The Core Curriculum   Three interrelated questions form something that is at once phenomenon and issue: what ultimately counts as knowledge, what is the explicit and formal curriculum, and who mandates that curriculum? Again, from the different camps, the theorists differ in their explanations on these three crucial questions.

Functionalists, for example, see the occurrence of a *core curriculum* as a reflection of society's consensus about which knowledge is important. Disputes over what is important knowledge are interpreted as attempts to reach consensus about what is important knowledge. For example, national concern over the mediocrity of educational foundations in the United States (Bell, 1983) led to reflection over what every child in the United States should know. E. Hirsch (1987) argues that the knowledge core has deteriorated. Knowledge facilitating literacy and basic skills in reading and mathematics is seemingly consensually (democratically) valued in United States culture. During the midtwentieth century, concerns about consensus arose over whether school curricula should portray the United States as a white-dominated society in which immigrants are expected to assimilate completely, or a multicultural society in which accommodation to differences is celebrated. The past several decades have witnessed a variety of adaptations of curricula, each reflecting what could be viewed as attempts to arrive at a new consensus. Recent concern over the lack of knowledge possessed by high school students (Ravitch and Finn, 1987; Bloom, 1987; Bennett, 1988) has been accompanied by a neoconservative movement espousing a core curriculum that would provide the same basic liberal arts education to all students. Former United States Secretary of Education E. William Bennett (1988) proposes a standard high school curriculum, a plan which relies primarily on an Anglo-Euro-American literary and educational tradition. It requires four years of literature, three years each of Anglo-Euro-American history and democracy, science (astronomy, geology, biology, chemistry, physics) and mathematics (algebra, geometry, trigonometry, statistics, calculus), two years each of foreign language and physical education and one year of art and music history. This proposal by Secretary Bennett has been criticized as catering to only the college preparatory segment of the high school student population, thereby ignoring the needs of a varied student body.

Unlike the functionalists, who interpret evidence of a standardized core curriculum as confirmation of consensus among society's members, interpretive and critical theorists view the principle of socialization in the case of the school curriculum as part of a sociology of knowledge and sociology of the curriculum approach (Berger and Luckmann, 1967). This approach assumes that knowledge is power and that various types of knowledge are provided or withheld according to one's place in the social structure. Because of their position in society, those in power are more able to use their influence to advocate the inclusion of certain kinds of knowledge in the schools. This approach (sometimes referred to as the *new sociology of education* [Giroux, 1983; Young, 1971]) emphasizes how different kinds of knowledge are provided for different groups of students. In contrast, the functionalist approach assumes the existence of a given body of knowledge that is objective and free from bias. In other words, knowledge is unbiased like neutral facts (Giroux, 1983).

Educational Productivity   Support for both the functionalist and conflict interpretations of curriculum content is found in a large body of research that indirectly indicates what counts as important knowledge through its definitions of *educational productivity*. What is considered to be academic productivity is measured by a uniform standard of performance such as standardized test scores in reading and mathematics. This knowledge standard can be seen as a shared agreement or one imposed by an elite and powerful few. In the United States two national achievement tests are given to college-bound high school students: the American College Test (ACT) and the Scholastic Aptitude Test (SAT). In New York City, beginning in the third grade, children are administered two nationally normed achievement tests: the Degree of Reading Power (DRP) and the Metropolitan Achievement Test (MAT).

Maureen Hallinan (1985) comments that consensus theory is implicit in the report of the National Commission on Excellence in Education, which criticizes the schools for not challenging students to attain their *intellectual potential* in order to make the greatest possible contribution to society. Potential is defined in studies on *educational productivity* that examine the factors that affect the academic productivity of students and its effects on their future educational and occupational attainments. Underlying these concerns is the belief that schools should equalize opportunities for learning and attainment for all students based on a uniform standard of performance. Research in this functionalist tradition is reflected in studies on *school effects* (the relationship between school characteristics and student outcomes) and *status attainment studies*. (This research is discussed in Chapter 7.)

Textbook Adoptions Theoretical explanation of how the principle of socialization operates in the case of the school curriculum has been applied to the issue of *textbook adoption*. One useful model of reproduction theory, according to Kathleen Bennett and Margaret LeCompte (1990), is the *hegemonic state reproduction model*. The term *hegemony* refers to a societal consensus or world view that is diffused by agencies of ideological control and socialization into every area of daily life. State and federal agencies play key roles in the production and dissemination of knowledge because they determine the curriculum as well as the ways in which that curriculum is presented in the schools. States require that school districts comply with a standard curriculum and some states require that districts select textbooks from state textbook adoption lists. Teachers are required by state law to teach the skills and concepts established in the curriculum; some states require that they must use the approved list when selecting their texts. Schools therefore reflect the ideology underlying the state agencies that regulate the schooling process. For example, if state officials have mandated that sex education, AIDS education, and driver education be taught in schools, districts must comply with those regulations. The weakness of this explanation is that the state agencies may reflect a consensus of societal values.

The Kanawha debate serves as empirical evidence about curriculum decision-making dynamics in protest over the *content of textbooks* used in public schools. Protests concerning textbook content lends itself to an interpretation of the principle of socialization that is not straightforward. Rather, this data suggests that both conflict and consensus are part of the dynamics. The Kanawha County textbook controversy is an issue over who controls the education of the young—the "moral orders which provide life meaning" (Page and Clelland, 1978). The resolution to the conflict was a compromise that resulted in alternative curriculum and materials within schools (Ballantine, 1989).

Other illustrations of issues over the school curriculum in the case of textbook publishing, adoption, and content lend more credibility to the theoretical interpretation that conflict and power is the basis of *what counts* as opposed to consensus. Since functionalists argue that schools transmit knowledge necessary for successful performance in the adult world (Parsons, 1959; Dreeben, 1968), and that children learn that this knowledge is deemed equally important and available to all, then we would expect that differences in material used by teachers and schools would reflect only differences in abilities. But further evidence suggests that the content of textbooks reflects consensus over what is important for society. For example, major *textbook publishers* determine what kinds of books are produced. Coverage of topics such as evolution and human reproduction are given attention by publishers when the promise of a market is enhanced by major adoptions by boards of education. The content varies sometimes, for the wrong reasons; while adoptions by boards of education indicate some consensus, differences are apparent at the regional level. Consensus and domination as dynamics explaining the operation of the principle of socialization in school curriculum content are indicated in content analyses of textbooks, which are conducted to investigate possible differences in political and gender socialization and in socialization into science. For example, Charles Harrington (1980) conducted research for the Fleischmann Commission and found that children in working-class districts were taught to be *subjects* while those in middle-class districts were taught to anticipate roles as *participants*. Lynn Mulkey (1985) found the content of science texts to be uniform across middle-class and working-class school districts. Differences in the depiction of male and female behavior have been examined in various content analyses (for example, Weitzman, 1979). Socialization practices that result in differential life outcomes along the lines of wealth, power, and prestige are evidence of the concurrent operations of the principles of socialization and stratification. (See Chapter 7 for coverage of gender socialization.)

When censorship by federal and state agencies of curriculum materials occurs, the principle of socialization can be interpreted as an act of consensus only when the governmental agency truly represents the values of the society at large; otherwise, it represents a decision based on the power of an elite few. Evidence suggests that efforts toward consensus about the value of academic freedom are preserved when federal and state governments avoid the censorship of textbooks and other curriculum materials. For example, according to Jeanne Ballantine (1989), textbook censorship (prohibiting book adoption) through court ruling is less frequent than decisions to bolster academic freedom. An exception to this, she says, concerns an issue over the separation of church and state; United States District Judge Learned Hand banned selected textbooks in Alabama, arguing that they did not present an accurate picture of religion in U.S. history. Laws related to presenting a curriculum that includes evolution have been considered by several states, including Georgia, Iowa, Florida, and Tennessee; these states have considered legislation to drop the teaching of biology in schools. Georgia has opted for equal teaching time devoted to creationism and evolution. The founder of the Creation Science Research Center in California sued the state arguing that it had violated the religious freedom of his children by teaching evolution as fact. The Superior Court judge ruled that the state does not violate rights by teaching evolution, but that it should be taught as a theory, not as dogma (*Newsweek*, 1981). Fundamentalists in several states advocate the teaching of *scientific creationism* alongside the teaching of evolution (*U.S. News & World Report*, 1980). The creationist viewpoint has been mandated in several states. In 1982, a federal judge ruled against including scientific creationism in the curriculum because it contained no scientific evidence in support of creationism and therefore violated the First Amendment of the separation of church and state. (See Ballantine, 1989, for further discussion on this topic.)

Still another curriculum content issue that sheds light on the operation of socialization in the schools concerns sex and drug education. Most adults in the United States support the teaching of *some* sex education in the schools (*Education Week*, 1985), although the controversy continues about whether these topics should be taught solely by parents. The growing consensus of Americans supporting the introduction of sex education in the schools is indicated, for example, by resources issued by the federal government that inform teachers about AIDS (United States Surgeon General, 1987).

These issues over what gets taught in schools contribute to our sociological understanding of how the principle of socialization operates because they reflect the degree to which curriculum choices are characterized predominantly by consensus or by domination. The characteristic federal decentralization of United States society is evidence that the principle of socialization operates more on the basis of consensus than on conflict.

How Knowledge Is Transmitted

Starting School   The issue of how, or under what conditions, knowledge is communicated can be addressed sociologically using the principle of socialization. Whether by consensus or coercion, whatever knowledge is deemed important must be communicated effectively. The effective transmission of knowledge has been investigated in a number of studies. Sometimes the evidence supports neither, and sometimes both, theoretical explanations of how socialization operates. Research from the functionalist perspective attempts to explain learning differences as the result of differences in intelligence. Studies that reveal to which degree differences in performance are attributed to gender, race, and social class lend support to the credibility of this argument. Research from the conflict perspective focuses on the mechanisms that ensure the replication of inequities that students bring to school. For consensus theorists, attention is devoted to those school mechanisms that equalize learning opportunities for all types of students.

The issue of how knowledge is transmitted includes consideration of *when* knowledge should be communicated to be effective. This issue can be addressed by way of a sociological analysis using the principle of socialization as it is observed in the case of the early childhood controversy (Ballantine, 1989). From a functionalist perspective, Talcott Parsons (1951) sees socialization (learning) as continuing throughout life, with its most significant impact occurring during childhood when the personality is formed:

> There is reason to believe that, among the learned elements of basic personality structure, in certain respects the stablest and most enduring are the major value-orientation patterns, and there is much evidence that these are laid down in childhood and are not on a large scale subject to drastic alteration during adult life.

Socialization is, for Parsons, accounted for by his theory of *functional prerequisites*, what is functional for society becomes represented and integrated into the child's personality. This model stresses the significance of the basic personality structure as a determinant of the adult's behavior. Research on whether placing a child in school or removing him or her from the family negatively influences the child's behaviors informs theory emphasizing the significance of early socialization. Consider: formal early childhood education (from ages three to five years old) is prevalent in half of all countries; enrollments in the United States from 1964 to 1984 increased from 4 to 28 percent for three year olds, from 15 to 45 percent for four year olds, and from 58 to 84 percent for five year olds (United

States Department of Education, 1985); the increased participation of women in the labor force is expected to increase use of early childhood daycare facilities (O'Connor, 1988). Accordingly, parents, educators, and researchers express much concern over formal early childhood education outcomes. Research on daycare effects on children have examined such concerns as the retardation of cognitive development, poor bonding of mothers and infants, aggressive or passive personality tendencies, and abnormal peer associations. Overall, without a detailed examination of each study, Donald Peters (1980) reports that early childhood education has no damaging effects on any of these aspects of the child's development. Other research (Etaugh, 1980) corroborates these findings that nonmaternal care of the preschool child is not injurious to the child's social-emotional behavior or intellectual and physical well-being. Children older than two placed in a good early childhood program show advanced social and intellectual skills without evidence of detrimental effects on their affective behaviors (Clarke-Stewart and Fein, 1983).

Research on programs such as Head Start, designed to make up for the long-term negative effect of poverty on academic performance, supports the view that the school's role is functional to society by equalizing learning opportunities for the young at a critical phase in their development. The evidence on early childhood education does not lend credibility to the view that early childhood education replicates class structure, nor does it necessarily indicate that young children at the cusp of the home-school transition learn a complacent role as student in an oppressive system.

One-Parent and Reconstituted Families   Another issue that concerns how the principle of socialization operates in the case of knowledge transmission and academic performance is that of students from one-parent households. How does the school best transmit knowledge to these students, and which theoretical explanations concerning the nature of socialization, in this context, are most powerful?

Are students with only one parent in the home less able to meet the school's demands for successful socialization, the transmission of school knowledge as measured by the student's academic performance? One study shows the effect is small and can be accounted for almost entirely by background attributes (race or ethnicity and parental educational level) of the student (Mulkey, Crain, and Harrington, 1992). This study shows that once background is controlled, the residual effect is explained more by student misbehavior than by family economic condition. This counters the expectation (Milne, Myers, Rosenthal, and Ginsberg, 1986) that the loss of a father's income, introduced as a mediating variable, is the main culprit in depressing student academic performance. These findings thus document how family structure is associated with schooling outcomes: In the absence of either a mother or father in the home, economic status plays less a role in educational performance than student misbehavior, once race and ethnicity and parental levels of education are controlled. In fact, the loss of income due to father-absence has virtually no effect on student grades or test scores. Given that for most children social class is a major predictor of educational and occupational achievement, the school, in this situation, does not reproduce the inequality generated by father-absence and reduced family income. Instead, the school responds, to a small degree, to student misbehavior, regardless of student social class standing, and in this sense does not allocate rewards on the basis of social class. (Similar effects have been found for students living in reconstituted families [Ware and Lee, 1988].)

One implication of these findings is for a cultural reproduction theory of the role of the school in relation to the home in the socialization process and the structure of opportunity. Income, as it relates to one-parent family structure, is only one aspect of class culture, and it does not influence the achievement demands of schooling. We gain an understanding of the relative contribution of noneconomic factors (patterns of family life such as kinship, socialization, and leisure activity) as a dimension of social resources and as they relate to mother- or father-absence and to academic performance. If secondary school rewards students on the basis of social resources, the rewards are based less on the economic dimension of cultural resources and slightly more on the behavioral dimension. Grade and test score demands of schools are only mildly dependent on these family life resources. Schools ask for very specific types of behavior on the part of students despite their economic condition, and not all class cultural resources are equally valuable to students for complying with the school's requests.

Working Mothers, Latch-Key and Homeless Children   Another issue of how school knowledge is most effectively transmitted concerns the relation between a mother's employment and children's achievement. The increasing proportion of mothers who work outside the home has created speculation about whether this sociostructural arrangement engenders poor development of offspring. Some contention exists. For example, Barbara Heyns and Sophia Catsambis (1986) assert that the effect of the mother's employment on student achievement is a complex phenomenon that we are just starting to untangle. They say certain patterns of employment are consistently related to student achievement, irrespective of background factors.

In particular, when other family characteristics are controlled, children whose mothers work briefly, during only one period of the child's life, or who decrease their commitment to work through time are one to two percentile points behind children whose mothers have never worked. This clearly suggests that women who are eager to increase their hours at work will not adversely affect their children's school achievement. This claim contrasts to that made by A. Milne et al. (1986), who say that, consistent with their review of the literature, the effect of the mother's employment varies by students' age, race, and family structure and by the intensity and duration of the mother's working. The significant effects of the mother's employment, they say, are primarily negative, except in the case of a positive effect on the achievement of black elementary school students from one-parent families. They found a cumulative negative effect of the mother's employment for the student's lifetime. Further, they suggest that certain behaviors mitigate the negative effect of the mother's employment, such as family size (with smaller families reducing the negative effect); further nvestigation of intervening variables (such as the mother's attitude toward her work, her degree of professionalism, and the quality of alternative daycare) will fill some of the knowledge gaps on this issue. Milne et al. (1986) refer to other studies that lend support to the view that mothers who work negatively affect their children's school performance. In another study (Myers et al., 1985), effects of the mother's employment on student's misbehavior and academic performance were estimated using both the baseline 1980 data and first follow-up 1982 data. For white sophomores, the mother's employment was related to high levels of misbehavior and low grades. An analysis of change for the two-year period showed that for the group still in school, the mother's employment was related to increases in misbehavior and to relative declines in academic performance. In an analysis of the effects of family background characteristics on values and high school success for a sample of 1980 sophomores in the High School & Beyond national survey, researchers found that among whites a mother's employment had a direct negative effect on time spent on homework, on GPA, and on changes in reading and math achievement (Hanson and Ginsburg, 1986).

Two issues concerning the effective transmission of school knowledge that are somewhat related to maternal employment are concerns over the numbers of *latchkey* and *homeless* children. As maternal employment has risen, the number of latchkey children, those who return from school to empty homes, has increased. National data indicate several million children, ages five to thirteen, are in such a situation (Rosenberger, 1985; United States Bureau of the Census, 1987). Despite these concerns, no significant differences in behavior between latchkey children and supervised children have been found (Bridgman, 1984). A review of the research on the school's provision of assistance to latchkey children showed too little is known about the delivery of services in before-and-after school programs, and controversy remains over the legal responsibilities of the parent versus the school in providing for the young (Strother, 1984). Although it is unclear whether the active participation of women in the workforce affects the transmission of school knowledge, what is clear is the increasing involvement of the public school in the socialization of the young. This observation could reflect either a democratically and consensually-oriented arrangement that results from the society's need and preference for women in the labor force, or a more coercive arrangement serving the needs of the dominant group.

A. Pavuk (1987) estimates that about three million children live among the homeless population. Research shows that these children attend school infrequently and perform poorly. Homeless children are characterized by high rates of absence; poor school enrollment, attendance, and achievement; and suffer from poor health as well as have learning disabilities (Goldberg, 1987; Pavuk, 1987). The issue of homelessness has only recently received attention as an issue of socialization and school performance.

Parent-Student-Teacher Relations   So far, the research findings presented document the conditions under which the status quo standards for school success are threatened by factors unrelated to the child's ability. Our understanding of the nature of the operation of the principle of socialization as it pertains to the transmission of school knowledge is advanced by looking at another factor. The home-school discontinuity in the operation of the principle of socialization is interpreted, as we might expect, differently by various theorists. The expectations of the family in socializing the child to be a productive member of society will affect the educational content of the home-school curriculum (Apple and Weis, 1986). Basil Bernstein (1974, 1975) propounds that an understanding of the curriculum content and what it means to be educated requires the application of a symbolic interaction approach in investigating language patterns. His work explains why the disjuncture between the language a child speaks at home (restricted code) and the language required of the child in school (elaborated code) is class based. Thus, the language of the curriculum serves to perpetuate the child's social class.

Cultural reproduction theory has been applied in an investigation of the principle of socialization as it operates in how knowledge transmission is affected by parent-student-teacher relations. Annette Lareau (1987) conducted ethnographic research on the social and cultural elements of family life that foster compliance with teachers' requests. The study suggests that the concept of cultural capital can be used to understand social class differences in children's school experiences. Specifically, the results indicated that schools have standardized views of the proper role of parents in schooling. Moreover, social class provides parents with unequal social resources to comply with teachers' requests for parental participation. Teachers participate with parents of the middle and working classes in a manner that perpetuates social class distinctions.

Peer Group Socialization   Another illustration of how school behavior can be understood by the application of a sociological analytical tool, the principle of socialization, and the various theories explaining the operation of this principle, concerns peer group activities in formal schooling. The dynamic of the peer group is that its members are likely to internalize the norms of their intragroup interaction so that particular objectives can be reached by the school's setting up conditions for specific kinds of relationships within and between peer groups (Sherif et al., 1961). The degree to which peer group knowledge transmission is compatible with school goals for knowledge transmission will tell us which theoretical interpretation is more credible in accounting for the principle of socialization in this case. One of the most dramatic changes that the introduction of formal schooling brings to the child is the replacement of the dominant role of the multiage children's group with that of the similar-age peer group (Valsiner, 1989). Schooling segregates different-age children into distinct groups, but many children, until their introduction to formal schooling, are accustomed to and develop in a group of multiage children. The major educational goal of this separation is to group children who have approximately the same knowledge base so that the teacher can develop their knowledge and skills further, as a group. This separation also minimizes the possible resistance that teachers may encounter from well-formed social groups. Because all the children in the same grade are approximately the same age and have approximately the same knowledge, the chance that group leaders will emerge on the basis of age (experience) is lessened. The school system effectively neutralizes possible opposition that multiage children's groups might present (see Rodgers, 1980, for a discussion of the introduction of age segregation in American education in the nineteenth century). Educators sometimes use interference in group activities (for example, separating children by age, race, or sex) to actively achieve society's educational and socialization goals. The United States educational system seems to take a noninterventionist approach, but in other countries peer groups are used for socialization purposes. In China, for example, the Cultural Revolution made explicit use of children's peer groups in promoting loyalty to the political leader (Valsiner, 1989).

N. Graves and T. Graves (1978) showed how, in a tribal society that had been characterized by interpersonal generosity and a minimum of rivalry among people, the introduction of a school corresponded with the spread of rivalrous conduct via competitive game strategies. In United States education, adults expect the peer group to function as a socializing agency to teach a child how to get along with others. The peer group teaches the child the prevailing standards of adult morality such as competition, cooperation, honesty, and responsibility. It also teaches children their sex roles (Eder and Parker, 1987). The influence of peers depends on a variety of factors, such as the type of behavior being examined. In a study of adolescents 12 to 15 years old, B. Biddle, B. Bank, and M. Marlin (1980) found that peer behavior was relatively more important than parental behavior in predicting adolescents' preference for and use of alcohol, but parental norms were more important than peer norms in predicting attitudes involving achievement in school.

A more theoretical understanding of how the principle of socialization operates in the case of peer group influence as a mechanism for the transmission of knowledge is found in a study of friendships (as a reference group) (Hallinan and Williams, 1990). These researchers present an alternate conceptualization of the peer-influence process that is based on Parsons's theory of influence (1963). Rather than deriving specific hypotheses from Parsons's conceptualization, the researchers use his framework to expand the understanding of peer effects. In contrast to reference-group and role theories, which do not explain how role model or reference group is selected, Parsons's theory contains two ideas which the researchers claim strengthen the existing conceptualizations of peer effects. Parsons asserts that a person can be influenced when he or she needs information to adapt to and interact in a particular situation. Parsons's emphasis on the importance of a relationship of solidarity in increasing the vulnerability to influence directs attention to a friendship tie as an important locus of peer influence. Also, Parsons's investigation of the role of trust in determining vulnerability to influence suggests that influence can occur in degrees—some friends are more trustworthy than are others and are more susceptible to influence by their more trustworthy friends. Thus, an extension of his theory, the researchers say, addresses the central role of friends in the peer influence process and the degree of trust as it affects a student's vulnerablity to influence. According to Parsons, the primary condition for influence is the need for information, and schools frequently place students in situations in which they must obtain information in order to act. For example, to make decisions about which courses to enroll in, students get information from other students. A student will get information or advice from others only under the condition of trust; parents, teachers, and other adults are usually available for counsel but are not always perceived as trustworthy. In the influence process, because friendships vary by their degree of solidarity, the vulnerability of a student to influence should vary across friends. A student would be more influenced by a close friend than by a casual acquaintance. Hallinan and Williams examined whether differences in the ascribed and achieved characteristics (gender, race, and other background characteristics as well as track placement in high school) actually result in different peer-influence processes and found that the influence of close friends on educational aspirations and outcomes varies with the racial and gender composiiton of the friendship, and that interracial friendships are beneficial to the aspirations of both black and white students. The study also showed the utility of applying Parsons's theory of influence to the study of peer influence in school. Future examinations of other areas of peer influence, the researchers believe, will help to determine how generalizable these findings are.

The amount of influence of the peer group is another issue that contributes to our understanding of how the principle of socialization operates. While the peer group operates informally, Sarane Boocock (1976) found that children have relatively weak ties with the larger society. Adolescents in American society are economically dependent on the family and are excluded for a prolonged period of time from participation in the adult world; youth therefore look to their peer group for affirmation and in this way the peer group takes on an increasingly larger role in the socialization process (Levine and Havinghurst, 1989). Part of this increasing influence is explained by the increasing number of female-headed households; the interaction between parents and children is reduced and parents exercise less influence over their children. James Coleman (1961) documents the influence of the adolescent peer group in his study of high school students. He found that academic achievement had low status in all of the eleven schools he examined, despite differences in parental background, community, and school type. The United States secondary school peer group's view of academic achievement is corroborated in more recent research (Cusick, 1983; Clasen and Brown, 1986). K. Tye (1985) found this pattern to be true for middle school peer groups. (The school's influence on students as a reference group is discussed in Chapter 8.)

The nature of socialization in the case of the peer group is unclear in terms of whose interests are being served. Some research on peer influence on the college plans and aspirations of high school students shows that influence operates through a mediating variable, curriculum placement. Students enrolled in a college preparatory curriculum come into contact with highly motivated peers who reinforce their own motivation to succeed in high school and go to college. Students in noncollege tracks associate mostly with less motivated peers and are not reinforced in their academic aspiration. Daniel Levine and Robert Havighurst (1989) point out that stress on curriculum placement as a factor influencing subsequent academic plans is compatible with data showing that peers play an important part in determining college plans and expectations. Middle-class students are more likely than lower-class students to enroll in college preparatory programs. Discriminatory placement seems to be a mechanism by which the middle class maintains its advantage over the working class (Vanfossen, Jones, and Spade, 1987; Alexander and McDill, 1976). Adam Gamoran (1986) disagrees and argues that curriculum placement gives little or no advantage to middle-class students after taking account of background, ability, and previous academic performance.

Another insight into the issue of the influence of the peer group on student achievement and educational plans and attainment is gained by studying student participation in extracurricular activities. J. H. Braddock II (1981) analyzed the National Longitudinal Survey of high school students and claimed that high school athletics has a positive effect on these outcomes regardless of ability and social class background (with a smaller effect for females as opposed to males; Hanks, 1979). Extracurricular activities have a positive and long-term effect on student outcomes and can be manipulated better than other variables related to educational outcomes, that extracurricular activities may be one important way to improve student aspiration and attainment (Holland and Andre, 1988; Otto, 1982). A review of other research on the influence of the peer group in the community, inner city, and as youth-serving organizations can be found in D. Levine and R. Havighurst (1989).

The influence of the peer group as a socializing agent relative to the family, the church, and the community has grown in the postindustrial United States. Lawrence Cremin (1977) discusses the transformation in the influence of a number of educative institutions. The empirical evidence suggests that under some circumstances, peer group socialization is an effective means of replicating social class disadvantage; under other conditions, the peer group facilitates a healthy adjustment into the society at large. Overall, regardless of whose interests are served, poor peer relations in elementary school and in high school are predictive of later psychological maladjustment (Johnson and Johnson, 1981; Nottelmann, 1982).

The Television as Educator   Another application of the principle of socialization to the school is in the interpretation of its role in the effective transmission of knowledge. The validity of theoretical explanations of how the principle of socialization acts in the effective transmission of school knowledge can be assessed by observing the influence of other socializing agencies, such as the media, as they complement or compete with the school for the attention of students (Ballantine, 1989). For example, although the evidence on the relationship between television viewing and school achievement is inconclusive, studies of television viewing tell us something about how and under what conditions the principle of socialization is a mechanism through which the general interests of society versus the interests of an elite are served.

Some studies, such as the one conducted by the National Assessment of Educational Progress (NAEP, 1984), have shown that students who watched more television demonstrated poorer reading proficiency than peers who watched fewer hours of television; however, the many factors that intervene in the process of television watching and school academic performance confound this finding. Other studies, such as one conducted by R. Hormik (1981), corroborate the findings that low reading scores are associated with excessive television viewing, but again, the correlational nature of these studies does not permit precise claims about the effects of viewing television on achievement. When the situation is considered in a multivariate manner so that parental socioeconomic background, supervision, student age, race, sex, and parental education level and intelligence are considered, the outcomes vary. Achievement also influences selective television watching (Gaddy, 1986). Stronger positive evidence shows that the effect of television watching on learning is mediated by parents who actively interpret or moderate what children watch (Singer and Singer, 1984).

An interesting exception is noted from a study (California Assessment Program, 1982) in which watching television for three to four hours per day actually benefited lower-class students, perhaps because the television environment is more productive of achievement than are working-class home and neighborhood environments. Beneficial effects of television watching also appear in 1977 studies by CBS on the effects of children's educational television (Levine and Havighurst, 1989).

The television as socializer in relation to the school also has an impact on social skills and peer relations, but again, the correlational nature of this research limits the claims about the impact of the television on school behavior. For example, one association between television and achievement may be that children who have poor interpersonal skills watch more television (to compensate for a lack of friends); on the other hand, maybe they watch too much television to develop skilled peer relations (Dorr, 1986). Some evidence shows that television socializes the young into aggressive behaviors; a small positive correlation between viewing violence and aggressiveness was found in a laboratory-experimental setting (Freedman, 1984).

Another interesting contemporary issue that illuminates how the principle of socialization operates in the context of the effective transmission of the school curriculum via the media is the videotaping of exemplary college lecturers. When Thomas Rollins was serving as Chief Counsel of the Senate Committee on Labor and Human Resources, one of the problems before the committee was the widespread public concern over the decline in quality of American public school education, especially in mathematics and science. Rollins recalled how the Irving Younger series of videotaped college lectures had saved him during his college days. He asked why the United States government couldn't track down the most brilliant math and science teachers, videotape their classroom presentations, and make the videotapes available to schools everywhere? At first, the idea was greeted with great enthusiasm, but it was soon apparent that development would face insurmountable legal difficulties; there were too many laws designed to prevent the federal government from having any influence over the content of public school curricula. Rollins began to realize that such a concept would have to develop as a private enterprise and that its real potential lay in recording and videotaping college lecturers for home audiences. In 1989, he left government service to found The Teaching Company (1990). This documentation reflects controversy of what counts as knowledge, but is used in this example to suggest the positive effects of the role of the media in college performance.

A survey of public school students (a total of 280 seventh and tenth grade students) in two midsized midwestern cities with typical socioeconomic characteristics examined differential socialization effects of four news media (television, radio, newspaper, and news magazines) on four types of political knowledge and behavior among several categories of youth on the basis of their abilities and predispositions (Garramone and Atkin, 1986). Broadcast news exposure is a better predictor of current events knowledge than of fundamental knowledge, but the overall pattern of findings across subgroups provides little evidence of unequal effects of exposure; the news media do not appear to produce knowledge gaps (or behavior gaps) between those adolescents who are brighter or more politically interested and those who are less scholarly or uninterested. The media seem to serve a compensatory function in some cases by more strongly stimulating the political orientations of exposed students scoring poorly on these background variables.

Overall, the evidence on the learning effects of television watching is variable, with negative outcomes only for extended viewing (six or more hours per day); only sparse support exists one way or the other that the television is extraordinarily beneficial or terribly devastating in affecting learning. The role of the media in effective socialization by way of videotaped college lectures is still exploratory. The mass communication of information by various types of news media seems to have similar socialization effects on student political knowledge and behavior. A small amount of data suggests a conflict interpretation of socialization in which the effective transmission of knowledge corresponds to the patterns of domination in the society at large.

Learning Strategies   Another way in which a school issue informs our understanding of how the principle of socialization operates is found in the literature on pedagogical approaches that improve learning.[7] The principle operates in this case so that cooperation versus competition, as a value, is transmitted through a student team learning approach. The positive learning outcomes reinforce cooperation, and cooperation, reciprocally, affects achievement and motivation. Cooperative learning as a method for transmitting knowledge is effective for increasing student achievement as well as improving intergroup relations (Slavin, 1983). Student Team Learning (STL) developed by Robert Slavin, places students in learning teams that receive rewards based on the extent to which all team members complete and master a common set of skills; thus, STL is effective in reinforcing the value of cooperation over competition. Students contribute to the team not by doing better than other members of the group but by improving on their own previous performance. STL has produced significant gains in student classroom participation, achievement, attitudes toward school, and self-concept. These gains have been found not only for minority students in desegregated classes but also in general. Modified versions of STL, such as Team Accelerated Individualization (TAI) and Cooperative Integrated Reading and Composition (CIRC), combine other strategies such as mastery learning to produce improvement in student attitudes and achievement (Slavin, Madden, and Leavey, 1984). Cooperative learning, as a technique that involves positive interdependence among students, face-to-face interaction, individual mastery of material, and the development of small group interpersonal skills, has been shown to improve college students' understanding of statistics (Borreson, 1990).

Other illustrations of how the principle of socialization operates in this case are the technique developed to transmit knowledge called Mastery Learning and the Degrees of Reading Power (DRP) test developed by the College Board (1983). Mastery Learning (Bloom, 1984) is an approach to knowledge transmission that has been successful in improving the achievement of disadvantaged students (Jones and Spady, 1985). Simply put, the process entails defining a specific learning objective; teaching the skills necessary to accomplish the objective; and using a criterion-referenced test to evaluate mastery (compared to the student's previous accomplishments). Additionally, corrective instruction is provided for those who do not achieve objectives, and acceleration is provided for students who master objectives. Students are then tested or retested, accordingly (Guskey, 1985). This illustration of the operation of the principle of socialization suggests that it mediates the effects of other socialization strategies that tend to replicate disadvantage.

The DRP approach to the development of reading comprehension is most effective at the secondary school level, while STL and Mastery Learning approaches are effective at the middle school and elementary school levels. The DRP approach is a criterion-referenced test (as opposed to norm-referenced which compared the individual's progress to that of the group), meaning that it indicates how well a student can comprehend everyday reading material and by fostering a general comprehension of reading material, helps students understand material in all aspects of the curriculum. Its effectiveness as a mechanism of socialization is documented by H. A. Sirois and R. L. Davis (1985).

Vocational, Liberal Arts, and Mass Education   The transmission of knowledge via vocational versus academic tracks (in high school) is also subject to sociological analysis using the principle of socialization. Transmission of vocational knowledge takes place in vocational education courses in comprehensive high schools or in vocational-technical high schools. By 1987, approximately ten million students 18 or younger were enrolled in vocational education courses. Researchers question whether knowledge transmitted in these courses facilitates better preparation for the job market or whether learning is restricted so as to impede later postsecondary education and occupational preparation.

Research shows that knowledge transmission of the vocational type benefits some students, such as potential dropouts. The vocational approach also is associated with better employment and higher earnings for female graduates of business and office programs than of general educational programs (Weisberg, 1983). This kind of socialization provides improved economic opportunity for students who do not want to attend college, but it also limits preparation for employment and inhibits the academic development of students with inadequate basic academic skills. Elizabeth Useem (1986) documents how corporate insistence on vocational education in high schools has been dropped in favor of a broad-based academic education. Corporate concerns emphasize the transmission of communication, science, and mathematics skills acompanied by problem-solving skills, which is deemed more adaptive for a rapidly changing work environment.

Vocational socialization outcomes are documented in other research. According to Natriello, Pallas, and Alexander (1989), the academic track is more effective in furthering gains in achievement than are the other curricula (general or vocational tracks). They state that such evidence seems to support calls for reforms that would make the entire high school curriculum more like the curriculum of the academic track. They caution that the intention of the nonacademic tracks, particularly the vocational track, may not be to develop the kind of cognitive skills that are captured in tests of vocabulary, reading, and mathematics. These tests are more likely to correspond to the materials from the academic track and may thus place students from the other tracks at a disadvantage. Even with this factor in mind, the researchers say, the results of their study indicate that the different school curricula, as constituted and under present conditions of selection and allocation, do make a difference in the academic achievement of students. (This evidence is also illustrative of how the principles of organization and stratification operate within the context of schooling.)

The debate over the value of vocationally oriented education in higher education as opposed to education for the well-rounded person has been interpreted by Max Weber's conflict perspective. In his work on the rationalization of education and training (1946), Weber discusses how rational education develops the specialist in contrast to the cultivated person (as described in his examination of educational systems in China). For example, the Harvard University Core Program for general education focuses on assuring that its graduates possess basic literacy in the major forms of intellectual discourse. All its graduates have a common core of courses constituting approximately 25 percent of their work toward graduation, educating them to be "cultivated" persons (Ballantine, 1989). Although it is clear that vocational socialization benefits some students who might not otherwise have some occupational success, in the long run students are less likely to be prepared to accommodate the changing occupational structure. Only the cultivated students are prepared to benefit from these changing demands.

Mass education has been interpreted by some scholars as an illustration of cultural reproduction at the national level. Worldwide understandings and conventions that legitimate some forms of social development and undermine others are exemplified in the last century by the dramatic rise in the authority and power of the national state. Research on the origins of state educational systems in Europe during the past hundred years and the institutionalization of mass education throughout the world shows the construction of a mass educational system is a major and indispensable component of every modern state's activity and mass state-sponsored schooling emphasizes the role of education in the nation-building efforts of states competing with one another in the European interstate system (Ramirez and Boli, 1987). Some conflict theorists (Bowles, 1972; Waller, 1965) view mass education as an instrument of capitalist society that controls entrance to higher levels of education through the selection and allocation function and manipulating the public. Willard Waller applies this view at the school and classroom level and portrays inter-group conflict as the battles between students, parents, and school boards (Ballantine, 1989). The same evidence, however, is amenable to a consensus interpretation.

Problem-Solving   The direct instruction of discrete skills unfortunately lacks those features that promote problem-solving as a higher-order skill (Anderson, Hiebert, Scott, and Wilkinson, 1985). Prescriptive teaching of skills inhibits the learning process when it comes to higher-order cognitive functioning, which implies the need for multiple modes of instruction and a repertoire of instructional models (Marzano et al., 1987). The gap between lower- and higher-order thinking skills in the school socialization process has consequences for students when they are confronted with later adult thinking demands (Sternberg, 1985). Apparently, these socialization strategies contribute to an unquestioning acceptance of society and its expectations.

Self-Development   Jaan Valsiner (1989), an anthropologist, has made some interesting observations in his work on the social nature of personality. He says that school systems in Western civilization socialize children with a strong emphasis on the separation of the personal self from its social context. Although no society exists in which an individual's actions and thoughts are unconstrained and absolutely free, the school promotes the illusion of unlimited personal choice. Western industrial society relies on the individual person's active pursuit of goals; hence the idea of personal freedom, the boundaries of which are usually unspecified in the socialization process. In the classroom, Valsiner says, this is furthered by providing students with limited freedom of choice between pregiven options. For example, multiple-choice questions and programmed (rote) learning methods have one point in common: the student's individual activity is used only to discover the correct answer, not to construct any novel answers. This method is appropriate for arithmetic problem solving in which the correct answers are unequivocally set, but when it is used to teach students about issues that have no single solution, the goal-directed nature of the socialization function of formal education is to prepare students to be independent in answering a given set of questions on their own but only in ways in which the correctness of the answers cannot be disputed.

Formal school socializes and contributes to children's self-development through cognitive development, particularly aspects of self-reflection, and the development of deductive reasoning. Valsiner claims that formal schooling leads to a reorganization of the child's understanding of himself or herself. Depending on the particular form of schooling, the child's self becomes either more differentiated from its surrounding social environment or more fused with the environment. Western-type formal schooling encourages the differentiation of the self from the surroundings. The role of Western formal schooling in the development of self-reflection involves replacing social roles and relationships as the criteria on which personhood is based with internalized and relatively context-free psychological criteria. For example, when asked what sort of a person they are, some students respond by describing themselves in terms of their surroundings: "I have three brothers and I work after school to help with the family income." These subjects display a context-dependent sense of self. For them, everything refers to the external conditions of life. When the subject is asked to comment on his or her temper or memory, the response, again, is a self-evaluation in terms of social behavior: "We would not have respect from anyone if we behaved badly." The subject cannot reason about himself or herself in terms of internal, context-free qualities; in contrast, children who internalize a context-free sense of who they are are less fused with their social surroundings and speak about their personality traits, for example: "I am smart, and I have a lot of patience."

In addition to self-reflection, Western formal schooling socializes children to encourage deductive reasoning. The major impact of schooling on children's cognition is its ability to promote the acceptance and internalization of knowledge that goes beyond the experiences and loyalties of the local community. School teaches children to accept the major premise of syllogistic reasoning tasks, thereby empowering them with a social mechanism of manipulating reasoning about important issues. For example, the socialized cognitive mechanisms of deductive reasoning promote the formation of stereotypes and prejudices (persons with whom the child never meets directly). This kind of abstract thinking contributes to the child's ability to solve complex scientific and technical problems and in this way is important for a modern work force. The school thus functions to prevent the subject's dominant inductive reasoning interference. The inductive reasoning cognitive process is characteristic of persons who rely on everyday life experience in the problem-solving process. But this tendency interferes with the subject's ability to reason deductively. For example, Valsiner presents the case of a child introduced to syllogism: All bears are white in the Far North. Jingles is a bear from the Far North. What color is he? The dominant-inductive respondent fails to deduce from the syllogism and replies, "Each locality has its own bears." Reliance on direct experience, Valsiner claims, is discouraged in formal schooling and is replaced with the emphasis on deductive reasoning skills. This is another way in which the school as an agency of socialization has profound impact on the personal orientation of individuals—on their personality, something they think is their own!

Summary

This chapter has dealt with the most fundamental way in which our behavior is influenced by others: through socialization. In fact, influence is not an appropriate word because being human is not possible without other people. Unlike other organisms that come into the world already equipped to relate to it, we are not born *human*; rather, being human is an ongoing process. Some of the rules about how to behave are not encoded in our genes; we make the rules and store them in our brains. Socialization is conditional upon the representation of societal rules as values, norms, statuses and roles, and the human capacity for internalizing society as behavioral directives through the vehicles of cognition and emotion (language and personality). While socialization enhances our capacity to develop adaptive modes of survival by our ability to assign meaning to events (how by definition we will respond to things and they to us), we must ask who makes the rules and what aspects of being human are not unfolded because of the rules. The principle of socialization is explained by various theorists, some who see becoming human as an active process and some as a passive process. Socialization has been illustrated in education wherever we see the transmission of knowledge (content and pedagogy). In viewing school issues related to curriculum and pedagogy from a sociological perspective, what counts are the curriculum and how to teach that curriculum. The principle of socialization operates generally on the basis of both consensus and conflict, as shown by theoretical and empirical investigations of

- The core curriculum;
- What is considered educational productivity;
- Textbook content, adoption–censorship, and publication;
- Sex education;
- Creationist-evolution subject matter;
- The early childhood controversy;
- Peer group socialization and other factors affecting the transmission of knowledge (school-starting age, one-parent effects, mother-working effects, being a latchkey or homeless child, parent-teacher-student relations, peer group learning, the media as educator, cooperative learning, mastery learning, DRP reading comprehension approach, vocation versus academic education, liberal versus practical college curriculum, mass education, instruction for self-reflection).

Specifically, through the school society replicates knowledge that it consensually agrees is important. Sometimes this knowledge is challenged and negotiated. In summarizing the evidence, it is difficult to discern whether socialization, as a mechanism to promote human survival, leaves much room for individuals to define their own ways for behaving. It appears, more often than not, that socialization is an act of replication or reproduction of the culture without our consent, a passive rather than an active process. The active process may be manifested as disagreements over what is taught and how it is taught in curriculum and pedagogy issues. The dominant interests, outlined by the conflict theorists, are observed especially in those instances in which optimal cognitive development in children is impeded through unequal provision of an intellectually stimulating environment. The passive appearance of what goes on in school befits the functional perspective only when socialization is primarily other than a consensual process (reflecting agreement on the maintenance of the system).

Vocabulary

externalization	role
internalization	society
norm	status
objectivation	theories of socialization
personality	value
principle of socialization	

Questions

1. What kind of behaviors go on in schools that can be explained by the concepts and theories of socialization?

2. Can you do a sociological analysis (interpretation) of the school phenomenon, known as "cooperative learning"?

References and Suggested Readings

Ainsworth, M., S. Bell, and D. Stayton. "Infant-Mother Attachment and Social Development: Socialization as a Product of Reciprocal Responsiveness to Stimuli." In Martin P. Richards, *The Integration of a Child into a Social World*. New York: Cambridge, 1974, p. 100.

Alexander, K. and E. McDill. "Selection and Allocation within Schools: Some Causes and Consequences of Curriculum Placement." *American Sociological Review*, (1976) 41:863–981.

Anderson, R., E. Hiebert, J. Scott, and J. Wilkinson. *Becoming a Nation of Readers: Report of the Commission on Reading*. Washington, DC: National Institute of Education, 1985.

Anyon, J. "Schools as Agencies of Social Legitimation." In Pinar, W. (ed.), *Contemporary Curriculum Discourses*. Scottsdale, AZ: Gorsuch Scarisbrick, 1988.

Apple, M. *Teachers and Texts*. New York: Routledge & Kegan Paul, 1988.

Apple, M. and L. Weis. "Seeing Education Relationally: The Stratification of Culture and People in the Sociology of School Knowledge." *Journal of Education*, (1986) 168:19–20.

Ballantine, J. *The Sociology of Education: A Systematic Analysis*. Englewood Cliffs, NJ: Prentice-Hall, 1989.

Bank, B., R. Slavings, and B. Biddle. "Effects of Peer, Faculty, and Parental Influences on Students' Persistence." *Sociology of Education*, (1990) 63:208–25.

Bell, T. *A Nation at Risk*. National Commission on Excellence in Education, April, 1983.

Bennett, E. *James Madison High School: A Curriculum for American Students*. Washington, DC: United States Office of Education, 1988.

Bennett, K. and M. LeCompte. *How Schools Work: A Sociological Analysis of Education*. New York: Longman, 1990.

Berger, P. *The Sacred Canopy: Elements of a Sociological Theory of Religion*. New York: Doubleday, 1967.

Berger, P. and T. Luckmann. *The Social Construction of Reality: A Treatise in the Sociology of Knowledge*. New York: Anchor Books, 1967.

Bernstein, B. *Class, Codes and Control*. Boston: Routledge & Kegan Paul, 1975.

———. "Sociology and the Sociology of Education: A Brief Account." In John Rex (ed.), *Approaches to Sociology*. London: Routledge & Kegan Paul, 1974, pp. 145–59.

Biddle, B., B. Bank, and M. Marlin. "Parental and Peer Influence on Adolescents." *Social Forces*, (1980) 58:1057–79.

Bloom, A. *The Closing of the American Mind*. New York: Simon & Schuster, 1987.

Bloom, B. "The Search for Methods of Group Instruction as Effective as One-to-One Tutoring." *Educational Researcher*, (1984) 13:4–16.

Blumer, H. *Symbolic Interactionism: Perspectives and Method.* Englewood Cliffs, NJ: Prentice-Hall, 1969.

Boocock, S. *Students, Schools, and Educational Policy: A Sociological View.* Cambridge, MA: Aspen Institute for Humanistic Studies, 1976.

Borreson, C. "Success in Introductory Statistics with Small Groups." *College Teaching*, (1990) 38(1):26–28.

Boudon, R. *Education, Opportunity, and Social Inequality: Changing Prospects in Western Society.* New York: John Wiley & Sons, 1974.

Bourdieu, P. and J. Passeron. *Reproduction in Education, Society and Culture.* London: Sage, 1977.

Bowles, S. "Unequal Education and the Reproduction of the Social Division of Labor." In Martin Carnoy, ed., *Schooling in a Corporate Society.* New York: David McKay, 1972, pp. 36–64.

Bowles, S. and H. Gintis. *Schooling in Capitalist America: Educational Reform and the Contradictions of Economic Life.* New York: Basic Books, 1976.

Braddock, J. "Race, Athletics, and Educational Attainment: Dispelling the Myths." *Youth and Society*, (1981) 12:335–50.

Bridgman, A. "Schools Urged to Seek Solutions to Troubles of Latch-key Children." *Education Week*, (1984) 3(10):15.

California Assessment Program. *Survey of Sixth Grade School Achievement and Television Viewing Habits.* Sacramento, CA: State Department of Education, 1982.

Camic, C. "Prolegomena to a Theory of Social Institutions: An Historical Prologue." *American Sociological Review*, (1990) 55:313–45.

Carnoy, M., ed., *Schooling in a Corporate Society: The Political Economy of Education in America.* New York: McKay, 1972.

Carnoy, M. and H. Levin. *Schooling and Work in the Democratic States.* Stanford, CA: Stanford University Press, 1985.

Cicourel, A. *Method and Measurement in Sociology.* New York: Free Press, 1964.

Clarke-Stewart, A. and G. Fein. "Early Childhood Programs." In M. Haith and J. Campos, eds., *Infancy and Developmental Psychobiology*, Vol. 2 of P. H. Mussen, ed., *Handbook of Child Psychology*, 4th ed. New York: Wiley, 1983, p. 980.

Clasen, D. and B. Brown. "The Relationship Between Adolescent Peer Groups and School Performance." Paper presented at the annual meeting of the American Educational Research Association, San Francisco, April 1986.

Coleman, J. *The Adolescent Society.* New York: Free Press, 1961.

The College Board. *Academic Preparation for College.* New York: The College Board, 1983.

Coser, L. *The Functions of Social Conflict.* Glencoe, IL: Free Press, 1956.

Cremin, L. *Traditions of American Education.* New York: Basic Books, 1977.

Cusick, P. *The Egalitarian Ideal and the American High School.* New York: Longman, 1983.

Dahrendorf, R. *Class and Conflict in Industrial Society.* Stanford, CA: Stanford University Press, 1959.

Dorr, A. *Television and Children.* Beverly Hills, CA: Sage, 1986.

Dreeben, R. *On What is Learned in School.* Reading, MA: Addison-Wesley, 1968.

Durkheim, E. *Education and Sociology* (trans. Sherwood D. Fox). Glencoe, IL: Free Press, 1956.

Eder, D. and S. Parker. "The Cultural Production and Reproduction of Gender." *Sociology of Education,* 60:200–213.

Education Week "Survey Finds Parental Suppport for Sex Education." *Education Week,* (Nov. 13, 1985) p. 6.

Etaugh, C. "Effects of Nonmaternal Care on Children." *American Psychologist,* (1980) 35:309–19.

Freedman, J. "Effect of Television Violence on Aggressiveness." *Psychological Bulletin,* 96:227–46.

Freire, P. *A Pedagogy for Liberation.* South Hadley, MA: Bergin & Garvey, 1987.

Gaddy, G. "Television's Impact on High School Achievement." *Public Opinion Quarterly,* (1986) 50:340–59.

Gamoran, A. "Instructional and Institutional Effects of Ability Grouping." *Sociology of Education,* (1986) 59:195–98.

Garfinkel, H. *Studies in Ethnomethodology.* Englewood Cliffs, NJ: Prentice-Hall, 1967.

Garramone, G. and C. Atkin. ' Mass Communication and Political Socialization: Specifying the Effects." *Public Opinion Quarterly,* (1986) 50:76–86.

Gesell, A. and F. Ilg. *Infant and Child in the Culture of Today.* New York: Harper, 1943.

Giroux, H. *Teachers as Intellectuals: Toward a Critical Pedagogy of Learning.* Hadley, MA: Bergin & Garvey, 1988.

_____. "Theories of Reproduction and Resistance in the New Sociology of Education." *Harvard Educational Review,* (1983) 53:257–93.

Goldberg, K. "Many Homeless Children Reported Out of School." *Education Week,* (1987) 6(26):6.

Gornick, V. "Introduction." In E. Goffman, *Gender Advertisements.* New York: Harper, 1976.

Gramsci, A. *Selections from the Prison Notebooks.* Q. Hoare and N. Geoff, eds., New York: International, 1971.

Graves, N. and T. Graves. "The Impact of Modernization on the Personality of a Polynesian People." *Human Organization,* (1978) 37:115–35.

Guskey, T. *Implementing Mastery Learning.* Belmont, CA: Wadsworth, 1985.

Hallinan, M. "Sociology of Education: The State of the Art." In Ballantine, J., ed., *Schools and Society: A Reader in Education and Society.* Palo Alto, CA: Mayfield, 1985.

Hallinan, M. and R. Williams. "Students' Characteristics and the Peer-Influence Process." *Sociology of Education,* (1990) 63:122–32.

Hamblin, R. et al. *The Humanization Processes: A Social, Behavioral Analysis of Children's Problems.* New York: Wiley, Interscience, 1971.

Hanks, M. "Race, Sexual Status and Athletics in the Process of Educational Achievement." *Social Science Quarterly,* (1979) 60:482–96.

Hanson, S. and A. Ginsburg. *Gaining Ground: Values and High School Success.* Final report to the United States Department of Education. Washington, DC: United States Department of Education, 1986.

Harrington, C. "Textbooks and Political Socialization." *Teaching Political Science,* (1980) 7:481–500.

Hartup, W. and B. Coates. "The Role of Imitation in Childhood Socialization." In R. Hoppe et al., eds., *Early Experiences and the Processes of Socialization.* New York: Academic, 1970.

Hearn, J. "Academic and Nonacademic Influences on the College Destinations of 1980 High School Graduates." *Sociology of Education,* (1991) 64:158–71.

Heyns, B. and S. Catsambis. "Mother's Employment and Children's Achievement: A Critique." *Sociology of Education,* (1986) 59:140–51.

Hirsch, E. *Cultural Illiteracy: What Every American Needs to Know.* Boston: Houghton Mifflin, 1987.

Hochschild, A. "The Sociology of Feeling and Emotion." In M. Millman and R. Kanter, ed., *Another Voice.* New York: Doubleday, 1979.

Holland, A. and T. Andre. "Participation in Extracurricular Activities in Secondary School: What is Known, What Needs to Be Known?" *Review of Educational Research,* (1988) 57:437–66.

Hormik, R. "Out-of-School Television and Schooling: Hypotheses and Methods." *Review of Educational Research,* (1981) 51:193–214.

Johnson, D. and R. Johnson. "The Key to Healthy Development and Socialization." *Character,* (1981) 2:1–8.

Jones, B. and W. Spady. "Enhanced Mastery Learning as a Solution to the Two Sigma Problem." In D. Levine, ed., *Improving Student Achievement through Mastery Learning Programs.* San Francisco: Jossey-Bass, 1985.

Kagan, J. et al. *Emotions, Cognition, and Behavior.* New York: Cambridge University Press, 1984.

Karabel, J. and A. Halsey, eds. *Power and Ideology in Education.* New York: Oxford University Press, 1977.

Kemper, T. "Toward a Sociology of Emotions." *American Sociologist,* (1987) 13:30–41.

Lareau, A. "Social Class Differences in Family-School Relationships: The Importance of Cultural Capital." *Sociology of Education,* (1987) 60:73–85.

Levine, D. and R. Havighurst. *Society and Education,* 7th ed. Boston: Allyn & Bacon, 1989.

Marx, K. *The Communist Manifesto.* Chicago: H. Regney, 1955.

Marzano, R., et al. *Dimensions of Thinking.* Alexandria, VA: Association for Supervision and Curriculum Development, 1987.

Mead, G. *Mind, Self, and Society.* New York: Morris, 1961.

Merton, R. *Social Theory and Social Structure.* New York: Free Press, 1967.

Milne, A., D. Myers, A. Rosenthal, and A. Ginsburg. "Single Parents, Working Mothers, and the Educational Achievement of School Children." *Sociology of Education,* (1986) 59:125–39.

Mulkey, L. "The Significance of the Relation of Principles to Theoretical Logic in Sociology: A Re-examination of a Field of Study." Working paper. Los Angeles: University of California at Los Angeles, Department of Sociology.

_____. "Science Textbooks Similar in Lower- and Higher-Income School Districts, New York State." *Sociology and Social Research: An International Journal,* (1986) 71:123–26.

Mulkey, L., R. Crain, and A. Harrington. "Academic Performance of Students from One-Parent Families: Economic and Behavioral Explanations of a Small Effect." *Sociology of Education,* (1992) 65:48–65.

Myers, D., A. Milne, K. Baker, and A. Ginsburg. "Student Discipline and High School Performance." Paper presented at the annual meeting of the American Educational Research Association, Chicago, March 1985.

National Assessment of Educational Progress. *The Reading Report Card.* Princeton, NJ: Educational Testing Service, 1985.

Natriello, G., A. Pallas, and K. Alexander. "On the Right Track? Curriculum and Academic Achievement." *Sociology of Education,* (1989) 62:109–18.

"New Battle Over Teaching of Evolution." *U.S. News & World Report,* (June 9, 1980) p. 82.

Nottelmann, E. "Children's Adjustment in School: The Interaction of Physical Maturity and School Transition." Paper presented at the annual meeting of the American Educational Research Association, March 20, 1982.

O'Connor, S. "Women's Labor Force Participation and Preschool Enrollment: A Cross-National Perspective, 1965–1980." *Sociology of Education,* (1988) 61:15–28.

Oster, G. and E. Wilson. *Caste and Ecology in the Social Insects.* Princeton, NJ: Princeton University Press, 1978.

Otto, L. "Extracurricular Activities." In *Improving Educational Standards and Productivity,* H. Walberg, ed. Berkeley, CA: McCutchan, 1982.

Page, A. and D. Clelland. "The Kanawha County Textbook Controversy: A Study of the Politics of Life Style Concern." *Social Forces,* (1978) 57:265–81.

Parsons, T. "On the Concept of Influence." *Public Opinion Quarterly,* 27:37–62.

_____. "The School Class as a Social System: Some of Its Functions in American Society." Harvard Educational Review (1959) 29:297–319.

_____. *The Social System.* New York: Free Press, 1951.

Pavuk, A. "Families with Children Constitute Third of the Homeless, Mayors Say." *Education Week,* (1987) 6:12.

Persell, C. *Education and Inequality: The Roots and Results of Stratification in America's Schools.* New York: Free Press, 1977.

Peters, D. "Social Science and Social Policy and the Care of Young Children: Head Start and After." *Journal of Applied Developmental Psychology,* (1980) pp. 2–27.

Piaget, J. *The Construction of Reality in the Child.* New York: Basic Books, 1954.

_____. *The Psychology of Intelligence.* London: Routledge & Kegan Paul, 1950.

Ramirez, F. and J. Boli. "The Political Construction of Mass Schooling: European Origins and Worldwide Institutionalization." *Sociology of Education,* (1987) 60:2–17.

Ravitch, D. and C. Finn. *What Seventeen Year Olds Don't Know*. New York: Harper & Row, 1987.

Robinson, P. *Perspectives on the Sociology of Education: An Introduction*. Boston: Routledge & Kegan Paul, 1981.

Rodgers, D. "Socializing Middle-Class Children: Institutions, Fables, and Work Values in Nineteenth-Century America." *Journal of Social History*, (1980) 13:354–67.

Rosenberger, L. "Letting in 'Latchkey' Children." *New York Times*, (August 18, 1985) sec. 5, pp. 12, 17–18.

Schutz, A. *The Phenomenology of the Social World*. Evanston, IL: Northwestern University Press, 1967.

" 'Scopes II' in California." *Newsweek*, (March 16, 1981) p. 53.

Sherif, M., O. Harvey, B. White, W. Hood, and C. Herif. *Intergroup Conflict and Cooperation: The Robbers Cave Experiment*. Norman, OK: University Book Exchange, 1961.

Simmel, G. *Conflict*. Glencoe, IL: Free Press, 1955.

Singer, D. and J. Singer. "Parents as Mediators of the Child's Television Environment." *Educational Media International*, 4:7–11.

Sirois, H. and R. Davis. *School Improvement through Instructional Design: Matching Teaching Strategies and Instructional Materials to Students*. New York: College Board, 1985.

Slavin, R. *Cooperative Learning*. New York: Longman, 1983.

Slavin, R., N. Madden, and M. Leavey. "Combining Cooperative Learning and Individualized Instruction: Effects on Mathematics, Attitudes, and Behavior." *Elementary School Journal*, (1984) 84:409–22.

Sternberg, R. "Teaching Critical Thinking: Are We Making Critical Mistakes?" *Phi Delta Kappan*, (November 1985) pp. 194–8.

Strother, D. "Latchkey Children: The Fastest-growing Special Interest Group in the Schools." *Phi Delta Kappan*, (1984) 66:290–3.

The Teaching Company. *SuperStar Teachers*. Arlington, VA: The Teaching Company in cooperation with the Resident Associate Program, Smithsonian Institution, 1990.

Tye, K. *The Junior High School: School in Search of a Mission*. Lanham, MD: University Press of America, 1985.

United States Bureau of the Census. *After-school Care of Schoolage Children: December 1984*. Series P-23, No. 149. Washington, DC: United States Government Printing Office, (1987) p. 145.

United States Department of Education. "Reports on Preprimary Enrollment." In *American Education*, (1984) 21:16–7.

United States Surgeon General. *Report on Acquired Immune Deficiency Syndrome*, Washington, DC, 1987.

Useem, E. *Low Tech Education in a High Tech World*. New York: Free Press, 1986.

Valsiner, J. *Human Development and Culture: The Social Nature of Personality and Its Study*. Lexington, MA: Lexington Books, D.C. Heath, 1989.

Vanfossen, B., J. Jones, and J. Spade. "Curriculum Tracking and Status Maintenance." *Sociology of Education*, (1987) 60:104–22.

Waller, W. *The Sociology of Teaching*. New York: Wiley, 1965.

Ware, N. and V. Lee. "Sex Differences in Choice of College Science Majors." *American Educational Research Journal*, (1988) 25:593–614.

Weber, M. "The Rationalization of Education and Training." in H. Gerth and C. Wright Mills, eds. and trans., *From Max Weber: Essays in Sociology*. New York: Oxford University Press, 1946, pp. 240–3.

Weisberg, A. "What Research Has to Say About Vocational Education and the High Schools." *Phi Delta Kappan*, (1983) 64:355–9.

Weitzman, L. *Sex Role Socialization: A Focus on Women*. Palo Alto, CA: Mayfield, 1979.

Weitzman, L. and D. Rizzo. *Biased Textbooks: A Research Perspective*. Washington, DC: National Foundation for the Improvement of Education, 1974.

Young, M. *Knowledge and Control: New Directions for the Sociology of Education*. London: Collier-Macmillan, 1971.

Zimiles, H. and V. Lee. "Educational Development Among Adolescents from Single-Parent, Remarried and Intact Families: Impact on Academic Performance and Educational Persistence." Paper presented at the annual meeting of the American Educational Research Association, New Orleans, Louisiana, 1988.

Notes

[1]The principle of *socialization* ensures survival of the individual in the group through his or her predisposition to behave cooperatively. Human infants, for example, seem to be wired or programmed for maximizing social interaction, suggesting an innate need to be social; they burrow into a person's arms, suckle, adjust their bodies to increase contact, and grasp adults. They do not have to be rewarded to make them want social interation; rather they are biologically preset to be social (see Mary Ainsworth, S. M. Bell, and Donelda Stayton, "Infant-Mother Attachment and Social Development: Socialization as a Product of Reciprocal Responsiveness to Stimuli," in Martin P. Richards, *The Integration of a Child into a Social World*. New York: Cambridge, 1974, p. 100). The essential sociality of the human to make and follow rules is a hallmark of organismic adaptive ability because there are a myriad of permutations possible in designs for cooperative living. Ultimately, however, the most elaborate form of cooperation is seen not in the social drama, but outside of it; that is, once the human develops a social self (locus of experience), or personality, ego, essential *sociality*, it can then realize that the social self is merely the form for expression of the "I" that makes it possible in the first place. Recognition of the authentic Self (alienated through the process of self-objectivation [Morris Rosenberg, "Self-Objectification Relevance for the Species and Society." *Sociological Forum*, (1988) 3:548–65]) enables the individual to be free of social self-defense. The individual detects that its true Self is *indestructible* to material and social threat. The logic here is that Self is by *grace*, so to speak; there is nothing to affirm or to defend, only to *be*. The *taking no thought* attitude is *love* because there is nothing to take, only to give out: self-preservation becomes preservation of selflessness, the optimal form of cooperation. The development of a social consciousness in the human organism is thus a precondition for becoming fully human through disidentification of the individual from his or her socially defined self (see references in Chapter 11 for Bernard McGrane's exercises in desocialization). The detachment is not indifference to the world, but rather the liberty to be in the world, but not of it—expressing through rather than equating with social roles. Freedom is having nothing to lose because everything

is already there. (For further discussion of the reciprocal relations between the individual and society and what constitutes individual freedom, the reader is directed to the author's work on "The Relation of Principles to Theoretical Logic in Sociology: A Re-examination of a Field of Study," also see references in this chapter and to Chapter 11 in this book.)

[2]Many arguments take place over what constitutes the social condition of the human being; just how much and how is the individual's behavior his or her own? This argument is especially expressed in the work of Talcott Parsons (Camic, 1990), who takes contention with the *Watsonian behaviorist* notion that patterns of social behavior in humans, such as institutional forms, result from the aggregate of individual tendencies or habits, a complex of relatively uniform behavior. Rather, he believes that it is normative consensus that accounts for and underlies the stable and recurring behaviors. He indicates a level of determinateness at the biopsychological level in terms of a general *values orientation.* The evolution of the explanation of uniform modes of behavior (determinate forms of social relationship) deserves an adjustment in the level of determinateness. A higher level of empirical precision is accomplished when principles are isolated on the continuum of social thought. The assumption of an inherent predisposition to act, not only as a values-oriented organism, but toward a qualification of what kinds of cooperation are valued, encourages accuracy in our predictions of human behavior. Parsons's (1951) *pattern variables,* basic social orientations, are less lawlike in their operation in contrast to the *principles of sociology* (socialization, organization, stratification, institutions, social control, and social change). The concept principles of sociology enhances our understanding of social determinants by specifying that at the biopsychological level is the *essential sociality* of the individual. The empirical evidence for essential sociality manifests itself as the observed laws or principles of social life, the orientation to make and to conform to rules. That is, a subjective state of consciousness becomes externalized as society in several forms of social phenomena (constraints) referred to earlier as the *principles of sociology.* We are predisposed to be social; we come to know what to expect from others and they from us through the shared agreements embodied in symbols. For example, at a fundamental level, human reproduction is an activity designed for two persons: the individual is characterized by features that orient it toward the other. Analogously, language is meaningful as a shared activity, but it becomes appropriated as an individual characteristic in the persons's language acquisition. While it can be found at the individual level, it is functional or fulfilled solely through group interaction; otherwise, it is like one hand clapping. Analogous to the idea of the human capacity to be social, to be a member of a group, to be predisposed to acquire shared rules, is the linguist's idea of *deep structure* of language. Just as the individual is wired to acquire language, he or she is wired to be *social*—to *socialize* (to receive and transmit the conventions of the group), to *stratify* (to rank and be ranked according to valued criteria concerning distribution of scarce resources), to *organize* (to arrange and be arranged with others to accomplish valued tasks), and so on. The principles of sociology are the individual's sensitivities to others in light of his or her self-preservation (rational action); society is the externalized form of this sensitivity. This formulation permits a concise statement of what constitutes the subject matter of sociology—society as the externalization of subjective consciousness and at a determinate level of the individual's inherent and essential sociality, the predisposition to group life, and thereby the orientation to make rules to socialize, stratify, organize, and so forth. The externalized societal forms of cooperative agreements reflect back on the individual as the principles of sociology to invoke rule-following behavior.

[3]Recall here from Chapter 1 that socialization is one of six general or universal principles of constraint (socialization, stratification, organization, institutions, social control, and social change). These constraints, or ways in which our behavior is influenced by other people, are the basis for how groups acquire their characteristic rules or properties. We mean here that the significance of sociology as an analytic tool for helping us to understand why people behave the way they do lies in its distinctive shift in emphasis from individual to group determinants of behavior. For example, a sociologist might expect that according

to the *principle of organization* individual behavior is affected by the group's characteristic arrangement of persons to accomplish a particular task. Some sociologists who attempt to explain how the principle of organization operates have theorized (explained) that when a group is characterized by rules for formal organization (as opposed to informal organization) the relations between persons are (among other things) *segmented*. That is, for example, two students sitting in a classroom are unlikely to tell each other what they had for breakfast or whether or not they brushed their teeth. The behavior is less attributable to the personality of the individual and more attributable to the rules for behavior for the group. Another example would be for the group (aggregate), women; the principle of socialization designates the value and normative expectations (role) for the status, woman, so that American women are more likely, on the average, to wear lipstick than American men. This behavior has no genetic explanation nor can it be attributed to slight variations in personality; this is the average personality.

[4]Some sociologists view their subject matter for study at the level of societal (collective) characteristics rather than at the level of the origins of societal characteristics in subjective consciousness.

[5]A more detailed discussion of how social learning is explained by other theorists through the processes of modeling [operant learning], problem solving, direct teaching, interaction, and other theories can be found in the Suggested Readings at the end of this chapter (Hartup and Coates, 1970; Gesell and Ilg, 1943; Mead, 1961; Hamblin, 1971).

[6]See Levine and Havighurst (1989) for detail on a useful summary and analysis of the arguments of the neo-Marxist thinkers and revisionist historians on education and society. For example, they note the monograph *The Revisionists Revised: Studies in the Historiography of American Education* by Diane Ravitch. Levine and Havighurst comment that an important strand of critical theory as it explores the relation of education to the economy is a school of revisionist historians of education that emerged in the 1960s. This group views the public school as a systematic attempt to miseducate citizens in ways that serve the interests of the upper middle class capitalists.

[7]One or more of the principles of sociology operate together to coordinate human interaction. For example, although it is clear that cooperative learning is primarily an example of socialization (transmitting the value of cooperation as opposed to competition), the principles of organization and stratification are also operating. When group arrangements have consequences based on the ranking of the individuals according to their wealth, power, and prestige, then the principle of stratification accompanies the principles of socialization and organization.

CHAPTER
7

Stratification

*Rules for Acquiring
the Desirable Things in Life*

Why do some people have more of the desirable things in life than others? Are some people worth more than others? Will the students in the photograph have an equal opportunity to acquire (achieve) the socially desirable things in life—wealth, power, and prestige—or will some attain more than others on the basis of their gender, race, or ethnicity (ascriptive characteristics)? R. Biehler (1978) provides an account of how society's rules for ranking individuals appear in our formal educational practices. He describes how Jane Elliott, a third grade teacher in a small town in Iowa, was so deeply affected by the assassination of Martin Luther King, Jr. that she devised a technique for providing her students with direct experience of the *principle of stratification*. Her basic technique, which is reported in the television documentary *The Eye of the Storm*, is to group students according to eye color and assign elite status to one of the groups. For instance, she told the students that brown-eyed people are better, cleaner, more civilized, and smarter than blue-eyed people. The superior brown-eyed students were given extra time at recess, allowed to go to lunch first and given preferential seating in the front of the room, and were praised extensively for correct answers. The inferior blue-eyed students were required to use paper cups rather than the drinking fountain, were not allowed to use the equipment on the playground, and were treated as stupid when they gave wrong answers. In a few hours brown-eyed students became convinced of their superiority, to the point of mistreating blue-eyed classmates and then demanding an apology; formerly confident blue-eyed children became tense and unsure of themselves. The following week the roles were reversed and the blue-eyed children were decreed superior and given all the privileges. Despite the fact that the now inferior brown-eyed children were aware that this was just a temporary game, they reacted intensely and seemed to become convinced that they now were inferior. The only difference between the two phases of the experiment was that the blue-eyed children who had experienced discrimination first were noticeably less vicious in their treatment of their inferior classmates.

Outline

I am always amazed when I am treated differently on the basis of whether people know that I have a Ph.D. Invariably, I get better service in restaurants, banks, stores, and so on when I am known to be a *doctor*. Granted, a credential is a symbolic denotation of the kinds of knowledge and skills a person has acquired, and for this reason is a signal to other persons about what to expect from that individual and how to react to him or her. The Ph.D. (in United States society) elicits a particular kind of response from others; it engenders respect, deference, and sometimes substantial monetary rewards. And here again, as with all human activity, we see our essential sociality: William Goode (1977) remarks that one of the earliest bits of wisdom that the infant obtains is an awareness that whatever it wants must be acquired through other people. Adults think of themselves, he says, as more independent than infants, but little they do, from making love to murder, is performed without enlisting the aid of others. We observe how another powerful and enduring principle of social life elicits the cooperation of human beings by mobilizing them to behave in certain ways as a response to rules for the allocation of desired resources.

Does this mean that some people are *better* than others? Why do some people have more of the desirable things in life than others? Does difference alone matter, or is it how the difference is valued? Many people in the United States believe in differences, in *inequality*, but they believe that the rules for obtaining society's rewards must be fair. Some people, for example, are rewarded on the basis of how many freckles they have, whereas others are rewarded when they work hard to achieve success, such as the ballerina who routinely practices four hours per day.

We, as society, sort people on the basis of some characteristic and then rank them so that some are at the top of the hierarchy and some are at the bottom. Society's structure includes this dimension of constraint in the name of cooperation: People who have unequal amounts of scarce but desirable resources or rewards form layers or *strata*—hence the term *stratification*. Also noteworthy (and true for all of the social forces, not only stratification, that operate on us) is the degree to which stratification is engrained as part of the social programming of individuals; that is, how little it is thought about, despite its profound influence. We react to stratification prescriptions in the same way we respond to gravity, matter-of-factly, and unfortunately with the consequence that we come to experience inequality and to perceive ourselves as better or worse (selves) than others based on our position in the social strata.

The Principle of Stratification

Is Stratification Inevitable?

The *principle of stratification* refers to the rules regulating who should have what of the *desirable things in life* (wealth, power, and prestige), and under what conditions. It operates in all human societies. Its pervasive influence is seen operating alongside the other social principles to sustain human life.[1] That is, all the other principles are usually explained in terms of their relative tendencies to operate on the basis of conflict and consensus (that is, coercively, serving the interests of a few, versus democratically, representing the interests of many). Perhaps what makes stratification one of the most important of the principles of sociology is that it has the severest of consequences for the well-being of the individual.

Sociologists ask why the stratification system exists at all (Goode, 1977).[2] Resources and rewards are distributed with a powerful regularity. Traditional sociologists do not ask why some people have more than others do so much as they ask why different rewards accompany different positions in the occcupational system in different societies. People evaluate tasks and rank some as more valuable than others. Furthermore, each country ranks occupations in strikingly different ways. The most general formulation is that a society will offer higher or lower rewards to people who enter different occupations depending on how highly they value those occupations and how big the supply is of people who might be willing or able to do them.

Donald Light and Suzanne Keller (1985), in their introductory sociology text, present examples of the universal nature of stratification, how some form of inequality exists in each group. They tell about Zhang Longquan, a twenty-five year old Chinese farmworker, who was tired of his ordinary status in Shanghai of the People's Republic of China (supposedly a classless society). Longquan presented himself as the son of a top-ranking general and, consequently, received first class accommodations in food, travel, entertainment, and so on. Another example is the Trappist monk who lived in a monastery where no economic distinction exists: the monks own no property or clothing; they share their food; they enforce absolute material equality. Nevertheless, the way in which prestige is allocated is evidence of stratification. Differences in rank appear in relation to the individual's degree of achievement of the ideals of the community: love, friendliness, simplicity, humility, spirituality, integrity. These examples illuminate the varying dimensions and forms of stratification.

Dimensions and Forms of Stratification

Beyond the assumption that the principle of stratification operates universally in all human societies, we can go a step further in describing the principle by introducing the three dimensions on which social strata are based, what are commonly referred to as the desirable things in life: wealth, power, and prestige. Wealth refers to economic status. These features are surrogate indicators of *social class* (Weber, 1946). They can be independent of each other, but they are usually closely related (Trieman, 1977; Davis and Smith, 1983). The term *socioeconomic status* (SES) is an index used by sociologists to represent a person's social position; the index comprises income, type of occupation, and years of education.

We can also talk, in a generic sense, about the forms of stratification: *open, closed,* or *classless,* which is neither open nor closed. In a closed system, the boundaries between the strata are very clearly defined and no possibility exists for persons to change their statuses. In a closed system, membership is based on *ascribed status*, one that is attached to people on a basis other than their earning it through merit (skin color, freckles, religion).

In an open system, the boundaries between the strata are more flexible and it is possible for persons to change their social status. Membership in an open system is based on *achieved status*, or merit. The possibility of movement from one status to another is referred to as *social mobility*. For example, sociologists investigate how frequently the child of a plumber becomes a lawyer. Social mobility is divided into two types. The first, *exchange mobility*, is when people in high status jobs lose their positions and people in lower status jobs are promoted to higher status. This mobility depends on whether the system is closed or open. The second type, *structural mobility*, refers to the changes in people's social statuses as a consequence of changes in the economic structure of the society—whether certain kinds of jobs are needed by the society. Most people, however, even in open societies, remain in the social class of their parents (Grusky and Hauser, 1984).

Stratification in Education:
Equality of Educational Opportunity

Educational issues are a context for understanding the principle of stratification. We know that stratification concerns the rules for acquiring the desirable things in life and the school plays a part in this process by preparing each generation for a place in society, particularly occupational position. The sociological analysis of the school as an institution in the preceding chapter bears this out. The issue of stratification as it occurs in schooling, however, concerns how the school goes about this process. In other words, do students have an equal chance for preparing for those positions in the society that are rewarded highly, or does the *status quo* benefit some but not others in a system defined by those in power? As we examine the pervasiveness of stratification in education, notice that this chapter is the longest: more issues pertain to stratification than to any of the other principles of society. The operation of the principle of stratification is illustrated in the case of the fundamental basis on which United States public schools consent to or are charged to act—*equality of educational opportunity*. Equality of educational opportunity refers to the concept of all students having an equal chance of achieving a high socioeconomic status regardless of *sex*, *race*, or *social class*. We will extend our examination to include a discussion of whose interests are served in stratification as it occurs in *higher education*.

Most Americans have believed, and continue to believe, the the school is the great equalizer (Mann, 1848), when in fact, without other fortuitous factors (such as a strong financial background or psychological motivation), the school makes a relatively meager difference in the life chances of the individual. It is true that in the past the *common schools* served to create a mainstream identity for immigrants; assimilation into American culture required the *mass education* of persons to provide them with the skills needed for working in industry. Today, resistance to assimilation and support for the preservation of subcultural identity is widespread. Although the school is not all that hopes make it to be (Hurn, 1978), 75 percent of primary-age children in the world are formally educated (UNESCO, 1983) and educational background, alongside race and ethnicity, as has been shown in the literature, will continue to have the greatest direct effect on the life chances of individuals (Boli, Ramirez, and Meyer, 1985).

Thus the main questions about the principle of stratification and education: Does the school equalize opportunity, does it replicate inequality, or does it do both?

Investigations of the Principle of Stratification in Education

Despite basic agreement among sociologists about the universal operation of the principle of stratification in all human societies, contention remains about aspects of the nature of this operation. We will attempt to interpret the nature of stratification as it is illustrated in issues concerning equality of educational opportunity.

Functionalist and Conflict Interpretations

Functionalists explain that stratification in education plays a role in selecting and training persons for occupational positions in society. They argue that stratification functions to match important roles with scarce talents. Conflict theorists argue that stratification arises from a struggle to control scarce resources. Social institutions such as education reflect the interests of those who control the economy. Education supports the status quo. The ruling class does not exercise malevolence through a conspiracy designed such that education protects its interests; rather, by forming social networks of upper class people, its members act in their mutual interest (Collins, 1974). The existing inequality is not maintained by force but by gaining *legitimacy* as being "just the way things are."

Furthermore, according to functionalists, stratification operates in education such that persons are motivated to fill occupational roles through allocation of extrinsic rewards. The value placed on a particular position and the scarcity of qualified persons to fill the role determines the wealth, power, and prestige afforded to people filling the role. The positions most valued are those that require the most talent and training—education—and are designated for the greatest rewards (Davis and Moore, 1945). The more education one has obtained, the more valuable one is to society; inequality results on the basis of more education and more valued occupational position. Talcott Parsons (1970) argues that it is by consensus of needs and values that the process occurs. Also it is on the basis of achievement (merit), not ascription (sex, race, SES) that selection and allocation take place and lower SES students are in this way afforded an opportunity to mobilize in the system. Some evidence suggests that minority students are completing more years of schooling and that perhaps this is indicative of the declining significance of inequality in education (Hauser and Featherman, 1976). Of course, years of schooling alone is offset by evidence showing that a credential is not necessarily an avenue to higher paying positions and that the standards for getting these jobs become exclusive on other counts (Collins, 1979). Other evidence shows a mismatch between placement and merit in most highly industrialized societies. The observed distribution of the labor force, according to Tadeusz Krauze and K. M. Slomczynski (1985), does not reflect very well the meritocratic ideal concerning status mobility, determination, and inequality.

The credibility of a functionalist interpretation of the operation of stratification in education is questionable on several counts. When it focuses on the maintenance of a system, it does not take into account the type of system; this perspective is partial to the integrative forces that preserve the existing social system regardless of whether it is one that perpetuates inequality (Gouldner, 1971). The functions of education may be determined by those individuals who have dominant and powerful positions in the society and who attempt to sustain their own interests (Levitas, 1974).

Conflict theorists (including revisionists, neo-Marxists, and reproductionists), we have seen, simply view educational systems as replicating the existing social class inequalities by controlling what it means to be educated and restricting access to educational resources and occupational positions (Carnoy, 1974). United States schools do not equalize opportunity on a meritocratic basis. Instead, they serve the needs of a capitalistic system and capitalistic employers (Bowles, 1977). Conflict theorists look to the school mechanisms that operate in behalf of those in power. For example, ability grouping and other forms of tracking manipulate the transmission of knowledge to reproduce the social class relationships (Young, 1971).[3]

We will now turn to an examination of a number of empirical studies that in varying degrees support both functionalist and conflict explanations of the operation of the principle of stratification in education. We can test the explanatory power of either position by observing how well the school gives students the tools to succeed in the system on the basis of merit regardless of ascriptive attributes such as social class, sex, and race.

Social Class and Equality of Educational Opportunity

Tracking and Ability Grouping

One issue that permits us to examine the nature of the operation of the principle of stratification in education is tracking and ability grouping. Do these mechanisms suggest that the principle of stratification operates in American society to reproduce social class or to provide students with opportunities for getting ahead on their merits? Some researchers believe that the greatest impedence to equal opportunity in American education is *tracking*, the classroom grouping of students according to their perceived (measured) abilities and career interests.

Conflict theorists argue that tracking *does* prepare students for the work force, *but* according to social class structure. Students from the lower echelons of the socioeconomic ladder (including many racial and ethnic minorities) have a much smaller opportunity for obtaining a quality education than those from the upper social strata.

In both the elementary and secondary school, ability grouping (homogeneous grouping) is used to bring about better teaching and learning (Passow, 1988). High achievers are placed in one classroom, low achievers in another, and average achievers in yet another. Tracking in high schools refers to the practice of enrolling students in college preparatory classes (and honors classes) or in general or vocational program tracks. Low achievers are in the nonacademic tracks. Research evidence shows that ability grouping and tracking corresponds to social class, racial, and ethnic status. Because economically disadvantaged students display lower average achievment scores than do middle-class students, they are found disproportionately in low-achieving classes and nonacademic tracks, while middle-class students are disproportionately represented in higher-achieving classes and college preparatory courses and tracks. Also, social class has an independent effect on track placement. Eighty percent of seniors high in SES were in an academic track compared with 52 percent of seniors who were high in achievement but low in status (Vanfossen, Jones, and Spade, 1987).

Although ability grouping purportedly has been introduced to facilitate teaching and learning, research findings indicate that it generally does not improve student achievement. D. Levine and R. Havighurst (1989) state that reviews of research on this topic have largely concluded that ability grouping has little or no consistent effect. Some studies indicate that homogeneous grouping does promote higher performance for high achievers (Kulik and Kulik, 1987), but further depresses the performance of low-achieving students (Dar and Resh, 1986; Sørensen and Hallinan, 1986). A. Gamoran (1986) says that not only do low achievers respond to their teachers' low expectations but they reinforce each other's negative attitudes and behaviors. Jeannie Oakes (1985) also reports detrimental effects of ability grouping and tracking. The rudimentary curriculum content in low-ability classes lock students in that track by the omission of knowledge needed for access to classes in higher tracks. She concludes that given the association between economically and socially disadvantaged background and low-track placement, ability grouping and tracking frequently serve as barriers to upward mobility for capable poor and minority students. Ability grouping and tracking only reinforce the low performance of disadvantaged students, and at the high school level, tracking further depresses low-status students' enrollment in postsecondary education (Vanfossen, Jones, and Spade, 1987). More often then not, ability grouping and tracking in the United States educational system reproduces rather than mediates inequality. Of course, the question remains of how to conduct instruction in a hetereogeneous class so that high achievers are challenged without frustrating low achievers. Another issue is how to maintain high teacher expectations of students in low-level classes so that remediation and assistance override the self-fulfilling prophecy effects of teacher expectations.

Public and Private Schooling

The operation of stratification in issues of equality of educational opportunity is illustrated in the case of public versus private schooling. Which type of schooling offers the best education? Does this structural difference help some students to maintain their privileged position in society, or does it more often help students obtain positions in society that would not otherwise be possible? Fair access to quality education is believed to improve life chances. Which type of schooling is better for the students? Research on how public and private schools affect student achievement shows that the qualities of a good school are found more often in private than in public schools (Ravitch, 1982). James Coleman et al. (1981) found that net of family background, students in private schools (predominantly Catholic) achieve at a higher level than do those in public schools. Private schools also tend to have smaller classes and more involvement of students. More discipline and orderly conduct is evident in private schools and the school climate is achievement oriented. More homework is required in private schools and attendance is better than in public schools. These conditions results in higher academic achievement.

Findings on student achievement of minority students indicate that a racially integrated group of students in private schools has higher levels of vocabulary and mathematics achievement than do similar types of students who attend public schools (Greeley, 1982; Bryk et al., 1984). J. Coleman (1968) argues that Catholic schools function in a manner like the American common school, in which children from different backgrounds are educated alike. That is, the private school mediates the effect of ascriptive differences better than the public school.

Other evidence (Falsey and Heyns, 1984) shows that minority students and students from lower socioeconomic backgrounds benefit the most by being in Catholic schools. Their verbal and mathematics achievement in high school are better than those of students in public schools. These differences are attributed to the rigorous academic program and homework assignments. Seniors in private schools receive academic advisement and are more likely to enroll in a college following graduation from high school.

Although these findings seem to suggest an overall pattern that public schools tend to reproduce inequality more than private schools and challenge American public schooling, they should be interpreted with some caution. For example, we need to think about what is meant by a significant difference in achievement and whether this is a valid basis for establishing the claim that private schools are better than public schools (Alexander and Pallas, 1983, 1984, 1985). Critics of federal support for private education in the form of tax credits argue that this policy would help a relatively small number of minority students and students from low-income families.

Family Background

Many parents are quite surprised to hear that it is the home, rather than the school, that accounts for who succeeds in the system. In addressing our question of whether the principle of stratification reinforces inequality or mediates it, we now turn to another extensive research literature. James Coleman, a sociologist who headed a team of sociologists for the United States Department of Health, Education, and Welfare (HEW), began his nationwide research project of 4,000 schools, 570,000 students, and 60,000 teachers as part of an effort emanating from the Civil Rights Act of 1964. His aim was to demonstrate the difference in the quality between black schools and white schools. Results were contrary to expectation; little difference was found between predominantly black schools and predominantly white schools on various characteristics, including class size, expenditure per pupil, teacher characteristics, curriculum materials, and library facilities. Furthermore, he discovered that these school attributes had little association with student achievement test scores. Coleman concluded that the school has little influence on a child's achievement that is independent of his or her background; the inequalities imposed on children by their home (neighborhood and peer environment) are brought to the school and confront students in adult life after they complete school. So we see that schools have little effect on student achievement: the family is the major educational institution! Families are an ascribed status that affects children's educational opportunities and long-term life chances. Coleman suggested that to achieve comparable outcomes among students, the disadvantaged youth would need to receive compensatory education.

Neo-Marxists such as Henry Levin (1976) see the school as part of larger system developed to produce disciplined workers for a position at the bottom of the social ladder. The schools accomplish this by emphasizing external discipline in teaching working-class children in the same way as does the family in which they are reared. This process is referred to as the *correspondence principle*, in which the social relations of schooling and of family life correspond to the social relations of production. The social relations of the larger society are reproduced in the school in a way that reproduces the social class structure. However, this neo-Marxist interpretation of the operation of stratification in the case of equality of opportunity, regardless of SES, is questionable. If the correspondence principle holds true, the data should show very little upward mobility and downward mobility between the working class and the middle class, and most working-class children should be attending predominantly working-class schools and be enrolled in vocationally oriented programs in which they are being trained to be disciplined workers for the capitalists. The evidence from a number of studies (Levine and Havighurst, 1989) suggests not only that considerable mobility occurs in the United States and in other western societies, but also that these societies seem to be growing more meritocratic and education seems to be accounting for an increasing share of mobility. Other research has challenged the correspondence principle hypothesis. M. R. Olneck and D. B. Bills (1980), for example, found that men from middle-class families who were rated as uncooperative by their teachers had higher initial occupational status than those who were rated cooperative. Also, no association was shown between teachers' rating of cooperativeness and initial job status (having better jobs right out of high school) among working-class youth. These findings are inconsistent with the contention that the same behaviors are rewarded at work as in school.

Christopher Jencks et al. (1972) conducted another landmark study on the determinants of school performance. Jencks's study reached the same conclusion as Coleman's study, that the effects of the family background have a much greater effect on school performance than school characteristics (although school composition is an important variable). He reported that family socioeconomic status is the most powerful predictor of academic performance. Family background accounts for more than half of the variation in education attainment.

Annette Lareau (1987) provides evidence that supports a cultural capital explanation of stratification as it operates in the school. Parental participation in schooling varies according to social class. Teachers relate differently to parents of middle-class students than to parents of working-class students so that students from middle-class families benefit from family resources more than students from lower-class families.

In an investigation of the cumulative disadvantage among the highly ambitious, Katherine McClelland (1990) says past research shows that while more young Americans want professional jobs, many will be disappointed. Based on a subsample of respondents to the National Longitudinal Study of the High School Class of 1972, McClelland examined the process by which high school seniors try, and some fail, to reach their goal of high-status professional jobs during the first seven years out of high school. She found that although a process of "cumulative disadvantage" occurs for everyone, controlling for differences in academic ability, males from upper-white-collar homes are more likely to survive and reach their initial goals. Marriage, on the other hand, is an especially strong disadvantage during this period for woman and the nonprivileged. However, going to an "elite" university helps everyone.

In sum, the theory and supporting evidence on social class background and equality of educational opportunity indicates that (as conflict theorists point out) talent selection results in the rejection of the disadvantaged and that cultural transmission and socialization result in different things depending more on social status than on merit. Social class is replicated through public versus private schooling, through tracking and ability grouping, and through the home environment characteristics that students bring to school. Despite the claim that United States schools make provision for equal opportunity for all children to develop their abilities, we see that certain categories of children finish at the bottom of the achievement hierarchy. By analyzing major dynamics in people's lives which usually go unquestioned, we have seen the way in which the principle of stratification operates in the case of the American school context.

Gender and Equality of Educational Opportunity

The principle of stratification operates in the school context as equality of opportunity. However, differences in opportunities according to the ascriptive attribute, *gender*, are found concerning the schools' perpetuation of gender stereotypes, the gender composition of schools, school activities, and in achievement and motivation to achieve.

Gender Stereotypes

Society's expectations of male and female children foster differential behavior. Stereotypes of gender behavior encourage girls' self-esteem to be linked with grades much more than is boys' self-esteem. Working-class girls' choices of business courses reproduce their class and gender status (Gaskell, 1985). Grade school textbooks have been found to be a source of gender expectations. For example, mathematics problems involving girls frequently show them jumping rope, sewing, cooking, or grocery tabulating (Federbush, 1974). These images and depictions limit what girls see as appropriate occupational roles. Gender expectations in society are reflected by the school: boys are competitive and ambitious, but girls are docile and cooperative (Delamont, 1980). School activities also reflect stereotypes. Six differences in the play patterns of boys and girls were observed by J. Lever (1978): boys play outdoors more than girls; boys play in larger groups; boys' play occurs in more age-heterogeneous groups; girls play predominantly male games whereas boys infrequently play girls' games; boys' games last longer than girls' games; and boys play competitive games more often than girls.

Gender Composition of Schools

Another occasion to witness how gender, as an ascriptive characteristic, typifies the operation of stratification in the educational context pertains to the gender composition of schools. In the United States, elementary school teachers are almost all female (86 percent). But at the high school level, 56 percent of the teachers are female, with increasingly fewer women in administration: assistant principal (22 percent), principals (14 percent), and superintendents (1 percent). The higher the status, the fewer the women. Socialization affects attitudes and structural barriers limit access (National Advisory Council on Women's Educational Programs, 1981). Women, because of socialization, tend not to seek administrative responsibilities; other barriers occur during recruitment and evaluation (Gupta, 1983). Sex-role stereotyping tends not to be reinforced in single-sex high schools and universities; the academic achievement and educational aspirations of girls in single-sex environments is higher (Lee and Bryk, 1986).

Gender Differences in Achievement and Motivation

Another clue as to how the principle of stratification operates in schools is found in issues of sex differences in achievement and motivation. Equality of educational opportunity would be indicated by similar patterns of achievement and motivation; girls, however, surpass boys in achievement in elementary school and in high school grades. By middle school, girls' perceptions of themselves begin to affect their career orientations so that by the time girls are seniors in high school, their occupational aspirations pattern like sex differences in occupations (Herzog, 1982). Other evidence of differential performance is in the case of mathematics and science achievement. Differences in mathematics achievement start to increase by adolescence, with males outperforming females (Fennema and Carpenter, 1981). Of course, the disproportionately smaller number of females who do not demonstrate achievement in mathematics are precluded from considering highly valued occupational positions in math- and science-related fields.

These differences by sex must be accounted for by explanations that are biological or social. Most research evidence discounts a biological explanation for male-female differences. The evidence is inconclusive because conducting research that rules out cultural and environmental confounding factors is difficult. Some evidence shows that boys tend to use both brain hemispheres for spatial and mathematical reasoning, whereas girls concentrate in the left hemisphere. Hormones may interact with brain functioning to cause differences that appear at adolescence (Sherman, 1977).

Concerning school-related social factors as explanations of gender differences in mathematics performance, some evidence indicates that the small differences in overall school math performance are associated with the number and level of mathematics courses taken, career expectations, and dating behavior. College and career plans are affected by whether girls have taken enough mathematics courses, and this varies according to their perceptions of discrimination against women working in certain fields and gender stereotypes about occupations (Vanfossen, 1987). Females have been shown to attribute success to external or unstable causes and failure to internal causes and the perception that teachers expect boys to be better and more aggressive problem solvers (Fennema, 1981). White males have been encouraged to be independent thinkers and to be creative in solving mathematics problems rather than following algorithms (Grieb and Easley, 1984).

Jeanne Ballantine (1989) states that a number of efforts have been taken by schools to combat sexism in the educational system. These range from teacher education concerning stereotypes to school regulations that enforce equal treatment of male and female students with regard to financial aid, counseling, course and program enrollment, and access to sports facilities. Apparently, the school reinforces society's expectations initially transmitted to students at home, but in so doing the school plays a part in prejudicing the availability of knowledge important for success in the United States system.

Race and Ethnicity and Equality of Educational Opportunity

Besides gender, the big divide in equality of educational opportunity is according to race and ethnicity. This ascriptive factor affects the educational opportunities of students and further illustrates the principle of stratification in operation.

Race, IQ, and Achievement Testing

Is it hard to believe that when people behave in unjust ways to harm others they tend to create beliefs to justify their harmful actions? As it pertains to the principle of stratification, this practice is known as *legitimation*. One attempt at legitimation is *racism*, the belief that some human races are inherently inferior to others. Arthur Jensen, an educational psychologist at the University of California at Berkeley, published a controversial article in the *Harvard Educational Review* in 1969 on race, heredity, and intelligence. Jensen reported that black Americans score ten to fiteen points lower than the average score for whites on IQ tests; he suggested that genetic factors account for the differences. Other social scientists (Scarr, 1981; Tumin, 1973; Scarr and Weinberg, 1975, 1976; Kamin, 1974) reject Jensen's interpretation of racial differences in IQ test performance. M. Tumin argues that racial prejudice and discrimination make it virtually impossible to equate blacks and whites; only if we could consider their life experiences equal (regardless of incomes, which are alike) could we make valid comparisons. Research findings generated by these scholars indicate that mathematical ability develops similarly in black and white preschoolers and that later differences exist mainly because blacks and whites have not had the same opportunities. They view support for a biological determinism explanation of racial differences in IQ from a conflict perspective. In this view, using the IQ test for educational and job placement guarantees that children of the dominant elite will secure the best occupational placement based on their IQ credentials.

The purported function of standardized testing is to select and allocate students according to their ability. Besides controversy over the validity of IQ tests for certain groups of students, testing in general concerns such issues as these: What is really being measured? To what extent do genetic or environmental factors influence test results? Is it possible to develop a culture-free test? Content validity, the match between curriculum and test items, is also an issue. Some educators criticize tests (like those produced by the Educational Testing Service) on grounds that they are invalid measures of classroom experience; nevertheless, in a society in which the principle of stratification operates on the basis of merit, giving tests seems to be the inevitable method for standardizing and evaluating knowledge deemed valuable by that society (Ballantine, 1989; Marlaire and Maynard, 1990).[4]

Race and Achievement Outcomes

Americans still find it difficult to believe that it is the home, not the school, that mostly accounts for the unequal distribution of success. Evidence from the Coleman (1966) study and the Jencks (1972) study (discussed earlier) provide major insights on the role of race in educational opportunity. Coleman's study, as mentioned, assessed the opportunities and performance of black and white students. The findings indicated that except for Asian students, minority students scored lower on standardized achievement tests at each level of schooling than did white students and the disparity increased from first to twelfth grades. Most of the students in the study attended segregated schools and teachers tended to teach students of their own race. The socioeconomic composition of the school was largely associated with students' achievement. Curriculum and school facilities had very little direct effect on achievement. These findings led to the recommendation that schools be integrated so as to create an environment that would foster in minority students the achievement motivation characteristic of white students. Busing was employed as a method for desegregating schools.

Jencks's et. al (1979) study of inequality corroborated the results of Coleman's study in that the school itself was found to make little difference in equalizing opportunity. He concluded that family background is the major determinant of school achievement (about 48 percent of the variance in occupational attainment is explained by family background). Ultimately, Jencks concluded that even when the educational attainment gap between minorities and whites is reduced, economic inequality among adults would continue; because schools are unable to achieve an egalitarian stratification structure, income should be redistributed according to a socialistic basis.

Despite these rather pessimistic results, efforts were taken toward reasonable reform rather than toward radical revolution of society's structure. We can examine the effectiveness of these modest attempts by the school to equalize opportunity.

Desegregation and Busing

In 1954, the Supreme Court ruled in *Brown v. The Board of Education* that schools must be desegregated. This intervention challenged traditional United States racial barriers in education (Orfield, 1983). Coleman had made known that blacks in middle-class schools performed better than blacks in ghetto schools. He argued that by immersing a low-income student in a middle-class environment, the achievement values of middle-class students would be internalized by the low-income student with a subsequent beneficial effect on school achievement. He advocated that the metropolitan school district include both disadvantaged children and privileged children and that students could be bused from one part of the district to another to accomplish a racial and socioeconomic balance in schools. Court-ordered busing has since reduced public school segregation. However, court-ordered busing has encouraged white parents to remove their children from metropolitan public schools by either sending their children to private schools or by engaging in the activity known as *white flight*, that is, moving to the suburbs. Some critics of busing have argued that busing has thus caused more segregation in city schools because it results in changes in the proportions of white and black students. But the evidence is otherwise. Most research indicates that white flight from urban areas does not, overall, appear to be the effect of desegregation (Daniels, 1983).

Research evidence on the effectiveness of desegregation in raising the academic performance of minority students is mixed. Some evidence suggests that achievement test scores of disadvantaged children have not improved as a result of desegregation practices alone (Rist, 1973). Some contradictory evidence exists that minority student achievement test performance was improved and white student performance remained the same (Daniels, 1983). Robert L. Crain and Rita Mahard (1982) argue that desegregation effects on achievement are fairly strong and positive. Blacks who attend desegregated high schools seem to have higher educational attainment and get better jobs than those from segregated schools (McPartland, Dawkins, Braddock, Crain, and Strauss, 1985). Blacks have made gains in educational attainment, but educational differences by social class continue.

Integration—Compensatory Education

Desegregation by itself has not been able to enhance the achievement of disadvantaged students. Other compensatory programs were implemented to facilitate equality of educational opportunity. In 1965, the Elementary and Secondary Education Act was passed as an effort to improve the education of poor and minority students, resulting in a number of compensatory education programs funded under the auspices of the government: early childhood programs, bilingual education programs, and high school programs to help students prepare for the college transition.

Head Start and Follow-Through are early childhood compensatory education programs. Head Start attempts to equalize opportunity for very young children so they are ready to start kindergarten with skills comparable to advantaged children. Program Follow-Through aims at sustaining this comparability, in the lower grades, of disadvantaged students who have been in the Head Start Program. A. H. Halsey (1980) has investigated the lasting effects of the early childhood programs and found that program participants are less likely to be assigned to remedial courses later in their educational experience. They are also less likely to be retained in grade (repeat a year in school) because of failing performance. Participants' achievement in mathematics and reading at fourth grade is improved by preschooling. Preschoolers in the program scored higher on the Stanford-Binet IQ test—for up to three years afterward—than did poor children who did not participate. Also, program children retain more achievement orientation, and their mothers tend to develop higher vocational aspirations for the children than the mothers have for themselves.

Bilingual education programs have been implemented, especially to teach English to children whose primary language is Spanish. The reasoning is that to have an equal opportunity in the system, children must be able to speak the dominant language of the system.

Bilingual education is criticized on grounds that students are disadvantaged when they are taught in a second language that does not reflect their cultural background, but some evidence shows that students who are instructed in the minority language perform as well in English academic skills as comparable students instructed totally in English (Cummins, 1986).

Other compensatory programs were designed to prepare students to make the high school to college transition by identifying students with college potential early in secondary school; by supplemental education; by accepting lower academic requirements for college admission; by using admission criteria that permit open enrollment; by assisting students once they have been admitted into college; and by making available financial assistance based solely on need (Ornstein, 1985). The Upward Bound Program is one such intervention program; however, Ballantine (1989) reports that statistics indicate a lack of lasting improvement in achievement for program participants overall. Benjamin Stickney and Virginia R. Plunkett (1983), in a historical review of the effectiveness of compensatory education programs, state that changes in the programs have resulted in postive and long-lasting effects. Critics, however, question whether compensatory education is able to make a valid contribution toward offsetting disadvantage. Martin Carnoy (1975), espousing a conflict interpretation of compensatory education, argues that educational achievement is not equalized simply by supplementing educational resources. He promotes a radical redefinition of schooling in which student performance is evaluated on a different basis, rendering all children equally acceptable.

Other Minorities

Another way to to detect inequality of educational opportunity is to examine the relative success of various minority students in the system. Hispanic children, on the average, perform more poorly than whites, but not as poorly as black students. Dropout rates for Mexican-American students are comparable to other groups (United States Department of Education, 1983). Asian students do better in school than other minorities. Asian students have taken more courses in mathematics, natural science, and foreign language than other students (National Center for Educational Statistics, 1985). The relative success of Asian students is explained by factors such as compatibility with American middle-class values, high performance expectations by teachers, and strong parental authority (Kitano, 1976). Native Americans now control their own schools rather than being under the control of the Bureau of Indian Affairs (Higher Education Research Institute, 1982). Last, special education students were ensured equal educational opportunities by the PL 94–142 legislation enacted by Congress in 1975. This was the Education for All Handicapped Children Act, which made provision for all handicapped children to be educated in a "least restrictive environment" (LRE). An LRE is one in which handicapped children are exposed, as frequently as possible, to the general educational environment. Some evidence shows that mainstreaming special education students has positive results (Wang, Reynolds, and Walberg, 1986).

Stratification in Higher Education

In this section, we are intent on looking at the role of higher education in equalizing opportunity. We will ask the same questions about the nature of the principle of stratification that was asked before when considering differences in equality of educational opportunity according to race, gender, and socioeconomic status. Does the school, in this case higher education, equalize opportunity, does it replicate inequality, or does it do both?

Before we examine specific issues of stratification in higher education, we need to consider the general issue of the declining significance of a college education.[5] In 1970 the median income of men with a college education was 42 percent higher than that of male high school graduates; by 1980 the advantage had declined to 25 perent (Guinzburg, 1983). For women, the decline was even greater, from 56 percent in 1970 to 31 percent in 1980. Educational inflation has reduced the significance of the bachelor's degree so that it is not worth as much as it once was in economic returns; more college degrees have been granted in relation to the number of occupational positions that require a college education. Jobs that were done by high school graduates are now being done by college graduates (Berg et al., 1978; Collins, 1979). Still, a college credential yields opportunity for upward mobility for most students, and we need to take a look at the differential allocation of this resource (Shavit and Kraus, 1990).

Equal Access: Selective and Open Admissions

Functionalists and conflict theorists have attempted to explain how the principle of stratification operates concerning the controversy over access to higher education. The functionalists argue that higher education is a mechanism that increases opportunities for people by enhancing their technical skills for specific occupational slots and for general participation in society. The conflict argument is that the expansion of higher education is associated with the needs of a capitalistic system and, as is true for primary and secondary education, the school is a mechanism that reproduces advantage and disadvantage. Samuel Bowles and Herbert Gintis (1976), for example, view higher education as a tracking arrangement in which, for the most part, students are not prepared for elite status jobs. Access to those institutions of higher education that prepare students for elite jobs is based on the admissions process—whether it is *selective* or *open* (Collier and Mayer, 1986).

Evidence on university admission "gatekeeping" is gathered on the basis of any one criterion or combination of criteria: test scores, high school grades, extracurricular activities, and references. United States college admission requires the student to answer all questions pertinent to these factors, but considerable debate continues about the fairness of national achievement tests (SAT and ACT) as a criterion for admission. Minority students, who constitute approximately 20 percent of those to whom the test is administered, do relatively poorly on the exam. Some argue that the tests are invalid measures of achievement for some groups of students (Crouse, 1986). For elite universities such as Oxford in England, entrance is based exclusively on examination performance. Students from lower SES categories attend less prestigous schools, and this social class disparity is an important consideration for entry into the British elite universities. In Japan, lower SES students simply decline to take the examination, which serves to perpetuate intergenerational inequality.

Critics of the *open door policy* (under which any high school graduate is eligible to apply for admission to the university) have argued that this arrangement compromises academic standards and quality of education, and in this sense violates the meritocratic structure of opportunity. Those in favor of the policy argue that the arrangement enhances minority opportunities for success in the system, thereby reducing social inequality (Lavin, Alba, and Silberstein, 1979). Conflict theorists caution that admissions alone are not a valid indicator of equality of opportunity in the stratification system; they suggest that attention be paid to the numbers who graduate compared to those who were admitted and to tracking arrangements within the system that ultimately tend to replicate inequality.

Some, like Joseph Ben-David (1972), claim that the growth of American higher education, especially in the 1960s, is reflected in the size of institutions and the fact that teaching quality has not declined and dropout rates have been stable. More recent data from the Center for Education Statistics (1986) show continuing enrollment increases. The evidence supporting the view that more people entering higher education does not compromise standards is offset by another argument: although more graduate, the college credential does not guarantee an elite job (Collins, 1979). Randall Collins says that the elite come up with new requirements, new standards, and new credentials, not as a consequence of the need for new educational knowledge, but to restrict access to elite positions. Of course, creating new standards deflates the value of the credential and serves the elite in perpetuating their status. The credential has decreasing correspondence to occupational requirements and, therefore, the functionalist argument that educational requirements match the economic and occupational demands of the society loses credibility. Conflict theorists would contend that increasing tensions could lead to change in opportunities afforded through structural mobility (the number and kinds of jobs, as well as the value placed on them in the system).

Equal Access: Affirmative Action

Equal access issues include the government's involvement in minority student admissions policy by making provision for special programs, by affirmative action ruling, and by denial of research monies for failure to comply with federal regulation of minority admissions and staff hiring (Ballantine, 1989). The complexity of the issue, according to Jeanne Ballantine, is illustrated by the 1978 Bakke case in which preferential treatment to minorities was challenged. Bakke contested the quota system at the University of California School of Medicine at Davis that admitted minorities with lower test scores than whites, calling the policy one of reverse discrimination. The court ruled that racial balance in admissions could be accomplished through admissions and affirmative action procedures, but that strategies other than quota systems that protected the individual rights of students (of nonminority status with higher tests scores) should be employed. The debate continues. As for evidence for deciphering how the principle of stratification operates in the context of higher education and equality of educational opportunity through equal access, we are left with good intentions but not data on outcomes; we do not know whether the arrangements undermine merit-based assignment of persons to valued positions in the society, or whether affirmative action legislation is a step toward advancing equality of opportunity.

Academic versus Business Interests

We have learned about the nature of the principle of stratification as it operates in higher education through examination of issues pertaining to equal access. Issues over the function of the university and whose interests are served in the process also lend support to competing explanations of the operation of stratification. Conflicts over functions of the university center around whether the school as a community (Kerr, 1963) caters to academic or business interests, whether the curriculum is liberal or practical education, and whether research or teaching is emphasized, including whether knowledge dissemination as public service is valued. Last, college type and occupational selection reveals something about who gets what and under which conditions. All of these issues, ultimately, concern equality of educational opportunity because they tell us about how social mechanisms impede a fair distribution of the desirable things in life.

Disputes over university governance on a bureaucratic or business model illuminate the operation of the principle of stratification in terms of whose interests are being served by this community organizational arrangement. The major debate is over providing quality education and administrating an economically efficient bureaucracy (Parelius and Parelius, 1978).

The Recruitment of Athletes   One empirical verification that seems to support the theoretical interpretation that people achieve more on the basis of ascription than on the basis of academic merit is the case of college athletes. Star high school players are recruited, but data on black athletes who enter college shows that 14 percent graduate in four years and 31 percent in six years (Ballantine, 1989). Attempts to equalize opportunity on a meritocratic basis for athletes have looked like a proposal to let athletes play for five years so that they have time to complete their schooling; also, freshman athletes must have a 2.0 high school GPA in core courses and an SAT combined score of 700 (or an ACT score of 15). Other program interventions such as counseling, tutoring, and restrictions on practice time suggest efforts to minimize business interests and to maximize equal educational opportunity.

Academic versus Administrative Hierarchies   Stratification also operates in higher education in the dual hierarchy of administration and academia. This issue again illustrates contention over the compromise between quality education and an economically efficient educational system. How are academic concerns negotiated for profit? The administrative and academic hierarchical structure is as follows: The *department* is an administrative unit with a chairperson who is elected or appointed for a given term. The position may even rotate among department members. The chair is accountable to both department members and to higher-level administrators. The position comes with an inherent role conflict, because a chair must both support faculty and sit in judgment of them for salary increases and promotions. Rank in the department hierarchy begins with instructor and proceeds from assistant professor to associate professor to professor. The department usually operates democratically in making decisions. At the *college* level, several related disciplines are grouped as a college (a group of departments) with a dean as administrator. Decisions at this level concern such broad areas as finances, salaries, scheduling, and new programs.

The *administration* consists of a president or chancellor, a vice-president, and deans and assistants who may or may not be faculty members. Responsibilites are for academic matters, student services, and finances. The faculty are advocates of academic freedom and this structural looseness undercuts centralized decision-making. Once faculty members are tenured, their independence from administrative decisions is further increased.

Faculty senates are composed of representatives from the various colleges and schools of the university and have decision-making power in academic issues. The

Board of Trustees is comprised of community lay persons. These members are appointed by state governors or elected by other board members. Trustees are usually white males, at least fifty years old, who hold or have held business positions (Jacobson, 1986). The Board of Trustees has ultimate control in decision making, thereby removing this power from faculty and prejudicing the decision making toward business interests (Clark, 1976). *Accrediting associations* are national associations that evaluate institutions of higher education, not to standardize practices, but to help each institution determine whether it has achieved its own goals. Action by the *federal government* in higher education is seen mainly in research funding, but a national policy, other than major concerns with such issues as "excellence in education" and failure to compete with other countries, does not exist. State and local governments provide more than half of the revenues for public and private institutions.

Professional Unions and Collective Bargaining   The operation of the principle of stratification in education as equality of educational opportunity, and in the case of higher education as business, is observable in the issues of *professional unions* and *collective bargaining*. Most faculty believe to some degree in the notion of academic freedom, autonomy over decisions related to their discipline. The American Association of University Professors (AAUP) has represented faculty interests by providing guidelines for salaries, promotion, and policies. Faculty at elite universities are less inclined to use union bargaining because their salaries are relatively higher than nonelite schools. Yet appeal of faculty unions and collective bargaining seems to be increasing to academics. Results of analyses of faculty salary gains at institutions with collective bargaining compared with those without have ranged from significantly increased faculty salaries and benefits (Morgan and Kearney, 1977) to no significant impact on salary and benefits (Brown and Stone, 1977). Other evidence indicates that academic governance and collective bargaining regularizes personnel procedures through a grievance system and includes policies for retrenchment in case of economic necessity (Kemerer and Baldridge, 1980). Perhaps the institution of higher education as a business gets in the way of promoting an equal learning opportunity for students. It seems that the evidence leans toward a conflict interpretation of stratification.

Academic control in the United States university shows little formal authority at the national level; at the state, multicampus, and university-wide levels, trustee and administrative authority predominates over faculty interests; at the lower college and departmental levels, faculty exert strong decision-making power over personnel and curriculum. Students also have varying degrees of power; although they are not primary decision makers, they influence change in the status quo. Because the decision-making power is with the trustees rather than with the faculty, the university appears to operate mostly on the basis of being a business, but with the intent to balance fiscal matters with the academic interests of faculty and student body. In public institutions of higher education, fundamental authority over finances is with the state Board of Trustees or Regents. In privately funded institutions, administrators depend on funds from alumni and other sources who will have say in making decisions.

In the language of stratification, these dynamics mean that although education's role is unilaterally the advancement and transmission of knowledge, as Ballantine (1989) comments, the commonness of purpose does not imply commonness of method or curriculum content and, further, dimensions of conflict and consensus operate within the university structure to benefit some and not others. Decision making in higher education varies by constituency in the institution. The combination of benefits, however, seems to be under the broader influence of societal economic and technological factors, and in this sense, institutions of higher education reflect competing national interests or consensus-based functional integration in a global system. (Recall from Chapter 5 how the principle of institutions operates at the macro level as a determinant of what goes on at the micro levels. A thorough understanding of the principle of stratification entails the consideration of conflict and consensus at both levels.)

Liberal versus Practical Education

Stratification operates in the case of higher educational curriculum as having a *liberal* or *practical* orientation. Knowledge for its own sake typifies a liberal education whereas job-oriented knowledge characterizes practical education (Millet, 1973). Elite schools are being pressured to introduce applied programs in addition to their pure arts and sciences focus. The degree to which the university emphasizes one purpose or other suggests a functional integration dynamic of stratification, but simultaneously, the economic value placed on certain types of jobs may represent the interests of an elite few. Educational purpose has functional correspondence with economic interests, but the interests may be those defined by a dominant few.

Research or Teaching Emphasis

The operation of the principle of stratification in higher education is visible in the issue of research versus teaching emphasis. The most prestigious institutions of higher education attract the most prominent faculty members; these faculty spend less time teaching than they do consulting, attending conferences, and working at other institutions as visiting scholars. Committee service and teaching are the responsibility of younger faculty members, and the university accepts this arrangement because having a well-respected faculty increases the prestige of the university, which in turn may attract other leading experts and students as well as more finances (Caplow and McGee, 1958). T. Caplow says that the trend away from teaching and toward research in the major universities is accompanied by minor shifts away from teaching and toward public service, and away from undergraduate and toward graduate instruction. The trend is also marked by less involvement of faculty in the curriculum and more interest in specialization. An increasing percentage of the faculty view teaching as a deterrent to their more essential responsibilities of research. Teaching is the primary obligation at two-year institutions and at four-year liberal arts colleges (McGee, 1971). *Cosmopolitan* faculty, those who maintain professional networks outside their institution, develop their research and writing in relation to a wider audience and attract more grant money and prestige. *Local* faculty attend to matters within their institution and are more loyal to that institution (Lemmers, 1974). Although attention to research indicates that the institution is fulfilling its goal by contributing to new knowledge on a theoretical level, the sociological question remains: whose interests does the new knowledge serve? If the goal of education is to offer the young equal opportunity in the work force, how does the emphasis on research ultimately benefit students?

Emphasis on teaching is indicative of the university's goal to *disseminate* knowledge and in this way prepare students for occupational roles. Many graduate schools and universities that have schools of medicine and law are criticized for giving inadequate attention to teaching. An empirical test of whose interests are served in this process is how well students obtain various occupations. Again, this must be viewed in light of who decides which occupations in the wider society are more valuable. If no differences in occupational attainment are shown between students who graduate from research-oriented schools and those who graduate from teaching-oriented schools, then differences in emphasis must reflect competing interests between faculty members; this, in turn, is a measure of stratification *within* the occupational group, college professors.

Another stratification issue related to knowledge dissemination is the university's involvement in the diffusion of knowledge in the wider community. What consequences will new knowledge have for the wider society? For example, in science, research related to the splitting of the atom had tremendous consequences: whose interests were served? A medical discovery has outcomes that are entrepreneurial in nature. The financial profits for the scientist making the discovery violate the norm in science that ensures knowledge production by making it available to everyone, not hoarding it for self-interest. Whose interests will be served? A continuing debate concerns the degree to which faculty should participate in using knowledge for social awareness; it is unclear how this would affect equal educational opportunity for students. We observe again that the principle of stratification operates, as in most situations, by both consensus and conflict. More empirical evidence on this issue will shed light on the relative contribution of each.

College Type and Occupational Selection

Institutions vary according to sponsorship, student composition, and types of programs and degrees offered. Students have long wondered whether it makes a difference in long-term success if they attend a public or private institution of higher education, or whether a small elite school is better than a large impersonal state institution. Evidence suggests that the college attended is more significant than college grades or job performance in predicting future status and earnings (Hurn, 1978). Students who have graduated from a prestigious school have a better chance for higher income (Tinto, 1979). Training in graduate school at a prestigious university by a productive faculty member enhances the graduate's productivity in his or her professional work (Reskin, 1979). Therefore, college type and quality are important determinants of occupational success. The gap between high school graduates and college graduates in terms of their beginning salaries is narrowing (Darling-Hammond, 1983), but it appears that the system is benefiting a few through restriction of access to prestigious schools of higher education. Junior colleges seem to filter out marginal students, who often are minority students (Velez, 1985). Burton Clark (1980) says that the two-year terminal degree was designed to dissuade students with academic weakenesses from transferring to four-year institutions. Junior colleges (with a population expanding more rapidly than that of four-year colleges) serve a "cooling-out" function for marginal students. These students with modest academic performance are channeled into occupational programs that prepare them for middle-level jobs. Career education and vocational training have helped move blacks into people-oriented and data-processing occupations (Campbell et al., 1982).

Issues of Race and Ethnicity, Sex, and SES in Higher Education

The influence of ascriptive factors on the life chances of students in the context of higher education are useful in interpreting the nature of stratification. The United States system provides, for the most part, *contest mobility*, characterized by open competition and rewards for high achievers with acceptance into the better academic institutions. *Sponsored mobility* sometimes impedes this process by favoring some students and preparing them for particular occupational positions (Turner, 1960). Of the 21 percent minority population in the United States, only 17 percent are enrolled in higher education. Many universities offer remedial and developmental services for low-achieving students with weak basic skills (Roueche, 1984). A profile (Mingle, 1987) of the participation of minorities in higher education during the past three decades shows that by the year 2025 they will make up nearly 40 percent of all eighteen to twenty-four year olds. Hispanics have the lowest high school graduation rates (62 percent), while whites have the highest (83 percent). College participation rates among black and Hispanic youth peaked in the mid-1970s and have declined since then. Asian-Americans now make up more than 3 percent of total enrollments, yet account for 2 percent representation in the general population. Except for Asian-Americans, the representation of minorities drops dramatically at the graduate and professional level. Blacks, who make up about 13 percent of college-age youth, comprise 9.5 percent of undergraduate and 4.8 percent of graduate students. Statistics on retention and success of minorities in higher education show that students on the fast track are those who achieve senior status four years after high school graduation. One of every three Asians in the class of 1980 was on the fast track, but only one in seven blacks and one in ten Hispanics. Minority representation in the professions is also disproportionate: only about 2.6 percent of employed engineers in the nation are black and their representation among such professional groups is far below their numbers in the population. The Hispanic population (Puerto Ricans, Mexican-Americans, and Cubans) are overrepresented in low-skill jobs.

The statistics on women completing college and entering graduate school show increases in their participation in nontraditional occupational roles (Giele,

1986). Many women are reentering college with more than one million in higher education (Billson and Terry, 1982). Women are less discriminated against in college and professional school admission, but once accepted, other forms of discrimination affect their achievement (Parelius and Parelius, 1987). Carol Gilligan (1979) argues that women have been judged by male patterns of success and there is little acknowledgement that other patterns result in success. Women, for example, may enter the professions after childbearing years.

Conclusion: Are We More than Our Position in the Social Structure?

We have examined how stratification operates in education to sort persons for differentially valued occupational roles in society. But we also need to consider who we are in relation to the social class status we occupy. Does our experience of having a self-identity exist apart from our social class status? Actually, sociology cannot answer the question of identity, of who we really are: it is not designed to address who we are *behind* our statuses and roles. Society is, however, only a part of the person; we *occupy* our statuses, we do not *become* them. But sometimes we confuse our occupying of a status with our *being* the status (Babbie, 1988). A good way to test whether you have let your social status determine your identity is when you react, emotionally, by getting angry at any comments made to you that denigrate any of your statuses, for example, "black," "female," "working class," "Democrat," or "fat." If so, you have identified with the status you occupy, but at the same time have probably lost sight of the totality of who you are. Chapter 6 begins with a comment about a young man who commits suicide because his identity was centered on being a good student, and he could not live up to that standard. This leads me to say he lost sight of the realization that we are more than just our statuses, we are more than just social beings. These statuses determine how others expect you to act and vice versa. But they are not you.

Peter Berger (1963) says that a nonhumanistic sociology equates persons with their socially assigned identities (a set of categories and roles that supply appellations to people: *Americans, students, the elderly*). This sociology emphasizes that a "black" is a person created by society so that the designation produces constraints that make the person behaviorally conform to a particular image or depiction. Others who interact with the "black" person might respond, therefore, as racist or racial liberal. Thus, the liberal as much as the racist is caught up in the socially taken-for-granted prescription, except that the liberal attaches opposite valuations to the role and status. That is, the liberal reaction to race is to simply reverse the signs attached to the category without fundamentally challenging the category itself. The real question of consequence for identity is whether the concept itself is useful as an avenue of expressing what it means to be a human being.

Berger says that all revolutions in society begin in transformations of consciousness and that detachment from one's own world transforms one's awareness of society in such a way that *givenness* becomes *possibility*. Berger refers to this detachment in *The Sacred Canopy* (1967) when he says that the true self is a consciousness that precedes socialization. Socialization is thus always partial and the consciousness shaped by socialization is the form known as the individual's socially recognizable identity. But this socially assigned identity estranges us from that part of our consciousness upon which it has been imposed. Berger also asserts that socialization is like an early development of consciousness and a cognitive *fall from grace*. Only primitive and infantile consciousness apprehends society in alienated terms, as facticity, as necessity, as fate, as reality. When, in the evolution of consciousness, society is grasped as a human product, this awareness becomes a precondition for finding the experience of the true self, of human freedom. The individual then has the capacity to act on society.

M. Rosenberg (1988) and E. Tiryakian (1968) concur that in the process of running with the herd in social conformity, the individual loses contact with the irreducible and everpresent ground of his or her *being*, his or her *self*. The self-alienated person is one who is separated from his or her existential experience, a direct experience of self as opposed to through the haze of self-objectivication. (This argument on the social self as a partial self is reiterated in Chapter 11.)[6] Roberto Assagioli (1964) says that the social self is not the pure self or self-consciousness and that the goal of human living is to disidentify, to disassociate from the *content* of consciousness rather than from consciousness itself. Some people get their identity from their feelings, others from their thoughts, others from their *social roles*. But this near-total identification with only a part of the personality destroys the freedom that comes from the experience of the pure "I."

In light of our discussion of the consequences of stratification as it is illustrated in education, does this mean that we should treat all of our social selves as illusory? No. But if our social status does not tell us *who we really are*, then nothing is gained by reacting to a definition that does not challenge our *authentic self*. However, neither does this realization get us "off the hook" concerning the problem of inequality. Two responses are possible: We can, let's say, help the ghetto child to recognize the inauthentic nature of his or her social identity; we can also, through our own recognition of an *authentic self*, change and create conditions that treat persons on the basis of a reflection of who they really are. Such changed social arrangements *reflect*, rather than create, conditions of consciousness. At the higher levels of individual human consciousness, statuses are the apparatus whereby we enact regard for others. The moral of this story is that stratification, as it operates in education, may be only in part egalitarian, but social structure does not have the final word on the conditions of consciousness. Social stratification operates in education, as in general, as a representation of consciousness. Its consequences for identity are up to the individual, first by his or her seeing that he or she is not simply a status, and second by doing what he or she can to make society a reflection of a state of mind that regards the other as one regards oneself.

Summary

The principle of stratification was discussed as it operates concerning the general issue of equality of educational opportunity according to race, sex, and socioeconomic status. The application of the principle of stratification as a conceptual tool for our understanding of these issues has illuminated "who gets what and under what conditions." Variations in the operation of the principle of stratification, as egalitarian and nonegalitarian, have been discussed as theoretical interpretations of the role of education in the allocation of wealth, power, and prestige. Thus, in the case of education, we have examined whether the school helps, hinders, or remains indifferent to the inequities that children bring to school. Investigation of issues of *equality of educational opportunity* included *social class* (tracking and ability grouping; public and private schooling; family background), *gender* (gender stereotypes; gender composition of schools; gender differences in achievement and motivation), *race and ethnicity* (race and achievement; desegregation and busing; integration; compensatory education; minority education), and *higher education*.

Theory and supporting evidence on social class background and equality of educational opportunity indicates that (as conflict theorists point out) talent selection results in the rejection of the disadvantaged and that cultural transmission and socialization cause different things depending more on social status than on merit. Social class is replicated through public versus private schooling, through tracking and ability grouping, and through the home environment characteristics that students bring to school. Despite the claim that United States schools make provision for equal opportunity for all children to develop their abilities, certain categories of children seem to end up at the bottom of the achievement hierarchy.

Efforts have been taken by schools to combat sexism in the educational system ranging from teacher education concerning stereotypes to school regulations that enforce equal treatment of male and female students with regard to financial aid, counseling, course and program enrollment, and access to sports facilities. Apparently, the school reinforces society's expectations initially transmitted to students at home, but in so doing the school plays a part in prejudicing the availability of knowledge important for success in the United States system.

Race and ethnicity research shows that although standardized tests are the inevitable method for standardizing and evaluating knowledge viewed as important by society, they are sometimes invalid measures because they are culturally biased. Other research on race and achievement outcomes, such as James Coleman's landmark study, indicates that the home, not the school, is the strongest determinant of student outcomes. Evidence is mixed on the effectiveness of efforts such as desegregation and busing made to equalize opportunity by boosting achievement test scores of disadvantaged children. Overall, black children have shown gains in educational achievement and attainment as a respond to interventions, but educational differences by race and ethnicity continue. Research on the effectiveness of efforts at integration to enhance school performance (compensatory education programs such as early childhood, bilingual education, and high school-college transition programs) also yields inconclusive evidence. Some positive and long-lasting effects of compensatory education programs exist, but critics question whether these programs make a valid contribution in mediating the effects of disadvantage. Documentation of the school success of other minority students (such as Asian-American, Hispanic, Native American, and special education) shows that some groups tend to do better than others, but that efforts made to equalize opportunity have had some positive effects.

The stratification of equality of educational opportunity in higher education according to race, gender, and socioeconomic status is again both fair and unfair; the rules both equalize life chances and replicate inequality. Research findings on equal access issues (selective and open admissions and affirmative action), on issues concerning the university as a business (the recruitment of athletes and administrative and academic hierarchies); on practical versus liberal arts education; on teaching- versus research-focus in institutions of higher education; and on college type and academic selection suggest that some mechanisms reduce differences in opportunity and that both conflict and consensus interpret how these differences emerge. It seems that the principle of stratification operates in education to equalize opportunity on the basis of merit, but also to reproduce the inequalities that students bring to the school.

The chapter concluded with consideration of the consequences of social stratification as it operates in education for individual human identity and suggested that society does not have the final say about our importance as human beings. We can occupy our roles without becoming them and in so doing are "free" to make educational institutions equitable.

Vocabulary

ascription	merit
equality of educational opportunity	occupying social roles
exchange mobility	open and closed systems of stratification
identifying with social roles	stratification
issues of stratification in education	structural mobility

Questions

1. What kind of behaviors go on in schools that can be explained by the concept and theories of stratification?

2. Can you analyze the issue of bilingual education from a sociological perspective?

References and Suggested Readings

Alexander, K. and A. Pallas. "School Sector and Cognitive Performance: When Is a Little a Little?" *Sociology of Education*, (1985) 58:115–28.

_____. "In Defense of 'Private Schools and Public Policy': Reply to Kilgore." *Sociology of Education*, (1984) pp. 56–8.

_____. "Private Schools and Public Policy: New Evidence on Cognitive Achievement in Public and Private Schools." *Sociology of Education*, (1983) 56:170–82.

Alwin, D. F. "Family of Origin and Cohort Differences in Verbal Ability." *American Sociological Review*, (1991) 56:625–38.

Assagioli, R. *The Act of Will*. New York: Viking, 1973.

Babbie, E. *The Sociological Spirit: Critical Essays in a Critical Science*. Belmont, CA: Wadsworth, 1988.

Ballantine, J. *The Sociology of Education: A Systematic Analysis*. 2nd ed. Englewood Cliffs, NJ: Prentice-Hall, 1989.

Barnhouse, R. W., D. R. James, and H. J. McCammon. "Accounting for Racial Inequality in Southern Education: A Reply to Ramirez." *Sociology of Education*, (1990) 63:145–50.

Ben-David, J. *American Higher Education*. New York: McGraw-Hill, 1972.

Berg, I., M. Freedman, and M. Freeman. *Managers and Work Reform*. New York: Free Press, 1978.

Berger, P. *The Sacred Canopy: Elements of a Sociological Theory of Religion*. New York: Doubleday, 1967.

_____. *Invitation to Sociology: A Humanistic Perspective*. New York: Doubleday, 1963.

Biehler, R. *Psychology Applied to Teaching*. Boston: Houghton Mifflin, 1978.

Billson, J. and M. Terry. "In Search of the Silken Purse: Factors in Attrition among First-Generation Students." *College and University*, (1982) pp. 57–76.

Boli, J., F. Ramirez, and J. Meyer. "Explaining the Origins and Expansion of Mass Education." *Comparative Education Review*, (1985) 29:145.

Bowles, S. "Unequal Education and the Reproduction of the Social Division of Labor." In J. Karabel and A. Halsey, eds., *Power and Ideology in Education*. New York: Oxford University Press, 1977.

Bowles, S. and H. Gintis. *Schooling in Capitalist America: Educational Reform and the Contradictions of Economic Life*. New York: Basic Books, 1976.

Brown, W. and C. Stone. "Academic Unions in Higher Education: Impacts on Faculty Salary, Compensation and Promotions." *Economic Inquiry*, (1977) 15:385–96.

Bryk, A., et al. *Effective Catholic Schools: An Exploration*. Washington, DC: National Catholic Education Association, 1984.

Campbell, P. B., J. A. Gardner, and P. Seitz. *High School Vocational Graduates: Which Doors are Open?* Columbus, OH: Ohio State University National Center for Research In Vocational Education, 1982.

Caplow, T. and R McGee. *The Academic Marketplace*. New York: Basic Books, 1958.

Carnoy, M. "Is Compensatory Education Possible?" In M. Carnoy, ed., *Schooling in a Corporate Society*. New York: David McKay, 1975.

_____. *Education as Cultural Imperialism*. London: Longman, 1974.

Center for Education Statistics. *Fall Enrollment in Colleges and Universities*. Washington, DC: United States Department of Education, 1986.

Clark, B. *Structure of Academic Governance in the United States*. New Haven, CT: Yale University Institute for Social and Policy Studies, 1976.

_____. "The Cooling-Out Function in Higher Education" *The American Journal of Sociology*, (1960) 65:569–76.

Clark, R. "Multinational Corporate Investment and Women's Participation in Higher Education in the Noncore Nations." *Sociology of Education* , (1992) 65:37–47.

Coleman, J. "The Concept of Equality of Educational Opportunity." *Harvard Educational Review*, (1968) 38:7–22.

Coleman, J., T. Hoffer, and S. Kilgore. *Public and Private Schools. Report to the National Center for Education Statistics.* Chicago: National Opinion Research Center, 1981.

Coleman, J., et al. *Equality of Educational Opportunity.* Washington, DC: United States Department of Education, 1966.

Collier, P. and C. Mayer. "An Investigation of University Selection Procedures." *Supplement to The Economic Journal*, Vol. 96, 1986.

Collins, R. *The Credential Society.* New York: Academic Press, 1979.

_____. "Functional and Conflict Theories of Educational Stratification." *American Sociological Review*, (1971) 36:1002–19.

_____. *Conflict Sociology: Toward an Explanatory Science.* New York: Academic Press, 1974.

Crain, R. and R. Mahard. *Desegregation Plans that Raise Black Achievement: A Review of the Research.* Santa Monica, CA: Rand, 1982.

Crouse, J. "The Time Has Come to Replace the SAT." *Chronicle of Higher Education*, February, 1986, p. 40.

Cummins, J. "Empowering Minority Students: A Framework for Intervention," *Harvard Educational Review*, (1986) 56:18–35.

Daniels, L. "In Defense of Busing." *New York Times Magazine*, (April 17, 1983) pp. 34–7.

Dar, Y. and N. Resh. "Classroom Intellectual Composition and Academic Achievement." *American Educational Research Journal*, (1986) 23(3):357–74.

Darling-Hammond, L. *Beyond the Commission Reports.* Santa Monica, CA: Rand Corporation, 1983.

Davis, J. and T. Smith. *General Social Survey File, 1972–1982.* Ann Arbor, MI: Inter-University Consortium for Political and Social Research, 1983.

Davis, K. *Human Society.* New York: Macmillan, 1949, pp. 366–8.

Davis, K. and W. Moore. "Some Principles of Stratification." *American Sociological Review*, (1945) 10:242–9.

Delamont, S. *Sex Roles and the Schools.* London: Methuen, 1980.

Duncan, G. J. and W. Rodgers. "Has Children's Poverty become More Persistent?" *American Sociological Review*, (1991) 56:538–50.

Entwisle, D. R. and K. L. Alexander. "Summer Setback: Race, Poverty, School Composition, and Mathematics Achievement in the First Two Years of School." *American Sociological Review*, (1992) 57:72–84.

Falsey, B. and B. Heyns. "The College Channel: Private and Public Schools Reconsidered." *Sociology of Education*, 57:111–21.

Federbrush, M. "The Sex Problem of School Math Books." In J. Stacey, et al., eds., *And Jill Came Tumbling After: Sexism in American Education.* New York: Dell, 1974.

Fennema, E. "The Sex Factor." In E. Fennema, ed., *Mathematics Education Research: Implications for the 80's.* Washington, DC: Association for Supervision and Curriculum, 1981.

Fennema, E. and T. Carpenter. "Sex-Related Differences in Mathematics: Results from National Assessment." *Mathematics Teacher,* October, 1981.

Fitzpatrick, K. M. and W. C. Yoels. "Policy, School Structure, and Socio-demographic Effects on Statewide High School Dropout Rates." *Sociology of Education,* (1992) 65:76–93.

Gamoran, A. "Instructional and Institutional Effects of Ability Grouping." *Sociology of Education,* (1985) 58:48–59.

Gaskell, J. "Course Enrollments in the High School: The Perspective of Working-Class Females." *Sociology of Education,* (1985) 58:48–59.

Giele, J., et al. "Changing Educational and Occupational Histories of Women College Graduates, 1934–1982." Paper presented at the American Sociological Association annual meeting, New York, 1986.

Gilligan, C. "Woman's Place in Man's Life Cycle." *Harvard Educational Review,* (1979) 49:431–46.

Goode, W. *Principles of Sociology.* New York: McGraw-Hill, 1977.

Goodson, I. F. "On Curriculum Form: Notes Toward a Theory of Curriculum." *Sociology of Education,* (1992) 65:66–75.

Gouldner, A. *The Coming Crisis of Western Sociology.* New York: Avon Books, 1971.

Greeley, A. *Catholic High Schools and Minority Students.* New Brunswick, NJ: Transaction Books, 1982.

Grieb, A. and J. Easley. "A Primary School Impediment to Mathematical Equity: Case Studies of Rule-Dependent Socialization." *Advances in Motivation and Achievement: Women in Science,* Vol 2. Greenwich, CT: JAI, 1984, pp. 317–62.

Grusky, D. and R. Hauser. "Comparative Social Mobility Revisited: Models of Convergence and Divergence in 16 Countries." *American Sociological Review,* (1984) 49:19–38.

Guinzburg, S. "Education's Earning Power." *Psychology Today* (1983) 17:20–1.

Gupta, N. *Barriers to the Advancement of Women in Educational Administration: Sources and Remedies.* Austin, TX: Southwest Educational Development Lab, March, 1983.

Halsey, A. "Education Can Compensate." *New Society,* (January, 1980) pp. 172–3.

Hauser, R. and D. K. Anderson. "Post-High School Plans and Aspirations of Black and White High School Seniors: 1976–86." *Sociology of Education,* (1991) 64:263–77.

Hauser, R. and D. Featherman. "Equality of Schooling: Trends and Prospects." *Sociology of Education* (1976), 49:99–120.

Herzog, A. "High School Seniors' Occupational Plans and Values: Trends in Sex Differences 1976 through 1980." *Sociology of Education,* (1982) 55:11.

Higher Education Research Institute. *Final Report of the Commission on the Higher Education of Minorities.* Los Angeles: Higher Education Research Institute, 1982.

Hoffer, T., A. Greeley, and J. Coleman. "Achievement Growth in Public and Catholic Schools." *Sociology of Education,* (1985) 58:74–97.

Hurn, C. *The Limits and Possibilities of Schooling.* Boston: Allyn and Bacon, 1978.

Jacobson, R. "Typical College Trustee, Survey Finds, Is a Middle-Aged, White Businessman," *Chronicle of Higher Education,* (February 12, 1986), p. 23.

Jencks, C., et al. "Who Gets Ahead?" *The Determinants of Edonomic Success in America.* New York: Basic Books, 1979.

Jencks, C., et al. *Inequality: A Reassessment of the Effects of Family and Schooling in America.* New York: Basic Books, 1972.

Jensen, A. "How Much Can We Boost IQ and Scholastic Achievement?" *Harvard Educational Review,* (1969) 39:273–314.

Kalekin-Fishman, D. "Latent Messages: The Acoustical Environments of Kindergartens in Israel and West Germany." *Sociology of Education,* (1991) 64:209–27.

Kamin, L. *The Science and Politics of IQ.* Hillsdale, NJ: Erlbaum, 1974.

Kemerer, F. and J. Baldridge. "Unions in Higher Education: The Going Gets Tougher." *Phi Delta Kappan,* (June 1980), pp. 714–15.

Kerr, C. *The Uses of the University.* Cambridge, MA: Harvard University Press, 1963.

Kitano, H. *Japanese Americans: The Evolution of Sub-Culture,* 2nd ed. Englewood Cliffs, NJ: Prentice-Hall, 1976.

Konrad, A. M. and J. Pfeffer. "Understanding the Hiring of Women and Minorities in Educational Institutions." *Sociology of Education,* (1991) 64:141–57.

Krauze, T. and K. Slomczynski. "How Far to Meriotcracy? Empirical Tests of a Controversial Thesis." *Social Forces,* (1985) 63:623–42.

Kulik, C. and J. Kulik. "Effects of Ability Grouping on Secondary School Students." *American Educational Research Journal,* (1982) 19(3):415–28.

Lamb, S. "Cultural Consumption and the Educational Plans of Australian Secondary School Students." *Sociology of Education,* (1989) 62:95–108.

Lareau, A. "Social Class Differences in Family-School Relationships: The Importance of Cultural Capital." *Sociology of Education,* (1987) 60:73–85.

Lavin, D., R. Alba, and R. Silberstein. "Open Admission and Equal Access: A Study of Ethnic Groups in CUNY." *Harvard Educational Review,* (1979) 49:53–92.

Lee, V. and A. Bryk. "Effects of Single-Sex Secondary Schools on Student Achievement and Attitudes." *Journal of Educational Psychology* (1986) 78:381–95.

Lee, V. E., R. F. Dedrick, and J. B. Smith. "The Effect of the Social Organization of Schools on Teachers' Efficacy and Satisfaction." *Sociology of Education,* (1991) 64:190–208.

Lee, V. E. and K. A. Frank. "Students' Characteristics that Facilitate the Transfer from Two-Year to Four-Year Colleges." *Sociology of Education*, (1990) 63:176–93.

Lemmers, C. "Localism, Cosmopolitanism, and Faculty Response." *Sociology of Education*, (1974) 47:129–58.

Lever, J. "Sex Differences in the Complexity of Children's Play and Games." *American Sociological Review*, (1978) 43:471–83.

Levin, H. "Educational Opportunity and Social Inequality in Western Europe." *Social Problems*, (1976) 24:148–72.

Levine, D. and R. Havighurst. *Society and Education*, 7th Ed. Boston: Allyn and Baron, 1989.

Levitas, M. *Marxist Perspectives in the Sociology of Education*. London: Routledge & Kegan Paul, 1974.

Liebrand, W., A. Henk, M. Wilke, R. Vogel, and F. Wolters. "Value Orientation and Conformity: A Study of Three Types of Social Dilemma Games." *Journal of Conflict Resolution*, (1986) 30:77–97.

Light, D., Jr. and S. Keller. *Sociology*, 4th Ed. New York: Alfred A. Knopf, 1985.

Mann, H. "The Twelfth Annual Report, 1848." In *Life and Works of Horace Mann*, Vol. 1. New York: C.T. Dillingham, 1891.

Marlaire, C. L. and D. W. Maynard. "Standardized Testing as an Interactional Phenomenon." *Sociology of Education*, (1990) 63:83–101.

Marsh, H. W. "Employment During High School: Character Building or a Subversion of Academic Goals?" *Sociology of Education*, (1991) 64:172–89.

McGee, R. *Academic Janus*. San Francisco, CA: Jossey-Bass, 1971.

McLelland, K. "Cumulative Disadvantage among the Highly Ambitious." *Sociology of Education*, (1990) 63:102–21.

McPartland, J., R. Dawkins, J. Braddock II, R. Crain, and J. Strauss. "Three Reports: Effects of Employer Job Placement Decisions, and School Desegregation on Minority and Female Hiring and Occupational Attainment." *Report 359, Center for Social Organization of Schools*. Baltimore: Johns Hopkins University, July, 1985.

Mehan, H. "Understanding Inequality in Schools: The Contribution of Interpretive Studies." *Sociology of Education*, (1992) 65:1–20.

Millet, J. "Similarities and Differences." In J. Perkins, ed., *The University as an Organization: A Report for the Carnegie Commission on Higher Education*. New York: McGraw-Hill, 1973, p. 3.

Mingle, J. *Trends in Higher Education Participation and Success*. Denver, CO: Education Commission of the States and State Higher Education Executive Officers, 1987.

Morgan, D. and R. Kearney. "Collective Bargaining and Faculty Compensation: A Comparative Analysis." *Sociology of Education*, (1977) 50:7–15.

National Advisory Council on Women's Educational Programs. *Title IX: The Half Full, Half Empty Glass*. Washington, DC: United States Department of Education, 1981.

National Center for Educational Statistics. *The Condition of Education*. Washington, DC: United States Department of Education, 1985.

Natriello, G., A. M. Pallas, and K. Alexander. "On the Right Track? Curriculum and Academic Achievement." *Sociology of Education*, (1989) 62:109–18.

Oakes, J. *Keeping Track*. New Haven, CT: Yale University Press, 1985.

Olneck, M. and D. Bills. "What Makes Sammy Run? An Empirical Assessment of the Bowles-Gintis Correspondence Theory." *American Journal of Education*, (1980) 89:27–61.

Orfield, G. *Public School Desegregation in the United States 1968–1980*. Washington, DC: Joint Center for Political Studies, 1983.

Ornstein, A. *Foundations of Education*, 3rd Edition. Boston: Houghton Mifflin, 1985.

Parelius, A. and R. Parelius. *The Sociology of Education*. 2nd ed. Englewood Cliffs, NJ: Prentice-Hall, 1987.

Parsons, T. "Equality and Inequality in Modern Society, or Social Stratification Revisited." In Edward O. Lauman, ed., *Social Stratification*. New York: Bobbs-Merrill, 1970.

Passow, A. "Issues of Access to Knowledge." In L. Tanner and K. Rehage, ed., *Critical Issues in Curriculum*. Chicago: University of Chicago Press, 1988.

Pettigrew, T. and R. Green. "School Desegregation in Large Cities: A Critique of the Coleman 'White Flight' Thesis." *Harvard Educational Review*, (1976) 46:1–53.

Pincus, F. "Customized Contract Training in Community Colleges: Who Really Benefits?" Paper presented at the American Sociological Association annual meeting, Washington, DC, August, 1985.

Pincus, F. "The False Promises of Community Colleges: Class Conflict and Vocational Education." *Harvard Educational Review*, (1980) 50:332–61.

Ravitch, D. "What Makes a Good School?" *Society*, (1982) pp. 10–11.

Reskin, B. "Academic Sponsorship and Scientists' Careers." *Sociology of Education*, (1979) 52:129–46.

Rist, R. *The Urban School: A Factory for Failure*. Cambridge, MA: MIT Press, 1973.

Rosenberg, M. "Self-Objectification: Relevance for the Species and Society." *Sociological Forum*, 3:548–65.

Rosenblum, G. and B. R. Rosenblum. "Segmented Labor Markets in Institutions of Higher Education." *Sociology of Education*, (1990) 63:151–64.

Roueche, J., et al. "College Responses to Low-Achieving Students: A National Study." *American Education*, (1984) pp. 31–4.

Sanchirico, A. "The Importance of Small-Business Ownership in Chinese American Educational Achievement." *Sociology of Education* (1991), 64:293–304.

Sanders, J. M. "Short and Long-Term Macroeconomic Returns to Higher Education." *Sociology of Education* (1992), 65:21–36.

Scarr, S. *Race, Social Class, and Individual Differences in IQ*. Hillsdale, NJ: Erlbaum, 1981.

Scarr, S. and R. Weinberg. "IQ Test Performance of Black Children Adopted by White Families." *American Psychologist*, (1976) 31:726–39.

_____. "When Black Children Grow Up in White Homes." *Psychology Today*, (1975) 9:80–2.

Sewell, W. and V. Shah. "Socioeconomic Status, Intelligence, and the Attainment of Higher Education." *Sociology of Education*, (1967) 40:1–23.

Shavit, Y. and V. Kraus. "Educational Transitions in Israel: A Test of the Industrialization and Credentialism Hypotheses." *Sociology of Education*, (1990) 63:133–41.

Sherman, J. "Effects of Biological Factors on Sex-Related Differences in Mathematics Achievement." In L. Fox and E. Fennema, eds., *Women in Mathematics: Research Perspectives for Change*. Washington, DC National Institute of Education, (1977) pp. 181–2.

Smith, H. L. and B. Powell. "Great Expectations: Variations in Income Expectations among College Seniors." *Sociology of Education*, (1990) 63:194–207.

Smock, P. J. and F. D. Wilson. "Desegregation and the Stability of White Enrollments: A School-Level Analysis, 1968–84." *Sociology of Education*, (1991) 64:278–92.

So, A. "The Math/Reading Gap among Asian American Students: A Function of Nativity, Mother Tongue and SES." *Sociology and Social Research: An International Journal*, 70:76–7.

Sørensen, A. and M. Hallinan. "Effects of Ability Grouping on Growth in Academic Achievement." *American Educational Research Journal*, (1986) 23:529–42.

Stickney, B. and V. Plunkett. "Closing the Gap: A Historical Perspective on the Effectiveness of Compensatory Education." *Phi Delta Kappan*, (December, 1983), p. 290.

Tinto, V. "Latent Sponsorship: Effects of College Origins upon Attainment among Professional and Managerial Occupations." Paper presented at the American Sociological Association, Boston, September, 1979.

Tiryakian, E. "The Existential Self and the Person." In C. Gordon and K. Gergen, eds., *The Self in Social Interaction*. New York: Wiley, 1968.

Tolbert, P. S. and A. A. Oberfield. "Sources of Organizational Demography: Faculty Sex Ratios in Colleges and Universities." *Sociology of Education*, (1991) 64:305–15.

Trieman, D. *Occupational Prestige in Comparative Perspective*. New York: Academic Press, 1977.

Tumin, M. *Patterns of Society*. Boston: Little, Brown, 1973.

_____. "Some Principles of Stratification: A Critical Analysis." *American Sociological Review*, (1953) 18:387–93.

Turner, R. "Sponsored and Contest Mobility." *American Sociological Review*, (1960) 25:855–67.

UNESCO. *Statistical Yearbook*. Paris: UNESCO, 1955–1983.

United States Department of Education. "High School Dropouts: Descriptive Information from High School and Beyond." *National Center for Educational Statistics, Bulletin NCES 83-221b*, Washington, DC: United States Department of Education, 1983.

Vanfossen, B. "Sex Differences in Mathematics Performance: Continuing Evidence." Paper presented at the American Sociological Association annual meeting, Chicago, September 1987.

Vanfossen, B., J. Jones, and J. Spade. "Curriculum Tracking and Status Maintenance." *Sociology of Education*, (1987) 60:104–22.

Velez, W. "High School Attrition among Hispanic and Non-Hispanic White Youths." *Sociology of Education*, (1989) 62:119–33.

———. "Finishing College: The Effects of College Type." *Sociology of Education*, (1985) 58:191–200.

Wang, M., M. Reynolds, and H. Walberg. "Rethinking Special Education." *Educational Leadership*, September, 1986, pp. 26–31.

Weber, M. *From Max Weber: Essays in Sociology.* In H. Gerth and C. Wright Mills, eds., New York: Oxford University Press, 1946.

Wrong, D. "The Functional Theory of Stratification: Some Neglected Considerations." *American Sociological Review*, (1959) 24:772–82.

Young, M., ed., *Knowledge and Control.* Middlesex, England: Collier Macmillan, 1971.

Notes

[1]Theories explain the nature of principles, particularly as to their stratification characteristics. Therefore the principle of stratification operates alongside (in conjunction with) all other principles and is discussion of the theoretical interpretation of the nature of other principles.

[2]For extended commentaries on this question, see Kingsley Davis and Wilbert E. Moore, "Some Principles of Stratification." *American Sociological Review*, 10 (April, 1945), pp. 242–9; see also Kingsley Davis, *Human Society.* New York: Macmillan, 1949, pp. 366–8. Also see Dennis H. Wrong, "The Functional Theory of Stratification: Some Neglected Considerations." *American Sociological Review*, 24 (December, 1959), pp. 772–82; and Melvin M. Tumin, "Some Principles of Stratification: A Critical Analysis." *American Sociological Review*, 18 (August, 1953), pp. 387–93.

[3]Based on the interpretive tradition, Hugh Mehan (in "Understanding Inequality in Schools: The Contribution of Interpretive Studies," *Sociology of Education*, 1992) says that ethnographic studies have drawn three connected contributions which may partially account for inequality within society. The first is that elements of culture have become part of the highly deterministic macrotheories producing a grid system of meaning which lays over social structure and human action. Second, individuals are not passive role players buffeted by structural forces beyond their control. Instead they make choices in often contradictory circumstances including on issues of inequality. Finally, schools are not black boxes spewing out students for pretermined roles in society. Rather, individual students make choices in response to competing demands—responses which sometimes help contribute to inequality.

[4]A study by Courtney L. Marlaire and Douglas W. Maynard ("Standardized Testing as an Interactional Phenomenon," *Sociology of Education*, 1990) suggests that students' scores on standardized tests are directly influenced by the teacher, or person, giving the test. Marlaire and Maynard looked at how an interaction develops between the test taker and test giver. They concluded that the three-part "instructional sequence"—testing prompts, replies, and acknowledgments—which has been seen in other learning situations, also applies to testing. Although contrary to a testing relationship based on the stimulus-response model, Marlaire and Maynard confirm that the final result of tests—the scores—may not be the student's achievement alone, which could have implications for research on bias in mental testing.

[5]For those interested in a description of higher education, see Jeanne Ballantine's (1989) discussion on the history and development of higher education.

[6]Social self means here that in the social realm each person is a rational actor whose actions in behalf of self-interest take others into account. By this definition, *self-interest* is equated with *cooperation*. The tendency to cooperate is a stable personality trait (Liebrand, Wilke, Vogel, and Wolters, 1986). This also presumes that each person will necessarily regard or value the other in order to guarantee that each will get what he or she needs. However, this is an ideal state of affairs. Self-interest takes on two forms of cooperation. In the first social cohesion is brought about through power and inequality; in the second, it is brought about through functional integration, interrelatedness, and, sometimes, equality based on merit.

Organization

*The Arrangement of Individuals into
Large and Small Groups*

How might a sociologist explain the behavior of the persons shown in the photograph above? The individuals are not acting as spontaneously and personally as you might think. Their behaviors are not unique and arbitrary, but result from their being constrained by others' expectations of how they should behave; they are behaving in response to a social force or *social fact* (Durkheim, 1959), that is, to *organization*. For example, agreements made about how persons should arrange themselves with others into groups affect how much they touch each other, what they wear, the similarity of their race, age, gender, income, and language, and how much they know about each other.

Outline

School Composition

School Culture

Classroom Characteristics

    Teacher Qualities

    Teacher Expectations

    Interaction Styles

    Physical Conditions

    Role Negotiations (Student Strategies)

    Ability Grouping

Social Constraints Do Not Explain Everything

Ritualism

Negotiated Order

Is Teaching a Profession?

Wasting Human Resources

Protection of the Inept

Iron Law of Oligarchy

Who Should Control the Schools?

Summary

Vocabulary

Questions

References and Suggested Readings

Notes

*I*f asked whether the photograph on page 162 is of a *group*, most persons would likely say yes. We are so accustomed to group life that we rarely, if ever, stop to ask what a group is and how it affects its members' behaviors. In this chapter we begin with the general concept of *social* to explain the particular constraint or set of others' expectations that affects a person's behavior. We will examine *organization*, the *arrangement of individuals into large and small groups*, define the meaning of *group*, and look at different types of groups. We will see how *organization*, as a type of constraint, helps explain why people act the way they do, particularly in the context of *schooling*.

Definition and Classification of Groups

The persons in the preceding photograph constitute a social group.[1] That is, they are not merely an aggregate of individuals who happen to be at the same place at the same time, such as people in a cashier's line or people waiting for a train. A social group is characterized by these activities:

- Its members interact with each other on a regular basis;
- They develop a structure;
- They adopt norms;
- They develop a sense of unity.

Four Characteristics of a Group

Groups share four main characteristics: scope, duration, rules, and boundaries. *Scope* and *duration* define the degree of ongoing interaction among persons. If a large proportion of an individual's daily activity takes place with others, such as in a family, then most likely that wide scope of activities and behaviors ensures that the interaction will tend to be repeated. *Duration* refers to the length of a relationship, of which one aspect is *continuity*. Groups have *real* as well as *expected* continuity. Another aspect of duration concerns how long people continue to belong to the group, and vice versa, how long the group exists. For example, groups may form for a specific purpose, such as raising money by having a bake sale. Then the duration of both the group and the members' interaction will be brief. Groups that last a short time do not command deep loyalty from members. Some groups are expected to last a long time, but the membership is expected to change constantly. Thus, a student may be a member of the debate team this year, but not the next, while the group continues through many generations of students. A family unit is expected to last through the lifetime of its members, but in reality may disrupt through divorce. Even then, we expect the relations between parents and children to continue.

In addition to the aspects of duration that characterize any group, all groups develop rules for behavior. A member of a medical team agrees that he or she cannot call his or her stockbroker during surgery. Groups vary with respect to the breadth of activity covered by the rules and to the degree of conformity required of the members. Some groups create an elaborate set of procedures and offices to deal with deviations; others do not. That is, "the rules" may be formal or informal. Formal rules are created by member vote or by the decision of an official leader and are or are not written and recorded. Informal rules might not be recorded anywhere; their origins are remembered by a few of the group's elite and passed on by an oral tradition. Some groups may have both formal and informal rules. For example, school attendance is a formal requirement, but teachers also have informal expectations about commitment to the group as indicated by presence in the classroom.

The group's boundaries are denoted by either an actual list of the group's members or determining membership by interviewing its members. For example, a list of the members of the American Sociological Association is easily obtainable, but it would be difficult to know all the people who are close friends in a neighborhood. Group boundaries may be distinct either because entrance is difficult or its members are outcasts; honorific societies like the school honor roll and a coalition of AIDS victims, respectively, are examples. Unity refers to the sharpness of the boundaries, the cohesiveness of the group, that is, how close members feel to and identify with one another. To the extent that the members are cohesive, people outside the group are likely to perceive the group as a unit. When boundaries are not distinct, this is harder to do. The members of a college sorority, for example, clearly define their boundaries by restricting their social relations to members of the group.

Types of Groups

The variety of groups is staggering. Some have two members, others two million. Some are secret, others open. Some are close-knit and affectionate. In other groups, members are distant from one another and do not share their feelings. Sociologists have not been successful in neatly classifying groups; however, some commonly discussed groups are in-groups and out-groups; peer groups; reference groups; hierarchical triads; small and large groups; friendship groups; and primary and secondary groups. Although these types of groups are those most often discussed, the analysis of primary and secondary groups is most useful to our understanding of behaviors in school settings.

Primary or Informal Groups

A primary group is any group in which social relationships, actual or expected, share the following characteristics; they are:

- Emotional—interaction features the expression of affect or feelings such as joy or displeasure;
- Diffuse—the breadth of the interaction or its scope covers many aspects of life;
- Particularistic—the relationship is specific to the persons within the group (my friend, my father), not to a class of persons (clerks, police officers);

- Collectivistic—members are expected to guide their behavior based on what is good for the group overall;
- Enduring—members expect duration in their emotional commitments.[2]

Primary groups are arrangements, in fact and in expectation, that permit people to express their *emotions*. Furthermore, members are not only permitted to express these feelings—whether love or hostility—but are supposed to do so. This dynamic contrasts to the relationship, say, between a shoe salesperson and a client. In business, the rule is that members should withhold personal feelings while carrying out their roles. We would not be interested in whether the shoe salesperson is a vegetarian, but we would be if the salesperson were our spouse.

Primary group members share many aspects of each individual's life with the other member or members. Primary groups are therefore *diffuse* in nature because they allow people to share many aspects of themselves rather than restricting interaction such that people limit what they share to a narrow part of who they are. It is highly unlikely that a student in a classroom knows whether the peers sitting next to him or her brushed their teeth that morning, had Cream of Wheat or oat bran cereal for breakfast, or wore colored underwear. Among family members, however, these facts would be shared, if not outright, at least by being willing to be unguarded in private moments or less guarded than with nonmembers.

Primary groups are *particularistic*; that is, our rights and duties with respect to the other person are determined by our special relationshp to that person, rather than to the class of roles or positions he or she occupies. For example, children kiss their own mothers, but not mothers in general. While the people in a primary group accept the general role obligations and duties that are part of being parents, spouses, or children, the unique or particular qualities of each person is also acknowledged. One child in a family might enjoy playing chess and another might be especially interested in heavy metal rock music. The particularistic quality of the primary group is also exemplified by saying that the people in it are *indispensable* or they are *not substitutable*; no one in the group is quite like the other. Each person with whom we have a love relationship is different from all others.

Primary groups are *collectivistic* because each member has the responsibility to regard not only other persons in the group, but also the group itself. The members view the group as an *end in itself*. One person's gain from the relationship is the enjoyment of the relationship itself, not merely because the situation is better than that available elsewhere. The members of the group also share *similar ends,* and when the ends of particular persons differ somewhat because of the unique value of each person in the group, then individuals must feel that they have *shared goals*. As an illustration, a brother might not have the same aspiration as his sister to win the 50-yard-dash in the track competition, but he will celebrate his sister's accomplishment if she wins or will share her regret if she loses.

In a primary group, especially in love and friendship relationships, members expect that their emotional commmmitment to one another will *endure*, even though the persons involved recognize that such relationships may be short-lived. In other words, duration has consequences for the primary group. If people do not care for one another, they are much less likely to continue the relationship; if they do continue, they are likely to share more of their lives with one another. We can observe that the primary relationship is characterized by the expectation of duration by the feelings of betrayal expressed by one member when the other member leaves the relationship.

Secondary or Formal Groups

Relationships within formally organized or arranged groups differ from relationships in primary groups. Secondary groups are:

- Emotionally neutral;
- Segmental, or narrow;
- Universalistic;
- Self-interested;
- Not enduring.

In a secondary group, people are expected to be *emotionally neutral.* The expression of love or hostility to one another is unacceptable. A gynecologist must withhold sexual feelings when examining patients. Relations between the two people are restricted or *narrowed* to the task at hand, so that the gynecologist would not share an affinity for fishing or a fondness for Chopin; the doctor's interaction is expected to concern only the physical examination. Secondary or formal group rules are expected to be *universalistic*: that is, the same rules apply to everyone. Gynecologists treat all patients with uniform rights and obligations; no one is given special privileges. Members of a formal organization are *self-interested* in that their participation is motivated by self-gain from membership in the group. Individuals do not sacrifice themselves for one another, and the assumption is that if the goals of the group do not serve the interests of the individual, the person will leave the organization. For this reason, members are *not expected to continue* indefinitely in their associations with the group. The group itself may continue for a long time; the university will continue to exist regardless of whether a particular student drops out.

Is the School Formally Organized?

As a sociological concept, *organization* refers to a constraint that determines, in general, what people do and how they act. If schools manifest the organization or agreed-upon relations typical of bureaucracy, much of what people do in schools can be understood by seeing the school as a formal organization that provides children with a "survival kit" designed to foster the attitudes and knowledge necessary for their well-being in the system or culture into which they are born (Durkheim, 1956; Gerth and Mills, 1958). Now, the question: can knowledge of how people arrange themselves formally help us explain the causes and consequences of human interaction in the school setting?

Modern American society is so large that thousands of persons may be interested in some specialized activity or goal, from mothers promoting breast-feeding to educators interested in formulating a standardized reading test that can be used nationally. When a group becomes large, such as a university, a hospital, or a department store chain, a special arrangement of people is required to coordinate the activities of the many people carrying out a variety of tasks. Sociologists refer to this type of formal organization as a *bureaucracy*. The purpose of bureaucratic organization is to maximize efficiency by achieving the most at the least expense. Members are arranged in a formal fashion so that relations between members are emotionally neutral, universalistic, self-interested, and not expected to continue indefinitely.

A Theory of Formal Organization

The German-born social theorist Max Weber (1864–1920) traced the evolution of authority from societies in which the relations between persons were based upon strong personal ties to societies in which the relations were based upon rules applied impersonally to all (Gerth and Mills, 1958). Weber claimed that in industrialized societies the role of formal education is to cultivate the technical expert, in contrast to feudal or patrimonial societies, in which education is based on participation in activities, such as tournaments, to foster heroism and honor or to obtain the rules and manners of an elite, respectively. Using the *ideal type* as an analytical construct that served as a standard by which to make comparisons in empirical cases, he classified three types of authority: charismatic, traditional, and rational-legal. *Charismatic* authority depends upon the appeal of leaders who accrue followers because of their extraordinary heroic, religious, or personality attributes. *Traditional* authority, which predominates in premodern societies, rests on the sanctity of tradition. It is not codified in impersonal rules, but inheres in particular persons who may either inherit it or be invested with it by a higher authority. *Rational-legal* authority, which characterizes relations in contemporary society, is based on rational grounds and impersonal rules that have been legally enacted or contractually established. Weber argued that in modern society rational authority accomplishes specific ends and is manifested as 1) the arrangement of persons so that work is divided into specialities, 2) rules and procedures developed by calculating the most efficient ways of doing things rather than by whim or tradition, 3) coordination accomplished by successively higher levels of management, and 4) jobs and promotions that are based on merit. Inherent in these arrangements are the formal characteristics of organization.

Functional Division of Labor

The activities of many persons are coordinated to accomplish a particular task through specialization. That is, quality and quantity of production (efficiency) are accomplished by dividing (differentiating) a task into more simple tasks. The labor is divided so that individuals specialize in performing a particular job (division of labor). This characteristic of bureaucratic organization is synonymous with what we referred to as the *segmented* nature of formal relations. Members do not relate to each other as whole person to whole person, but only to a particular aspect of the person. Emotion is withheld so that the task at hand can be performed effectively.

Rules of Procedure

In the bureaucracy the nature of a task and how it should be carried out are explicitly expressed in written rules. Behavior is predictable and can be maintained despite changes in personnel; as we recall from our definition of formal organization, persons are not indispensable and unique, as in informal organization; they merely fill *prescribed slots*, defined in writing as a set of procedures. Individual members will not remain in the group if the group's rules do not serve the individual's interests.

Hierarchy of Authority

Workers are arranged so that each person is responsible to the person directly above in a chain of command. Rank and authority increase in a pyramid-shaped manner. Each position consists of specific responsibilities and is rewarded with a particular salary. Authority is in the office, not in the person who occupies it. Again, we can see the restricted nature of relations between individuals.

Roles

Ideally, employees do not let feelings about someone affect how well they work with that person; the boss does not give promotions to those who are liked; inquiry about employees' personal lives is unauthorized unless it can be shown to be related to their performance on the job. Positions are awarded only on the basis of technical qualifications as measured by tests, college credentials, and other objective criteria. Everyone doing the same job should be treated the same. (This is the universalistic nature of formal organizations.)

Although formal organization is an arrangement that accomplishes many things well, it fails at accomplishing others. When a solution can be used for large batches of similar cases, such as applications for telephone service, receiving income taxes, or mailing grade reports each college semester, a secondary group organization works well. However, formal organization is relatively ineffective in giving love or friendship; it cannot promote attention to the uniqueness of individual members. Can you imagine the school registrar having to deal with all the students' likes and dislikes in every aspect of their lives? Yet neither primary groups nor secondary groups function well without the other in contemporary society. Now that we know that formal or bureaucratic arrangements of persons constrain individuals to behave in specific ways, we can understand human interaction in school settings by seeing it first as a response to the school as a formal organization, then by examining the school as an informal organization.

Charles Bidwell (1965) and David Goslin (1965) describe how qualities of contemporary school systems match Weber's model of bureaucratic arrangements and formal arrangements in general (as nonemotional, segmented, universalistic, self-interested, and not enduring). The functional division of labor is exemplifed in the allocation of instructional and coordinative tasks to the roles of teacher and administrator. Staff roles as offices is illustrated by recruitment according to merit and competence, legally based tenure, functional specificity of performance, and universalistic, affectively neutral interaction with clients. The hierarchy of authority is exhibited by the legally defined and circumscribed power of officers and the regularized lines of communication. Rules of procedure set limits to the discretionary performance of officers by specifying in a legal document both the aims and modes of official action. Gerald Moeller (1964), in a study of St. Louis elementary and secondary schools, showed that schools generally adhere to the bureaucratic model with some variations. He constructed an index based on eight characteristics: 1) uniform course of study, 2) communication through established channels, 3) uniform hiring and firing procedures, 4) secure tenure for nonteaching personnel, 5) explicit statement of school policies, 6) clearly delimited areas of responsibility, 7) specific lines of authority, and 8) standard salary policies for new teachers.

Evidence on the School as a Bureaucracy

Allocation of School Tasks

Figure 8–1 shows that schooling is a "bureaucratic" arrangement with allocation of instructional and administrative tasks.

School Staff Roles

How well do school roles correlate with Weber's observation? We recall from our discussion of *role* in Chapter 6 that the position or location a person occupies is called a *status*. Father, electrician, a happy person, an overweight person, a Guardian Angel, freshman: each of these statuses represents a function to be carried out. The function refers specifically to a set of activities that comprises the role associated with the status. Each status is like a mask we hold up when we interact with others so that we can predict what to expect from others and they know what to expect from us (Babbie, 1988). If you occupy the status of *shopper* you are not expected to lean over the counter and tell the cashier that you had a difficult day at school, you didn't eat breakfast, and you have a headache. When a teacher meets a student, they behave toward each other in ways that both agree are expected for each status. If a teacher walks into English class on the first day of school wearing scuba gear, the students may walk out.

School roles not only have formal characteristics but also have intended and unintended consequences for the school system. How are these roles universalistic, segmented, not enduring, and self-interested? Weber's bureaucratic model

New York City Public Schools
Table of Organization

Board of Education
- Secretary
- Counsel

Occupational Education Advisory Council

Strategic Planning

Board of Education Retirement System

Hearing Unit

Counsel Legal Affairs

Public Affairs

State Legislative Office

Parent Involvement

Chancellor
- Equal Opportunity
- Special Investigations
- Auditor General

Office of Budget

Chief Executive for School Facilities

Deputy Chancellor for Operations

Chief Executive for Monitoring & School Improvement
- Monitoring Field Operations
- Monitoring Bilingual Gen. & Sp. Ed.

Support Services (Food, Trans., Supplies)

Business & Administration

Human Resources

Labor Relations

School Safety

Computer Information Svcs.

Chief Executive for High Schools

Deputy Chancellor for Instruction

Multicultural Education

Instruction & Prof. Development

Student Support Services

Funded Programs

Bilingual Education

Special Education

Special Ed. Citywide Prog.

Adult & Continuing Educ.

Source: New York City Public Schools, June 1992.

helps us to identify these characteristics. In simplified structure, faculty staff roles are to be based on merit and competence, resulting in tenure; they have functional specificity of performance; and they are characterized by affectively neutral relations to others. We know from theory that if roles fit this description, then certain outcomes can be predicted. Weber said this structure of human relations accomplishes efficiency. Let's see if school organization fits this prediction.

School Board Members

The status *school board member* is accompanied by a specific formal and legal role. The state, to establish democratic lay control over schools, authorizes schools to set up a board (Ballantine, 1989; Brookover and Erickson, 1975). The segmented relations of people having this role are in terms of the school board members' duties for the hiring of superintendent, principal, and teachers; determining salaries and contracts; providing transportation for students; formulating the school budget; deciding the length of the school term; building new schools and facilities; changing school attendance boundaries; selecting textbooks and subjects to be taught; and serving as arbiters for maintaining school discipline. The school board also legitimizes the actions of the superintendent to the community (Kerr, 1973). The decision making of the school board is restricted by state and national regulations of curriculum content, supplementary educational programs for the disadvantaged, and testing and graduation standards. School boards typically are appointed or elected (National School Boards Association, 1975).

District Superintendent

The superintendent is an official elected by the community to be the top administrator, the chief executive officer of the school district. Although school boards establish overall policy, ratify the budget, mandate curricular and instructional directions, and oversee the hiring of personnel, the superintendent implements the educational policy, representing the community. The responsibilities of a superintendent include generating budget reports, meeting with school principals and staff, reporting to the school board and to federal and state agencies, and maintaining curriculum evaluation. Superintendents are usually hired because they reflect the educational philosophy that is acceptable to the board. The board members rely on the superintendent for his or her knowledge of educational issues. The authority of the superintendent is over a variety of line and staff offices. Line offices are teachers, students and principals; staff offices are those persons who provide noninstructional services. The superintendent also controls finance, maintenance, personnel, security, transportation, records, maintenance, and procurement (Bennett and LeCompte, 1990).

Principals

Another example of the functional specificity of performance (division of labor) is the role of the principal. The segment of behaviors which defines this role concerns middle level administrative responsibilities between the superintendent and teachers. Principals hire and fire teachers, manage the budget, decide on classroom scheduling and placements, and serve as mediaries between the school and the community. They also counsel and discipline teachers and students (United States Department of Education, 1978).

Research, however, shows that the principal's role in relation to the teacher's role is conflictive or dysfunctional for the school system. Teachers are resistant to the principal's suggestions for change because of their sense of autonomy fostered by their primary responsibility in the classroom (Hargreaves, 1984). The principal's role functions efficiently, however, when the role specification indicates emphasizing instruction, communicating views on instruction, being responsible for decisions related to instruction, coordinating instructional programs, and emphasizing academic standards (Wellisch et al., 1978). The role of the principal varies somewhat according to school level, social class composition of students, school district size, and rural or urban setting. For example, the role of the principal as disciplinarian is important at the middle and high school levels. High school principals are preoccupied with enforcing the accountability standards for graduating students (Ballantine, 1989). The delineation of the principal role is further documented in empirical work on the androgynous characteristics required for effective administrators (Shakeshaft, 1986).

Teachers

The status *teacher* is accompanied by a specific role aimed at promoting learning. The obligations of teachers can be identified in a civil service job description:

> Duties of Teachers. Teachers shall take charge of the division of classes assigned to them by the principal. They shall be held responsible for the instruction, progress and discipline of their classes and shall devote themselves exclusively to their duties during school hours. Teachers shall render such assistance in the educational program in and about the buildings as the principal may direct, including parent-interviews, pupil-counseling, corridor, lunchroom, and playground supervision, and attendance at professional staff meetings.
> (Ballantine, 1989)

The formal agreements about the teacher status and role are shown in the extensive certification regulations, personnel policies, hiring committees and procedures, and equal opportunity regulations. The competencies are so clearly defined that only those acquiring these competencies will be hired for the job. Ideally, favoritism shown toward friends and relatives is not permissible; only those who are competent according to the prescribed criteria are eligible for the status. Training institutions are organized to equip persons with the necessary job skills and must be carried out in compliance with federal and state regulations. Promotion and salary are also based on merit. Salary schedules are linked to the individual's level of education and number of years of service. For example, in New York state teachers with thirty credits beyond the master's degree get a substantially greater salary than those with only a master's (New York City Board of Education, 1988). Pay raises, however, are given more on the basis of years of service than for improving student behavior (Kohl, 1967).[3]

Students

According to Talcott Parsons (1959), students are expected to achieve cognitive learning and moral learning. Cognitive learning refers to the skills, frames of reference, and factual information about the world while cooperation, respect, initiative, leadership, and responsible citizenry comprise moral learning. Role expectations are further standardized by grade so that the student's success in meeting the role criteria is monitored in terms of standardized test scores and grade reports. The segmented nature of formal relations is evident in that children are reduced to two narrow segments of identity: grades and test scores.

Bureaucratic or formal roles are typified by affectively neutral role relationships. Close relationships typical of informal organization in which ties are emotional and persons know a lot about each other are discouraged. Efficiency, or getting the job done, is the result of obedience to rules that carefully prescribe the allowable degree of personal intimacy. The impersonality apparent in the roles of students in relation to teachers is exemplified in standardized test administration (Ballantine, 1989). Children sit in rows and are to told when to begin, when to stop, when to turn pages, when to close the test booklet, when to talk, when to write, and so on.

Service Personnel

Weber's theory of formal organization also tells us something about the behaviors of service personnel. These staff roles include counselors, program specialists in areas such as mathematics or reading, librarians, school nurses, janitors, and food service personnel. The segment of behavior for each of these positions in the school system is formally outlined in school policy. For example, the American School Counselor Association describes the gatekeeping functions or responsibilities of the school counselor (Bernard and Fullmer, 1977).

The School's Hierarchy of Authority

The school as bureaucracy can be illustrated by one other salient feature, its hierarchy of authority. Typical of hierarchical arrangement of authority is that communication is from the top down. Those with higher rank in the hierarchy are identified by their formal status. The formal title acts as a signal of how to relate to that person. A teacher would not take a personal complaint directly to the district superintendent, but would likely complain to fellow teachers and then to the principal, who would relate the problem to the district superintendent. Teachers also have relatively low status in the school-role hierarchy; consequently they have little control over their working conditions (Corwin, 1970) and they receive pay raises for years of service rather than for improving student behavior (Kohl, 1967). Students are at the bottom of the role hierarchy even though they comprise the majority group in the school (Dodd, 1965). Students have little say in decision making about what is good for them.

How is the School Informally Organized?

Think about a college course description. It illustrates formal expectations: what the content of the course is supposed to be, how the teacher should be addressed, what the required tasks will be. The informal organization, not communicated in the outline, is what the course is really about. Does it cover everything it mentions in the description? Do we have to refer to the teacher as professor, or can we use his or her first name? Will we have to read the whole textbook? Do we have to buy the supplementary books? Do we have to attend every class session? How will the instructor prepare us for taking the examinations? By recognizing the school's aspects of informal organization, we can understand more about why people behave as they do and schools operate as they do.

A Theory of Informal Organization

Alongside the formal structure exists an informal structure, a structure of arrangements that enables people to accomplish what cannot be accomplished within the constraints of formal regulations. Formal organization actually encourages informal organization. The impersonality of formal organization results in individuals seeking the emotional relationships typical of informal organization (Blau and Meyer, 1971; Evans, 1983.) For example, workers at the central office of the New York City Board of Education (1989) organize birthday parties, baby showers, and other congratulatory parties after work or during lunch hour to offset the emotionally sterile environment characteristic of scheduled working hours.

Where, in schools, can we observe the expectations for behavior typical of informal arrangements operating, structuring, or constraining individual behavior? These informal aspects of schooling are not part of the explicit rules and procedures of formal organization, but they certainly exist as social facts. The term *hidden curriculum* (Snyder, 1971; Hurn, 1978) refers to the informal constraints that operate to govern behavior in school environments. Jeanne Ballantine (1989) has referred to these informal aspects of schooling as the *educational climate*, which includes several dimensions: 1) school composition, including the SES of the children attending the school and the family structure; 2) school culture, the unique set of values and norms typical of that system; and 3) classroom characteristics (including teacher qualities, expectations and interaction styles), role negotiations (the implicit rules or strategies that individuals develop to survive formal group demands), classroom size, ability grouping, seating arrangements, and other arrangements concerning the physical conditions of the classroom, extending to such seemingly mundane items as wall color.

Some Empirical Investigation of the Educational Climate

School Composition

The first informal organizational characteristic that can be identified in schools is *school composition*. School composition refers to the type of students enrolled in the school. The type of student depends upon family background features such as race, income, and family structure. Formal regulations do not explicitly define roles according to these characteristics, but evidence shows that these implicit, and therefore informal, factors are determinants of student outcomes. For example, every year the New York City Board of Education (1989) publishes a report on the rank distribution of schools according to reading scores. We might ask why there are differences among schools if schools organize students to promote efficient learning. What informal arrangements account for the variable performance?

James Coleman (1966), under the auspices of the Department of Health, Education, and Welfare, conducted a national investigation of black and white student differences in educational opportunity and performance. The results of the study indicated that minority students scored lower on tests than did white students, and the differences increased as grade level increased. Contrary to popular opinion, Coleman concluded that family background factors were more important than school factors in explaining students' achievement. Family background factors structure a school atmosphere, or values climate, that is either conducive or not conducive to achievement. Christopher Jencks (1972) also explored the question of the role of the school in equalizing learning opportunities for children and found that the school does not do much to change a person's chances in life. His findings confirmed those of Coleman: students' academic performance depends upon their families.

A later study, known as the Wisconsin Social Psychological Model of Status Attainment (Sewell and Hauser, 1964), found that SES has no effect, independent of measured ability, on high school performance. It does have strong direct and indirect effects on significant other's influence and on educational and occupational aspirations and, through these variables, on educational attainment and occupational status. These results suggest that deficits in family background can be overcome through schooling and that the process of social mobility and status attainment in the United States is a meritocratic one. Another study conducted by James Coleman, Thomas Hoffer, and Sally Kilgore in 1981 showed that private schools mediate the effect of background on learning. Approximately 60,000 high school students from public, private, and parochial schools in the United States were tested in vocabulary and mathematics. Students in racially integrated private schools showed a higher performance than students integrated in public schools.

The increasing occurrence of single-parent families and concurrent increases of women in the labor force have raised the question of the impact of single-parent houshehold structure on student academic performance. The effects that schools have on children are affected by factors unmentioned in formal school policy. Children from single-parent and reconstituted families show significantly poorer achievement than those who come from intact households. (Milne et al., 1986; Mulkey, Crain, and Harrington, 1992). Other factors that can be called informal in that they are not considered in explicit school regulations but are related to school outcomes are the number of hours worked by female heads-of-households (Heyns and Catsambis, 1986). No conclusive evidence has been gathered on the effects of these informal aspects of school groups.

School Culture

A second informal charcteristic of schools not appearing in formal school guidelines is the *culture* of the school apart from any individual student's, teacher's, or administrator's qualities. Schools have a distinctive culture that consists of the values and norms of those making up the system. That is, the average or normal type of joke, style of clothing, language, game, rule about hanging out, or commitment to excellence differ from school to school (Waller, 1932). The school culture is a reflection of the geographical community in which the school is situated. Expectations about the school culture are reproduced in each generation of newly entering students.

Classroom Characteristics

Another set of constraints as they relate to informal organization is classroom characteristics. Classrooms are conceptualized as collectives with variable properties (school resources and facilities) including, for example, differentiation of instructional technology, delegation of authority, and interdependence of work arrangements (Cohen, Lotan, and Leechor, 1989). That is, the properties of the classroom constrain individual behavior through teacher qualities, expectations, and interaction styles, student strategies (role negotiations) and ability grouping, and through physical characteristics of the classroom such as class size, seating arrangements, color of the walls, lighting, ventilation, and so on.

Teacher Qualities

Other informal classroom interaction arrangements, not spelled out in the formal rules, affect children. What teachers expect of students varies according to teacher characteristics. When teachers have had more experience teaching or when they are trained in the subject area in which they are teaching, students tend to have better performance than when teachers are less experienced or teach in an area in which they have no credentials (Averch et al., 1974).

Teacher Expectations

Another encounter with informal social constraint is with teacher expectations. Research shows that teacher expectations affect student performance (Braun, 1976). Teachers make false judgments about students on the basis of such characteristics as gender, race, ethnicity, parental occupation, verbal communication, previous test results, and the student's appearance. A false definition of the situation by the teacher evokes a new behavior from the student that makes the original false conception come true (Merton, 1968). Robert Merton referred to this phenomenon as a *self-fulfilling prophecy*. Theories of deviance, such as Edwin Lemert's labeling perspective (1951), define primary and secondary deviance. Primary deviance is a violation of a norm; secondary deviance occurs when people define themselves as deviant and undertake life patterns as a reaction to their being labeled as deviant. This point of view derives from the *symbolic–interaction* theory (Mead, 1934) in which the person imagines or imputes meaning to himself or herself in response to interactions with others. For example, teachers have unwritten rules that determine how they and other children relate to each other in the classroom. In a study conducted by Ray Rist (1970), permanent seating assignments were made on what the teacher perceived as the kindergarten students' differing scholastic abilities. Three tables were arranged so that the middle-class children were in the front of the room and the poorer children in the back of the room. When standardized reading tests were employed at the end of the year, the children at the first table became the high group in first grade and were designated as the Tigers, while the second and third table children became the Cardinals and Clowns—despite the children's comparable scores on intelligence tests.

Another test of informal organization in the case of the self-fulfilling prophecy was made by Robert Rosenthal and Lenore Jacobson (1968). The experimenters hypothesized that children from whom the teacher expected greater intellectual growth would show greater growth. The children in the experimental and control groups were the same but for a single distinction: the students in the experimental group were identified to teachers as those who would show unusual gains. The children from whom the teachers had been led to expect greater intellectual gains (as indicated by test scores) did, indeed, show greater gains.

Other studies, replicating the Rosenthal and Jacobson design, subsequently tested the self-fulfilling prophecy hypothesis and did not confirm the findings (Finn, 1972; Braun, 1976). However, other types of studies that examined the effects of race and SES (Leacock, 1969; Harvey and Slatin, 1975) and physical attractiveness (Clifford and Walker, 1973) all suggest that teachers can affect students' actual achievements. Studies conducted at Johns Hopkins (Entwisle et al., 1974; Cohen, Lockheed, and Lohman, 1976) demonstrated that students' attitudes and behavior can be changed in desirable directions.

Interaction Styles

Classroom patterns of interaction constitute another dimension of the informal arrangements of individuals in schools. Teacher styles, student friendships, classroom participation, and male-female interaction are informal organizational characteristics of classrooms.

Some of the research on classroom interaction has focused on the the development of observational instruments for measuring interaction. The Interaction Analysis Scale (Flanders, 1965) has been used to test the hypothesis that learning is greatest when teacher influence is indirect. The Observation Schedule and

Record (OScAR) was developed to measure teacher *warmth* in relations with students. Warmth is indicated, for example, when a teacher accepts and clarifies the feelings of the students in a nonthreatening manner or when a teacher praises or encourages student action or behavior. Teachers whose classroom management style was warm were found to be the most effective.

Friendship patterns, another informal classroom arrangement, reveal something about behavioral outcomes of students. Open, democratic classrooms focus on the emotional development of students. Affective classrooms are those with increased interaction and shared activities, more uniform distribution of popularity among students, and an increased opportunity for students to be good at some task (Hallinan, 1976). Open classrooms decrease isolation and increase the length of friendships. Students in open classrooms also have fewer best friends (Hallinan, 1979). In contrast, ability grouping limits the pool of students with whom friendship is possible (Damico and Sparks, 1986). At the college level David Karp and William Yoels (1976) found three informal organizational characteristics encouraged rates of classroom participation: the consolidation of responsibility such that students rely on a select few of the class to respond to questions; the unlikelihood that instructors will call on students; and infrequent testing. Achievement effects are found when male teachers are partial to students who are obedient versus students who are independent and assertive (Good, Sikes, and Brophy, 1973).

Physical Conditions

In elementary and college classrooms, students sitting in the front or center of the classroom participate more and demonstrate higher levels of achievement (Brooks, Silven, and Wooten, 1978). The physical characteristics of the school classroom are manipulated to bring about predictable relations between students. This informal imposition on student behavior might include the size of the school and classroom, the shape and temperature of the room, the number of windows, the number of plants, and the amount of noise. All affect how students act and, furthermore, all represent determinants over which students personally have no choice (Ballantine, 1989).

Perhaps the most obvious physical determinant of behavior is the size of the classroom and school. Students in lower grades with lower academic performance learn more when they are in smaller classes. Overall, however, larger class size is positively related to gains in student achievement. Why larger groups are more effective is unclear, but perhaps smaller groups require adequate supervision of a situation in which students are given more autonomy (Boocock, 1980). James Coleman (1974) recommended smaller school size because students are able to interact more informally with teachers and administrators than in larger schools. Students have also been shown to participate less in drama, athletic, and musical activities in larger schools because only a small percentage of students can participate (Morgan and Alwin, 1980).

Last, the architecture of schools influences the interaction of individuals. Giancarlo De Carlo (1969) says that the school building is unique for its function in society, but it also isolates the students from interaction with the community at large.

Role Negotiation (Student Strategies)

When the explicit rules become unbearable, the implicit rules about how to break the formal rules govern our behavior. We can observe these hidden prescriptions in how to break the rules in *student strategies* (Ballantine, 1989).

One major informal arrangement for coping with formal demands is the student peer group. This is an age- and grade-related subculture in which students develop a unique set of behavioral prescriptions. Coleman (1961) found the influence of peer group expectations to be almost as great as parental expectations. Coleman also found that academically outstanding students are not rewarded for their achievement by the peer group. D. Hargreaves (1967) reported that high schools have two main subcultures, one that reinforces school values and another that does not.

Other student strategies for meeting school demands are described by Merton (1968) in his discussion of *types of individual adaptation*. According to this typology, some students conform by accepting school goals and the means for attaining them; other students retreat by rejecting the school goals and means for attaining them. Still other students are ambivalent or are indifferent. Last, some students rebel, replacing school goals and means with their own.

Formal organizational demands are negotiated as student strategies in the case of *cue-taking*. Research on college students who are able to pick up cues from professors about the kinds of knowledge that will enhance their test performance was conducted by C. M. Miller and M. Parlett (1976). Cue-conscious students pick up only a limited number of cues and rely on hard work and luck; cue-seeking students seek information from teachers; and the cue-deaf students study everything and pick up no cues.

Another informal organization feature under the rubric of student strategies is *student learning style*. Anthony Grasha (1975) developed an inventory that helps students to identify their learning style. Some students learn more efficiently from auditory stimulation than from visual or tactile stimulation. A cooperative learning setting facilitates learning for the same students who would not learn as well in a competitive learning context.[4]

Ability Grouping

Ability tracking, the major formal organizational mode of horizontal differentiation within schools, also has an implicit organizational aspect. It is strongly correlated with students' race and SES. It has been criticized because little evidence points to learning gains associated with tracking and because it produces a stratification system with stigmatizing effects for those at the lower levels (Boocock, 1980). A study of the antecedents and consequences of curriculum tracking (using longitudinal survey data from a national sample of students contacted in the ninth, eleventh, and twelfth grades) concluded that tracking affects educational aspirations and achievement, and that in a variety of ways, sorting processes within high school substantially affect later socioeconomic attainment (Alexander, Cook, and McDill, 1977). James Rosenbaum's research suggests that different socialization processes occur in the upper and lower tracks, so that students of otherwise similar characteristics come to feel differently about themselves and their school experience.

We have seen, then, that just when we imagine we are unique individuals and believe we personally have our lives under control, along comes the sociologist and says, *No, we don't!* Informal social agreements constrain our behavior so that contrary to what might appear to free choice, things are already decided. Hidden and subtle rules make it possible to deal with the formal demands made upon us. These rules exemplify informal organization because they make people respond in more emotional, diffuse, particularistic, collectivistic and enduring ways as opposed to the emotionally neutral, narrow, universalistic, self-interested, and not enduring ways of formal organization.

Social Constraints Do Not Explain Everything

The writings of the great classical theorists have disclosed the principles by which social forces constrain our behavior, but these early formulations are clearly inadequate in explaining some contemporary phenomena and challenge sociologists of education to refine and extend their theories. The problem of the inadequacy of theory on formal organization concerns several critical issues about the unintended outcomes of formal organization for the school system. By applying general social theory on organization, we have been able to link specific outcomes to their causes; yet, for example, whether bureaucratic organization is actually efficient remains unclear. Weber's insight that the outcome of the formal arrangement of people into groups is in the efficient realization of goals is questioned by some social scientists. Some insightful scholars claim that Weber did not go far enough in investigating the unintended consequences of formal arrangements. They maintain that formal arrangements also create inefficiency. Several investigators have identified the inefficiencies created by formal organization: ritualism (Merton, 1968); negotiated order (Strauss, 1964); waste of human resources (Parkinson, 1957); protection of the inept (Goode, 1967; Peter and Hull, 1969). These are all illustrated in the case of the school as a bureaucracy. Efficiency is questioned in the case of whether teaching, as a staff role, is a profession, or whether the school operates *better* when governed by a local district or by a central school board. Certain research findings add to the explanatory power of Weber's theory on bureaucracy by qualifying and extending under what conditions certain types of goals are efficiently attained.

Ritualism

Robert Merton (1968) questioned whether bureaucratic organization maximizes efficiency. In his discussion of the bureaucratic personality, he says that persons focused on procedures frequently do not think about the aims the procedures were intended to accomplish. Jobs become like rituals to the extent that employees perform tasks unthinkingly. The ritualism becomes obsessive and inhibits people from adjusting to new situations, thus impeding efficiency. Ritualism is illustrated when decision making and autonomy in carrying out one's role are affected through the centralized regulation of the schools. Although the central control is an attempt to standardize procedures concerning curriculum, staffing, budgetry, and supplies, this arrangement stunts innovation and flexibility (Rogers, 1969).

Negotiated Order

Others, like Anselm Strauss (1964), see bureaucratic procedures as conditions for negotiation rather than inflexible rules and view organizational behavior as predominantly informal in nature. The concept of negotiated order is illustrated in the issue of whether teaching is a profession. Professionals see themselves as having autonomy over their own area of expertise; this perception creates pressure to get away from the classic bureaucratic model. When the job calls for more craft or esoteric skill, it is difficult to have clear lines of authority, a high degree of division of labor, rules and procedures for everything, or an exact specification of duties and responsibilities (Perrow, 1979). The more teaching is defined as a highly trained profession, the more likely negotiations will go on because the work cannot be routinized.

Is Teaching a Profession?

The unintended consequences of formal agreements that limit relations among persons toward attaining particular goals concern whether teaching is a profession. Although formal agreements protect teachers from irrational requests and decisions (Moeller, 1964), the self-regulation or autonomy that typifies the professions is different for teachers than it is for other professional statuses. Disagreement continues about whether teaching-defined-as-a-profession is more efficient than teaching-defined-as-a-nonprofession. Sociologists seem to agree that the characteristics that distinguish an occupation as a profession (Goode, 1957; Jencks and Riesman, 1968; Friedson, 1973) include highly specialized and esoteric knowedge, extensive university training, considerable autonomy in making professional judgments, an ideology that stresses service and commitment rather than personal gain, and membership in nationwide organizations of fellow practitioners (Parelius and Parelius, 1987).

Formal organization imposes strict regulation on teachers, that is, it limits teacher autonomy, and autonomy is one of the characteristics of the professional. Professionals are not subject to the judgments or control of outsiders when practicing their profession. For example, lawyers and medical doctors reach consensus more easily than teachers in defining their expertise. Teachers do not have control over what constitutes their own training or the procedures by which they are licensed; school boards, not teachers, have formal control over curriculum, textbooks, and teaching methods. Additional formal constraints exist in the form of state and federal laws, policies established by local and state boards, administrative decisions handed down by superintendents, and informal pressures exerted by parents and community groups. Despite this bureaucratization, informal social norms have developed that tend to offset these formalities and teachers do exercise some autonomy in the context of the classroom itself.

The growth of teachers' unions during the 1960s is attributed to the powerlessness teachers felt in educational decision making (Jessup, 1978). The number of union members and strikes increased dramatically during the 1960s and 1970s; collective bargaining has become the norm because of teachers' quest for professional status and because of the resistance of the general public and the school boards to grant this privileged position (Cox and Elmore, 1976). Sixty-five percent of public school teachers in the nation are members of a labor organization (United States Census Bureau, 1982). The National Education Association (NEA) and the American Federation of Teachers (AFT) are the major teachers' unions. At the university level, the American Association of University Professors (AAUP) is a union for full-time faculty. The implications of unionization for the professionalization of teachers are disputed. Some argue that collective bargaining can strengthen the position of faculty who do not have the credentials that provide the basis of autonomy for those in more prestigious schools, while others argue that unionization will undermine the meritocratic reward structure in higher education and will eventually lower faculty quality.

Charles Bidwell (1965) suggests that the role of teachers differs from other professional roles partly because there is no comprehensive, identifiable body of knowledge, such as "law" or "medicine," that all teachers can be taught and on which they can be evaluated. As teachers have attempted to change their image from dedicated, low-paid public servants to full professionals, they have had to show accountability to fulfill their responsibilities in a professional role. Incentive pay to teachers for teaching in high-priority schools, for teaching subjects during a staff shortage, for extending professional training, and for increasing student gains on standardized tests has resulted in higher status and more pay (Say and Miller, 1982). Nevertheless, despite some gains toward professional status, obstacles to the further professionalization of teachers remain. Compared to law and medicine, teaching is a "semi-profession" (Meyers, 1973). Sociologists therefore suggest that teaching may never be fully professionalized unless teacher training is improved by on-the-job training, extended training, and conformity to professional scientific and social norms (Lortie, 1975). The Carnegie Commission Task Force on Teaching as a Profession proposed a plan to professionalize teaching that included the following recommendations (Carnegie Task Force on Teaching as a Profession, 1986):

- Create a national board, similar to those serving the professions of law and medicine, that would be responsible for establishing high standards of pedagogical practice and certifying those who meet them;

- Eliminate the undergraduate education major and strengthen master's of arts degree programs in education;

- Upgrade teachers' salaries to make them competitive with other professions;

- Shift many responsibilities from principals to teachers, including selection of instructional methods and materials, class scheduling, staffing structure, and student placement;

- Create a new position for a lead teacher who will have the responsibility for facilitating collegial interaction among teachers;

- Increase teacher accountability for student performance.

Unionization has definitely played a major role in the professionalization of teaching but many critics consider unions unprofessional because they believe them to destroy the meritocratic distribution of rewards that now encourages maximum development of faculty talent. Collective bargaining levels the differences among faculty teaching within the same bargaining unit; they are egalitarian because they oppose merit increments and other benefits that are otherwise unequally distributed among members.

The feminization of teaching has also contributed to its perception as a non-profession (Parelius and Parelius, 1988). Women have traditionally assumed the responsibility for child care; teaching, probably because it involved the care of children, was not viewed as intellectually taxing. Teaching also permitted relatively easy movement in and out of the labor market with different life cycle stages, particularly childrearing. A teacher could work for a few years, stop to care for her young children, and return again to teaching later. Teaching is also a careerless profession (Lortie, 1975) because the rank and responsibilities of beginning teachers are essentially identical to those of very experienced classroom teachers. Research shows that men are more likely than women to enter teaching with the move into administration already in mind as an avenue of mobility (Gross and Trask, 1976).

Wasting Human Resources

Other critics of bureaucracy (such as Parkinson, 1957) claim that bureaucratic procedures contribute to waste making rather than to getting tasks performed efficiently. Work expands to fill the time available for its completion. Bureaucrats appear busy in order to justify their jobs and create extra tasks for themselves; then they find they need to hire other personnel to manage the workload. For example, a college president, dean, assistant dean of students, and a clerk might handle admissions procedures until enrollment doubles. The administrative personnel increases so the work formerly done by four secretaries is done by several deans, assistant deans, and assistant vice presidents.

Protection of the Inept

Another characteristic of bureaucratic organization that Weber believed fostered efficient goal attainment is its hiring and promotion on the basis of merit. William Goode (1967) says that organizations are not likely to demote or fire incompetent employees. Instead, they protect these less competent employees by retaining them in the organization on the basis of their loyalty. The organization benefits from this approach because of the high turnover of personnel. Administrators also tend to promote employees who are very competent; people are promoted until they reach their level of incompetence or inability (Peter and Hull, 1969). Good teachers might be promoted to principals and then to superintendents (Knezevich, 1971). At this higher ranking position their performance may be inadequate, but they remain at this level and others at lower levels carry out the tasks the the superintendent is not able to manage.

Iron Law of Oligarchy

Bureaucratic organization is, according to Weber, characterized by staff roles as offices so that authority rests in the office, not in the person who occupies it. The authority of persons rests in the role that is explicitly defined by rules and procedures. This aspect of bureaucratic organization results in a concentration of power among those individuals who use their positions in the organization to advance their personal interests (Michels, 1949). Although Weber's theory of formal organization as a social instrument for coordinating the behaviors of large numbers of persons finds general support, it is inadequate to account for the dysfunctional consequences of the misuse of power, as illustrated in the case of issues over control of the schools.

Who Should Control the Schools?

It is clear from our observations of schools that both formal and informal organization facilitate the attainment of basic school goals (socialization and selection and allocation). While functionalists and conflict theorists would probably agree about the basic classification of constraints, how they see these constraints differs as related to outcomes. Are schools organized for an efficient pursuit of educational opportunity by provision of equal facilities, finances, and availability of schooling for all children (Coleman, 1968)? Or do schools represent arrangements to maximize the needs of capitalist employers for a disciplined and skilled labor force (Bowles and Gintis, 1976)? That is, conflict theorists and functionalists have alternative explanations of the uses of formal organization to achieve social integration, selection of talent, and the development of skills. In a functionalist view of education, schools are formally organized to teach what every American should know, the skills and beliefs important to participate in the mainstream culture. Schools are also organized to give children equal opportunity to identify their talents, so that under optimal conditions people are selected for jobs according to their abilities, regardless of personal characteristics such as gender, race, ethnicity, or wealth.

Aspects of school behavior fit our model of formal organization, but it is unclear whether the outcomes of these arrangements (central versus local control of schools; public versus private schooling; racial integration versus segregation; ability grouping and bilingual education) are oppressive or lead to opportunity. As a sociological concept, the application of the concept *bureaucracy* to schools explains some behavior, but it does not tell us exactly whose interests are served, only how efficiently they are carried out. Research on the relative contribution of formal versus informal organizational factors will perhaps clarify how and which school goals are attained. For example, studies on the effects of public and private school outcomes show that private schools mediate the effect of social class better than public schools. The formal organization of private schools includes strict regulations about doing homework, whereas the role of the student in the public school does not include as rigid an expectation (Coleman, Hoffer, and Kilgore, 1981). When private school children are racially mixed, minority students do better in mathematics and vocabulary than do minority students in public schools (Greeley, 1982; Bryk et al, 1984).

Let us examine more closely the controversy over who should control the schools. The role of the school board may appear to accomplish the American ideal of community representation in the governance of its schools, but some researchers argue that, empirically, such is not the case. K. Goldhammer (1964) found that communities have six role expectations of school board members: to promote public interest in education; to defend community values; to hear complaints and grievances; to supervise school personnel; to conserve resources; and to promote individual rights and interests within the school. N. Kerr (1964) claims that the chief contribution of school boards in the continuance of our educational system is their legitimation of the schools' policies, rather than their representation of the community. He argues that the community's ignorance of the school board's job fosters the board's alienation from the community. For example, school board members rely on the knowledge and expertise of professional educators when making decisions. They receive carefully selected information on issues from teachers and administrators. The interdependence between roles such as the superintendent and the board influences board decisions. According to Jeanne Ballantine (1989), in a survey of school board presidents and superintendents, the National School Board Association reports that more than half of the 3,240 respondents said their communication was excellent.

Another feature of school boards has also led conflict theorists to believe that minority views are not represented or influential in decision making (Ballantine, 1989). The composition of school boards has been shown to be predominantly white male homeowners with some college or graduate school and middle- to high-income white collar or professional occupations. The number of women increased from 10 percent in 1974 to 37 percent in 1983. The evidence does not necessarily support the view that minority interests are not represented because the volunteer members of the school boards have been shown to have a genuine interest in a cross section of community interests (Useem and Useem, 1974).

The degree to which the school board represents the community depends on whether the board is elected or appointed. David Rogers (1969), for example, studied the case of the New York City Board of Education and found that the appointed board was private and operated in isolation from the wider population and insensitive to community interests. Today, thirty-two school boards exist in New York City that are elected by their districts under a system of decentralization (New York City Board of Education, 1990). Adherents of conflict theory, who propound that educational institutions serve the interests of those who dominate the capitalist economy (Bowles and Gintis, 1976), would view appointed school board members as more likely than elected members to represent the interests of an elite. The vested interests of the powerful few would conflict with those of community interest groups.

Ongoing evaluations of the outcomes of decentralized versus centralized control help determine whose interests are being served. For example, the New York City Board of Education has encouraged decentralized control of its special education programs; many of the programs implemented to serve children in special education are evaluated at the local level rather than from the headquarters's Office of Research, Education, and Assessment (New York City Board of Education, 1990). The school board serves as a liaison between the school and the wider community on current issues such as drug use, disproportionate representation of black children in special education programs, and the use of condoms to prevent AIDS. Functionalists believe that bureaucratic organization concerning role expectations is efficient in maintaining the system, whereas conflict theorists would say that roles are effective for those who hold more powerful roles to dominate those in subordinate roles. Controversy over which explanation is better does not undermine Weber's claim that formal organization, as a generic term, represents the structuring of relations among people to bring about desired goals; instead, it allows further qualification about which specific type of formal arrangment most efficiently accomplishes a particular goal.

In sum, the school as a bureaucracy is probably similar to other bureaucracies in its characteristics. While the rights and obligations for particular roles can be identified in all bureaucracies, disputes about staff roles as they apply specifically to the teacher are not about whether the rights and obligations of teaching are clearly outlined. The question is, is the role that of a *professional?* The changing role of the teacher has focused on disagreements over the consequences of the role for teachers and the system depending upon whether the tasks for the role are viewed as professional or nonprofessional.

Summary

This chapter introduces the concept *organization* as a type of constraint or agreement by persons about how individuals should behave. By defining organization as the arrangement of people into large and small groups, we had to consider what a group is. Then, even though all groups have fundamental characteristics, we focused on two of many types of groups, *primary* and *secondary groups.* The expectations about how people should arrange themselves formally and informally are especially effective in meeting specific human needs. Using the concepts of formal and informal organization, respectively, we see schools as bureaucratic organizations and as informal structures with hidden curricula. Schools manifest formal group characteristics such as a functional division of labor, staff roles as offices, a hierarchy of authority, and rules of procedure. Informal constraints appear as the educational climate (school composition and culture and teacher characteristics), classroom characteristics (ability grouping, class size, and teacher expectations), and role negotiation (student strategies and teaching styles). Schools are formal and informal arrangements that bring about desired ends for the society by getting students to learn and to prepare for jobs, but they also have undesirable consequences. The bureaucracy is not as efficient as we expected; when we consider teaching as a profession, some things that occur in schools do not fit this model of behavior. We must qualify Weber's theory to explain what types of formal arrangement function efficiently in accomplishing a particular goal, as in the case of central versus decentralized school control. The distinctive sociological insight, however, is that individuals do not have an inherent biological predisposition that programs them to attend school. Schooling is an arbitrary agreed-upon arrangement about how to learn and how to prepare for a job. As Earl Babbie (1988) points out, "bee and ant corporations work more effectively because all the individuals are aligned by instinct." Humans make agreements about how to behave formally and informally to accomplish their goals.

Vocabulary

bureaucracy	organization
classroom characteristics	particularlistic
diffuse	primary group
educational climate	role
emotional	role negotiation
enduring	school composition
formal organization	school culture
functional division of labor	secondary group
group	staff roles as offices
hidden curriculum	student strategies
hierarchy of authority	teaching style
informal organization	Max Weber

Questions

1. What kind of behaviors go on in schools that can be explained by the concepts and theories of formal and informal organization?

2. What are the properties of a group?

3. Describe the two major types of arrangements that characterize groups and identify where these can generally be found in the school context.

3. Analyze school behavior as a response to formal and informal organization.

References and Suggested Readings

Alexander, K., M. Cook, and E. McDill. "Curriculum Tracking and Educational Stratification: Some Further Evidence." *Report 237, Social Organization of Schools.* Baltimore: Johns Hopkins University, 1977.

Astone, N. and S. McLanahan. "Family Structure, Parental Practices and High School Completion." *American Sociological Review,* (1991) 56:309–20.

Averch, H., et al. *How Effective Is Schooling? A Critical Review of Research.* Englewood Cliffs, NJ: Educational Technology Publications, 1974.

Babbie, E. *The Sociological Spirit: Critical Essays in a Critical Science.* Belmont, CA: Wadsworth, 1988.

Ballantine, J. *The Sociology of Education.* Englewood Cliffs, NJ: Prentice-Hall, 1989.

Bennett, I. and M. LeCompte. *How Schools Work: A Sociological Analysis of Education.* New York: Longman, 1990.

Bernard, H. and D. Fullmer. *Principles of Guidance,* 2nd Ed. New York: Thomas Crowell, 1977.

Bidwell, C. "The School as a Formal Organization." In James G. Marsh, ed., *Handbook of Organizations.* Skokie, IL: Rand McNally, 1965.

Blau, P. *The Dynamics of Bureaucracy.* Chicago: University of Chicago Press, 1955.

Blau, P. and M. Meyer. *Bureaucracy in Modern Society,* 2nd Ed. New York: Random House, 1971.

Blau, P. and R. Scott. *Formal Organizations.* San Francisco: Chandler, 1962.

Boocock, S. *Sociology of Education: An Introduction,* 2nd Ed. Boston: Houghton Mifflin, 1980.

Borman, K. and J. Spring. *Schools in Central Cities: Structure and Process.* White Plains, NY: Longman, 1984.

Bowles, S. and H. Gintis. *Schooling in Capitalist America.* New York: Basic Books, 1976.

Braun, C. "Teacher Expectations: Sociopsychological Dynamics." *Review of Educational Research,* (1976) 46:185–213.

Brookover, W. and E. Erickson. *Sociology of Education.* Homewood, IL: Dorsey Press, 1975.

Brooks, D., S. Silven, and M. Wooten. "The Ecology of Teacher-Pupil Verbal Interaction." *Journal of Classroom Interaction,* 14:39–43.

Bryk, A., P. Holland, V. Lee, and R. Carriedo. *Effective Catholic Schools: An Exploration.* Washington, DC: National Catholic Education Association, 1984.

Carnegie Task Force on Teaching as a Profession. "A System of Pay, Autonomy, Career Opportunities." *Education Week,* May 21, 1986, 11–18.

Clifford, M. and E. Walker. "The Effect of Physical Attractiveness on Teacher Expectations." *Sociology of Education,* (1973) 46:248–58.

Cohen, E., M. Lockheed, and M. Lohman. "The Center for Interracial Cooperation: A Field Experiment." *Sociology of Education,* (1976) 49:47–58.

Cohen, E., R. Lotan, and C. Leechor. "Can Classrooms Learn?" *Sociology of Education,* (1989) 62:75–94.

Coleman, J. *The Adolescent Society.* New York: Free Press, 1961.

Coleman, J., et al. *Equality of Educational Opportunity.* Washington, DC: Department of Education, 1966.

Coleman, J., et al. *Public and Private Schools.* National Center for Educational Statistics. Washington, DC: United States Government Printing Office, 1981.

Coleman, J., et al. *Youth: Transition to Adulthood.* Chicago: University of Chicago Press, 1974.

Coleman, J., T. Hoffer, and S. Kilgore. *Public and Private Schools: Report to the National Center for Education Statistics.* Chicago: National Opinion Research Center, 1981.

Corwin, R. *Education in Crisis: A Sociological Analysis of Schools and Universities in Transition.* New York: Wiley, 1974.

_____. *Militant Professionalism: A Study of Organizational Conflict in High Schools.* New York: Appleton-Century-Crofts, 1970.

Cox, H. and J. Elmore. "Public School Teachers: A Sociological View of their Status." *Contemporary Education,* (1976) 47:247.

Damico, S. and C. Sparks. "Cross-Group Contact Opportunities: Impact on Interpersonal Relationships in Desegregated Middle Schools." *Sociology of Education,* 59:113–23.

"Databank." *Education Week.* October 22, 1986, p. 16.

DeCarlo, G. "Why/How to Build School Buildings." *Harvard Educational Review,* (1969) 39:26.

Dodd, P. "Role Conflicts of School Principals." *Final Report No. 4, Cooperative Research Project No. 853.* Graduate School of Education, Harvard University, 1965.

Durkheim, E. *Moral Education: A Study in the Theory and Application of the Sociology of Education.* New York: Free Press, 1973.

_____. *The Rules of Sociological Method.* New York: Free Press, 1959, pp. 2–13.

_____. *Education and Sociology.* Glencoe, IL: Free Press, 1956.

Entwisle, D., M. Webster, and L. Hayduk. *Expectation Theory in the Classroom.* Report to United States Department of Health, Education and Welfare, Department of Social Relations, Johns Hopkins University, 1974.

Evans, O. "Friendship: On the Job and After Five." *New York Times,* August 1, 1983, p. 13.

Finn J. "Expectations and the Educational Environment." *Review of Educational Research,* (1972) 42:387–410.

Flanders, N. *Teacher Influence, Pupil Attitudes, and Achievement.* Washington, DC: United States Department of Education, 1965.

Friedson, E., ed., *The Professions and Their Prospects.* Beverly Hills, CA: Sage, 1973.

Garner, C. and S. Raudenbush. "Neighborhood Effects on Educational Attainment: A Multilevel Analysis." *Sociology of Education* (1991) 64:251–62.

Gerth, H. and C. Mills, eds., *From Max Weber: Essays in Sociology.* New York: Galaxy, 1958.

Goldhammer, K. *The School Board*. New York: Center for Applied Research in Education, 1964.

Good, T., J. Sikes, and J. Brophy. "Effects of Teacher Sex and Student Sex on Classroom Interaction." *Journal of Educational Psychology*, (1973) 65:74–87.

Goode, W. "Forms of Social Organization: Groups Large and Small." *Principles of Sociology*. New York: McGraw-Hill, 1977.

_____. "The Protection of the Inept." *American Sociological Review*, (1967) 32:5–19.

_____. "Community within a Community: The Professions." *American Sociological Review*. February, (1957) 22:194–200.

Goslin, D. *The School in Contemporary Society*. Glenview, IL: Scott, Foresman, 1965.

Grasha, A. *Grasha-Reichmann Student Learning Styles Questionnaire*. Faculty Resource Center. Cincinnati, OH: University of Cincinnati, 1975.

Greeley, A. *Catholic High Schools and Minority Students*. New Brunswick, NJ: Transaction Books, 1982.

Gross, N. and A. Trask. *The Sex Factor and the Management of Schools*. New York: John Wiley and Sons, 1976.

Hallinan, M. "Structural Effects on Children's Friendship and Cliques." *Social Psychological Quarterly*, (1979) 42:43–54.

_____. "Friendship Patterns in Open and Traditional Classrooms." *Sociology of Education*, (1976) 49:254–65.

Hargreaves, A. "Experience Counts, Theory Doesn't: How Teachers Talk about their Work." *Sociology of Education*, (1984) 57:244–53.

_____. *Social Relations in a Secondary School*. London: Rutledge and Kegan Paul, 1967.

Harvey, D. and G. Slatin. "The Relationship Between Child's SES and Teacher's Expectations: A Test of the Middle-Class Bias Hypothesis." *Social Forces*, (1975) 54:140–59.

Heyns, B. and S. Catsambis. "Mother's Employment and Children's Achievement: A Critique." *Sociology of Education*, (1986) 59:140–51.

Horan, P. and P. Hargis. "Children's Work and Schooling in the Late Nineteenth-Century Family Economy." *American Sociological Review*, (1991) 56:583–96.

Hurn, C. *The Limits and Possibilities of Schooling*. Boston: Allyn & Bacon, 1978.

Jencks, C. et al. *Inequality: A Reassessment of the Effects of Family and Schooling in America*. New York: Basic Books, 1972.

Jencks, C. and D. Riesman. *The Academic Revolution*. Garden City, NY: Doubleday, 1968.

Jessup, D. "Teacher Unionization: A Reassessment of Rank and File Motivations." *Sociology of Education*, (1978) 51:44–5.

Karp, D. and W. Yoels. "The College Classroom: Some Observations on the Meanings of Student Participation." *Sociology and Social Research*, 609:421–39.

Katz, F. "The School as a Complex Social Organization." *Harvard Educational Review*, 34:428–55.

Kerr, N. "The School Board as an Agency of Legitimation." *Sociology of Education*, (1964) 38:34–59.

Knezevich, S. *The American School Superintendent*. Washington, DC: American Association of School Administrators, 1971.

Kohl, H. *Thirty-Six Children*. New York: Signet Books, 1967.

Leacock, E. *Teaching and Learning in City Schools*. New York: Basic Books, 1969.

Lemert, E. *Social Pathology: A Systematic Approach to the Theory of Sociopathic Behavior*. New York: McGraw-Hill, 1951.

Lortie, D. *Schoolteacher: A Sociological Study*. Chicago: University of Chicago Press, 1975.

Mead, G. *Mind, Self, and Society*. Chicago: University of Chicago Press, 1934.

Medley, D. "Experience with the OScAR Technique." *Journal of Teacher Education*, (1963) 267–73.

Merton, R. *Social Theory and Social Structure*. New York: Free Press, 1968.

Meyers, D. *Teacher Power—Professionalization and Collective Bargaining*. Lexington, MA: D.C. Heath, 1973.

Michels, R. *First Lectures in Political Science*. Minneapolis: University of Minnesota Press, 1949.

Miller, C. and M. Parlett. "Cue-Consciousness." In M. Hammersley and P. Woods, eds., *The Process of Schooling: A Sociological Reader*. London: Open University Press and Routledge & Kegan Paul, 1976, pp. 143–9.

Milne, A., D. Myers, A. Rosenthal, and A. Ginsburg. "Single Parents, Working Mothers, and the Educational Achievement of School Children." *Sociology of Education*, (1986) 59:125–39.

Moeller, G. "Bureaucracy and Teachers' Sense of Power." In R. Bell and H. Stub, eds., *The Sociology of Education*. Homewood, IL.: Dorsey Press, 1964, pp. 236–50.

Moore, K. and N. Snyder. "Cognitive Attainment Among Firstborn Children of Adolescent Mothers." *American Sociological Review* (1991) 56:612–24.

Morgan, D. and D. Alwin. "When Less Is More: School Size and Student Social Participation." *Social Psychology Quarterly*, 43:241–52.

Mulkey, L., R. Crain, and A. Harrington. "One-Parent Households and Achievement: Economic and Behavioral Explanations of a Small Effect." *Sociology of Education*, (1992) 65:48–55.

National Education Association. *Status of the American Public School Teacher, 1985–86*. National Education Association, 1987.

National School Boards Association. *The People Look at Their Schools*. Evanston, IL: National School-Boards Association, 1975, 1–47.

New York City Board of Education. Division of Research and Strategic Planning; Office of Research, Evaluation, and Assessment, Brooklyn, NY, 1990.

Parelius, R. and A. Parelius. *The Sociology of Education*, 2nd Ed. Englewood Cliffs, NJ: Prentice-Hall, 1987.

Parkinson, C. *Parkinson's Law*. Boston: Houghton Mifflin, 1957.

Parsons, T. *The Social System*. New York: Free Press, 1951.

Parsons, T. "The School Class as a Social System: Some of Its Functions in American Society." *Harvard Educational Review*, (1959) 29:222–3.

Perrow, C. *Complex Organizations: A Critical Essay*, 2nd Ed. Glenview, IL: Scott, Foresman, 1979.

Peter, L. and R. Hull. *The Peter Principle*. New York: Morrow, 1969.

Rabow, J. and T. Robischon. "The Public School: Organizational and Teacher Goals." *Education and Urban Society*, (1972) 4:468.

Rist, R. "Student Social Class and Teacher Expectations: The Self-Fulfilling Prophecy in Ghetto Education." *Harvard Educational Review*, (1970) 40:411–51.

Rogers, D. *110 Livingston Street: Politics and Bureaucracy in the New York City School System*. New York: Vintage, 1969.

Rosenbaum, J. "The Stratification of Socialization Processes." *American Sociological Review*, (1975) 409:48–54.

Rosenthal, R. and L. Jacobson. *Pygmalion in the Classroom*. New York: Holt, Rinehart and Winston, 1968.

Say, E. and L. Miller. "The Second Mile Plan: Incentive Pay for Houston Teachers." *Phi Delta Kappan*, December (1982) 270–71.

Sewell, W. and Hauser, R. "The Wisconsin Longitudinal Study of Social and Psychological Factors in Aspirations and Achievements." *Research in Sociology of Education and Socialization*, (1964) 1:59–99.

Shakeshaft, C. "The Female World of School Administrators." *Educational Horizons*, (1986) 44:117–22.

Shavit, Y. and J. Pierce. "Sibship Size and Educational Attainment in Nuclear and Extended Families: Arabs and Jews in Israel." *American Sociological Review*, (1991) 56:321–30.

Sills, D. "Preserving Organizational Goals." In Oscar Grusky and G. Miller, eds. *The Sociology of Organizations: Basic Studies*, New York: Free Press, 1970, pp. 227–36.

Snyder, B. *The Hidden Curriculum*. New York: Knopf, 1971.

Strauss, A. et al. *Psychiatric Ideologies and Institutions*. New York: Free Press, 1964.

United States Bureau of the Census. "Unionization and Work Shortages Characterize Educators." *Phi Delta Kappan*, (1982) April 571.

United States Department of Education. *High School '77: A Survey of Secondary School Principals*. Washington, DC: United States Department of Education, 1978.

Useem, E. and M. Useem, eds., *The Educational Establishment*. Englewood Cliffs, NJ: Prentice-Hall, 1974.

Waller, W. *The Sociology of Teaching*. New York: Wiley, 1932.

Weber, M. *The Theory of Social and Economic Organization*. Glencoe, IL.: Free Press, 1947.

Wellisch, J., et al. "School Management and Organization in Successful Schools." *Sociology of Education*, (1978) 51:211–26.

Notes

[1]The following discussion of groups is derived from the insights of two prominent sociologists, Robert K. Merton and William J. Goode. For a more detailed analysis, see Merton's "The Classification of Types of Membership Groups," in *Social Theory and Social Structure*, enlarged ed., New York: Free Press, 1968, pp. 362–80 and Goode's "Forms of Social Organization: Groups Large and Small," in *Principles of Sociology*, New York: McGraw-Hill, 1977, pp. 174–207.

[2]Goode, in "Forms of Social Organization," *Principles of Sociology*, New York: McGraw-Hill, 1977, p. 188, uses the descriptive concepts (called the *pattern variables*) of Talcott Parsons, except for the last one. His fifth concept, he says, is *ascriptive–achieved*, but in primary relations no specification demands that relations should be either one. He suggests that for a discussion of these ideas, see Talcott Parsons, *The Social System*, New York: Free Press, 1951, pp. 55–88. The terms are an elaboration of the concepts *Gemeinschaft* and *Gesellschaft* discussed in the latter part of the chapter on "Forms of Social Organization."

[3]The persons who fill these formal roles are described as follows: Approximately 3.2 million teachers staff American primary and secondary schools (*Education Week*, "Databank." Oct. 22, 1986). Selected demographic characteristics of public school teachers in the past twenty years indicate that teachers are predominantly female. The average teacher is a white, married woman in her midthirties, with two children. She comes from a middle to upper-middle class family, teaches in a suburban elementary school, and was educated in a public university; fifty percent have a master's degree (Statistical Abstracts of the United States, Washington, DC: U.S. Department of Commerce, Bureau of the Census, 1987, p. 125).

[4]An extensive literature exists on the nature and consequences of cooperative learning, but it is not reviewed here.

CHAPTER
9

Social Control and Deviance

Getting People to Conform

As we look this time at the preceding photograph of kindergarten children, we will attempt to understand their behavior as a response to yet another principle of sociology—social control and deviance. The children in the photo above have the appearance of conformity: the question is, why aren't they acting more idiosyncratic in their behavior? Are the few children who are not smiling like the other children disobedient? Society decides which behaviors are normal and which are deviant. Yet rarely do we ask why we punish certain behaviors and reward others. In other words, deviance, behavior that is bothersome to most people, is not inherent: it is a relative phenomenon. We must ask whether deviant acts are defined through a general consensus of values or whether a conflict of values stands between those who have the power to apply definitions of deviance and those who do not. For example, in the past the Gallup (1987) education opinion polls have found that the public's major concern about schools is the lack of discipline. Recently, *A Nation at Risk* (National Commission on Excellence in Education, 1983) and other national reports have called attention to the implications of the decline in test scores for the nation's youth. Policy analysts hypothesize that poor academic performance is associated with student misbehavior. More specifically, researchers cite lack of discipline in the classroom as a significant cause of poor academic performance. Some scholars, educators, and parents advocate more discipline in schools and encourage physical punishment of students by public school teachers. In other words, we find ourselves at the point of endorsing either the old-fashioned authoritarian methods, which tend to make us forget about the freedom of the child, or following the lead of others, who attempt to show the benefits of a radical negation of the use of force.

Outline

Given that we are—each and every one of us—inclined to think we are unique and individual, it is remarkable that the world stays together. In other words, haven't you ever wondered, when driving on a busy two-lane highway, "What's to keep the next oncoming driver from crashing into me head-on?" Perusing the daily headlines, haven't we all offered silent thanks that we weren't in that burger joint when the mass murderer struck—and then wondered why, given society's widespread social ills, that mass murder is not the norm? To borrow an example from popular culture, perhaps John Lennon said it best when comparing the two biggest rock'n'roll bands of the Baby Boom generation: "The amazing thing is not that the Beatles broke up, but that the Rolling Stones didn't."

Surprisingly enough, we are able to believe in ourselves as individuals by taking our connections to others for granted. We are very obedient to society's rules, so much so that we only notice this when someone breaks the rules. Americans emphasize the notion of the unique individual, the self, but most people follow others and fulfill their roles in accordance with society's expectations. School begins at 9:00 a.m. tomorrow regardless of whether a few teachers decide they are bored and tired and don't want to teach that day. This chapter gives attention to the orderliness and predictable nature of our human world by pointing out some of the rules that make it so. Most important, we are now concerned with how societies decide what counts as deviance and what actions are taken to exact conformity.

How do theories tell us about whose interests are served when some acts are defined as deviant and some are not? We will investigate how the principle of social control and social deviance operates by looking at theories such as strain theory, cultural transmission theory, labeling theory, and control theory. These explanations are put forth to account for many of the issues involving school and classroom discipline. What counts as deviance in this context? What fosters conformity? This chapter examines the application of the principle of social control and deviance as it concerns several major school issues; reciprocally, these issues reveal something of the nature of the principle of social control and deviance.

Conceptualizing Social Control and Deviance

The *principle of social control and deviance* is one of the six principles of sociology. *Deviance* refers to socially disapproved violations of important norms and expectations. *Social control* refers to those mechanisms designed to align behavior. The principle operates, at the individual, subjective level, as a predisposition to make and comply with rules that in some way ensures the survival of the individual in the group. When the principle operates at the societal level (as shared, collective agreements), the mechanisms of social control and deviance are codified or objectified as part of the social structure so that individuals belonging to various positions (groups according to statuses and roles), are expected to act in specific ways. Students, for example, are expected to graduate; dropouts are those students who deviate from this standard role prescription for students. The principle of social control and deviance, like the other sociological principles, is a version of the more generic principle of organization. It is elaborated as those behavioral prescriptions that are transmitted (via the principle of socialization) to specifically articulate the boundaries of what are considered severely deviant acts (those bothersome to most people) and to define those actions necessary to prevent their occurrence.

To repeat, the principle of social control and deviance operates to maintain order and stability in society. In an ideal community in which each individual relates to others on the basis of complete self-giving, no laws are required to manage individual behaviors so that all members of the group are preserved. However, most people do not love their neighbors as themselves, and prescriptions for appropriate behavior must be reinforced to balance the rational, instrumental, and self-seeking characteristics typical of human action. The principle of social control and deviance acts as those behavioral directives that orient people to act in particular ways, and it defines the significance of these expectations through various degrees of rewards and punishments. Individuals are then able to fit into society in those ways needed to maintain both society and the individual.

Social Control and Deviance in Schools

During the past decade or so, *discipline* has been the major concern of parents and teachers. Teachers also report that student misbehavior interferes with delivery of instruction (Baker, 1985). Discipline in the school is manifested as several issues that can be understood from a sociological analysis, beginning with identifying it as a response to the principle of social control and deviance. Theoretical and empirical studies on classroom discipline, dropping out of high school, student drug abuse, adolescent sexual behavior, school violence, and special education as the medicalization of deviance provide an idea of how the principle operates in the school context—and, thereby, also offer a basis for comparison of its operation in other contexts.[1]

Investigations of School Discipline

No single theory adequately explains the nature of social control and deviance. The starting point is not to understand why a person becomes deviant, but to account for the labeling of a behavior or an activity as deviant in the first place. Cultural transmission theory views deviant behavior as learned through differential association with other deviants, and it implies that persons socialized in a particular group may become deviant by learning the norms of that particular subculture. For instance, a ghetto child may learn patterns of behavior that the mainstream culture defines as deviant. Structural strain theory, which locates the source of deviance in social structure rather than in the deviants, posits that deviance arises from a discrepancy between socially approved goals and the availability of socially approved means of achieving them. Control theory explains deviance as the outcome of inadequate social control over the behavior of people who have weak bonds to the community. Labeling theory accounts for deviance as a process by which some people come to act in accordance with the label people assign to them.

However, in the accounting of the causes and effects of deviance, we must consider whose interests are served in the process of defining which acts are deviant. These theories must therefore be considered under the rubric of conflict and consensus (functionalist) paradigms, in which functionalist argue that the phenomenon exists because it provides some effect or function that contributes to the maintenance of society as a whole. (Note that in Chapter 6 conflict theory is considered in a different manner, as alongside critical theory, while cultural reproduction theory is considered under the rubric of "active" theories of socialization.) Conflict proponents are critical of this approach and see a "deviance as functional for society" interpretation as an example of functionalist bias in favor of the status quo. In the conflict interpretation, in contrast, the deviant behavior reflects the power relationships in the society and the phenomenon benefits certain groups and persons but not others.

Approaches to Student Discipline

The evidence on school and classroom orientations to student discipline suggests something about the operation of the principle of social control and deviance; this evidence should be examined for how effectively it serves as a means for ensuring conformity to those behaviors that are important to most people. Other questions must be considered: Does broad consensus exist over the behavior being enforced? Or, perhaps more importantly, does the broad consensus about what is normal and what is deviant mirror compliance to a powerful few who benefit from the arrangement? Or does the agreement occur through democratic participation? The evidence suggests that of the two orientations (consensus and conflict), one ensures compliance by encouraging unreflective conformity to the status quo and the other by reflective consent. Disciplinary strategies that encourage unthinking conformity to the status quo also seem to be social class based. Thus, the nature of the principle of social control is to limit deviance and, at the same time, to reproduce social order. However, for limited periods some groups within a society may benefit more than others on grounds considered unfair by the majority of people. Labeling theory accounts for this process whereby students are rewarded or punished in accordance with the labels of *obedient* or *self-reflective*.

One issue that illustrates the operation of the principle of social control and deviance concerns techniques employed for discipline in schools. Two approaches characterize disciplinary strategies on a continuum; at one end is a *humanistic* approach; at the other is an *authoritarian* approach.

Evidence indicates that teachers fall into a range of categories on the continuum of disciplinary approaches (Glickman and Tamashiro, 1980): a humanistic noninterventionist strategy in which students are given freedom to solve their own problems and to explore personal values; an interactionist strategy in which the teacher limits the choices; an interventionist strategy in which clearcut standards of behavior are articulated and reinforced with rewards and punishments; or an eclectic strategy, in which the teacher incorporates a variety of approaches. Techniques for control vary from corporal punishment, expulsion or suspension, detention, transfer to another class or school, loss of privileges, the use of drugs to calm children, or special education classes (Ballantine, 1989).

The use of authoritarian techniques with corporal punishment and expulsion or suspension seems to be the choice of federal administrations to protect the rights of teachers and students (Bauer, 1985). Humanistic approaches avoid strict discipline (Agnew, 1985). All states, except for Massachusetts and New Jersey, permit corporal punishment (Cryan and Smith, 1981). Corporal punishment has been shown to be ineffective as a behavioral control mechanism; it increases disruptive behavior and hinders learning (Jones and Tanner, 1981). Educators responsible for the well-being of students of necessity emphasize obedience to rules and regulations designed to ensure orderly conduct (Jackson, 1968; Goodlad, 1984; McNeil, 1986; and Mergendoller, 1988). W. Doyle (1986) documents how this emphasis on order goes against higher order learning because while tasks such as those involving recall of algorithms go well, higher level tasks are difficult to carry out.

In contrast to high-status schools, low-status schools tend to emphasize external discipline. Teachers in high-status schools emphasize independent work and self-discipline more than do teachers in low-status schools. K. A. Wilcox (1978), for example, reports that teachers used more authoritarian control mechanisms in working with lower-status classrooms than they did with higher-status classes. J. Anyon (1980) observed that in working-class schools, children were asked to follow steps of a procedure in a mechanical manner involving rote behavior. Information was written on the board for students to copy. As schools varied from middle-class to affluent professional to executive elite, the degree of creative activity carried out independently by the student increased. These findings and those from other studies (Havighurst, 1964; Bernstein, 1975) suggest that schools can be classified according to the types of students they enroll and the type of discipline they use; discipline in middle-class schools tends to be informal compared with the strict discipline imposed on working-class students. Emphasis on openness versus control in family discipline patterns were found to be correlated to school experience in a national sample of high school students (Howell and McBroom, 1982). These findings suggest that elementary and secondary schools reinforce family background in the mobility process for students.

Other evidence supporting the social-class–based association with school discipline concerns *student rights*. The issue of student rights centers on the claim that arbitrary disciplinary measures have been used disproportionately on minority students, and thus schools contribute to the replication of race- and class-based inequality of opportunity. Constitutional rights (especially due process and First Amendment rights) have been neglected when they relate to students (Glasser, 1969).

The issue of school disciplinary strategies can be understood through the application of the principle of social contol amd deviance. Moreover, the characteristic operation of the principle in this case suggests conformity through domination (and perhaps mostly through the process of labeling) in contrast to conformity through representation.

Dropping Out

Another issue that tells us how the principle of social control and deviance operates in education is that of dropping out of high school. Although the research on this topic is atheoretical, its post hoc evidence lends some support to aspects of the major theoretical interpretations of deviance.

The high dropout rates of students in urban secondary schools is considered a national problem that is embedded in the broader concerns for the quality of American education (Rumberger, 1987; Burch, 1988). Research on high school dropouts shows that, generally, they are lower in SES than their peers who graduate. The academic performance of most dropouts is poor, and before dropping out they have attended school less and misbehaved more than those who go on to graduate (Mensch and Kandel, 1988; Pallas, 1986). Researchers have identified how disadvantage plays a role in dropping out for inner city students (Wehlage and Rutter, 1986). These students see no association between schooling and a future income; they often leave school because of family economic obligations. Social control interventions implemented to decrease drop out rates include: early intervention to develop positive attitudes in elementary and middle schools (Pallas, 1986); alternative schools (for example, storefront schools and magnet schools) (Wehlage, Rutter and Turnbaugh, 1987); smaller schools and classes (Reinhard, 1987); vocational education opportunities (Hamilton, 1986); job placement (Fortenberry and White, 1987; Hamilton, 1988); counseling (Mann, 1986); and reform in curriculum and delivery of instruction (Ekstrom, Goertz, Pollack, and Rock, 1986). Research on the effectiveness of these interventions in enhancing scholastic persistence shows some support for antidropout programs (Hamilton, 1986).

A general explanation of social control and deviance dynamics drawn from the preceding evidence is that, for the most part, the schools play a role in reproducing the inequities that students bring to school, yet this tendency is countered by the school's provision of resources that attempt to mediate the negative effect of social class background. The more specific details of these general dynamics are understood through the following theoretical interpretations: structural strain thinking accounts for the deviant behavior as a rejection of culturally approved goals and culturally approved means. Cultural transmission theory explains that the school does not provide the skills necessary to survive in the lower-class subculture. Control theory says that students deviate because their ties to the community at large are weak; the commitment and involvement elements of a strong bond to society are threatened. Labeling theorists focus on deviant behavior as the outcome of the successful definition the school gives to these students as deviants.

Adolescent Sexual Behavior

Adolescent sexuality is another issue that lends itself to sociological analysis by application of the principle of social control and deviance. Adolescent sexual behavior has been dealt with as deviant by sociologists who advocate a control theory approach to understanding the phenomenon (Reiss, 1970). From this theoretical interpretation of how social control and deviance operates, *everyone wants to do it*, and, without social control, would engage in socially undesirable sexual activity. The question of importance is not why they *do* it, but why they *don't* do it (Hirschi, 1969). T. Hirschi proposes a control theory explanation of deviant behavior that takes motivation for granted and explains that investment in the traditional institutions of society restrains the deviant behavior of adolescents. Although he does not specifically address sexual behavior, other studies show that sexual behavior belongs to a class of adolescent norm violations that are both intercorrelated and predicted by such social control factors as parental attitudes, family structure, respondent's religion and church attendance (Thornton and Camburn, 1987), neighborhood characteristics (Hogan and Kitagawa, 1985), and peer effects (Udry and Billy, 1987). J. Udry (1988) explored the relative contribution of biological predisposition (hormones) and social control mechanisms in explaining adolescent coitus. He says that a sociological model by itself is incomplete without controlling for differences in hormonal levels of adolescents at different ages. The study found that when conventional norms are weakened, adolescent sexual behavior is more prevalent, but that this varies somewhat when biological factors are considered. For girls, only sociological variables control or suppress androgenic hormone effects. For boys, hormones mediate the effect of social controls.

The evidence explaining adolescent sexual *inactivity* as a response to social controls supports control theory. Control theory says that the principle of social control and deviance operates to suppress an activity that threatens the maintenance of society and its individuals. It is functional in that it aims at exacting conformity to formal educational requirements and the selection and occupational allocation process.

Cultural transmission theory is adequate to explain how the principle of social control and deviance operates in the case of teen pregnancy and motherhood. What is commonplace in the subculture of poverty is deviant in the mainstream culture. Contemporary black youth are relatively accepting of early coitus and out-of-wedlock parenthood (Moore, Simms, and Betsey, 1986). G. Furstenberg, J. Brooks-Gunn and S. Morgan (1987) report that researchers have noted a sizable racial difference in the prevalence and timing of premarital sexual behavior. In a national sample of youth (ages fifteen to sixteen years) blacks were about four times more likely than whites to report having had intercourse. Three explanations were considered: (1) a demographic composition explanation that stresses differential socioeconomic position; (2) the consequences of low socioeconomic position, a higher incidence of female-headed households, or differences in school performance or educational aspirations; and (3) a contextual explanation based on differences in subgroup attitudes or norms. Results provided limited support for the demographic composition argument and stronger support for a contextual subgroup argument. Attitudinal differences between whites, blacks in segregated schools and blacks in racially homogeneous schools characterized different normative contexts.

The same phenomenon is interpretable as a structural strain theory of the operation of the principle of social control and deviance. When persons do not have adequate means to accomplish goals they deviate from the normal expectations for behavior. Gangs consist of lower-class boys who, being deficient in social and educational resources, are unable to attain success by way of mainstream channels (Cohen, 1955). Therefore they get approval of their peers through behaviors that conform to gang norms. In this way, the gang whose members are unable to obtain respectable status find other sources of achievement not acceptable to the wider mainstream society. The relationship between teen motherhood and later-life disadvantage is well-documented, and this association seems to be reciprocal.[2] Young women who are poor and have limited opportunity are more likely to have babies at an earlier age, but having a baby also reduces the future opportunities of these young mothers (Sonenstein, 1985). Longitudinal research working with low income teenage black females has found that motherhood had a negative impact on their subsequent careers. Early pregnancy interfered with the intended life course by disrupting schooling and creating eonomic hardship. Poorly educated, unskilled women ages twenty to twenty-one had become resigned to a life of economic deprivation and, although they wanted to complete high school, most had not found inspiration to return to school.

These dynamics suggest that for young inner city women, the principle of social control and deviance reinforces their underclass status. The principle of social control and deviance, as it applies to teen pregnancy, suggests a consensus of values in contemporary society about the dysfunctional nature of teen sex, but the fact that the regulation of teen sex is restricted to a subgroup of the overall population shows that regulation also perpetuates the problem by making provision for an alternative for groups who cannot attain success by status quo avenues. Conflict proponents see this as an example of functionalist bias in favor of the status quo. Teen pregnancy, as deviant behavior, more reflects the power relationships in society and benefits a certain few.

Evidence to the contrary which supports a functionalist argument shows how social control mechanisms ensure equal life chances in the system. The evidence comes from studies of fertility control practices. The success of preventive educational services is inconclusive: determining any significant effect on adolescent sex, pregnancy, or abortion is impossible (Jaffe and Dryfoos, 1980). Other researchers (Sonenstein, 1985; Zabin et al., 1986; Buie, 1987) report positive outcomes of public school programs to reduce teen pregnancy. The United States House of Representatives Select Committee on Children, Youth, and Families conducted a survey on teen pregnancy (1986) and reported that the problem required more support. The report of the National Research Council Panel on Adolescent Pregnancy and Childbearing (1986) made several recommendations, including the broad distribution of contraceptives to teenagers; beginning sex education at an early age; establishment of more school-based clinics; life-planning courses as part of the curriculum; mass media campaigns help to emphasize sexual responsibility; and availability of abortion to teenagers.

Other evidence that lends itself to a functionalist interpretation of the principle of social control and deviance accommodates structural strain theory as well: given the socially approved goal of restricting adolescent sexual activity, and that contraception is socially disapproved as a means to support the goal (because contraception implies sexual activity), adolescents cannot conform and adapt through rebellion. Teen pregnancy is not necessarily related to race and social class; international data found that the United States has a higher rate of teen pregnancy and illegitimacy than other Western industrialized nations (Jones et al., 1986). Promiscuity alone does not account for the situation, for rates of teen sex are about the same in other nations. Welfare benefits for unmarried mothers are not less generous in other societies, so lower social aid cannot account for the matter; neither do other countries have higher abortion rates than the United States. The best explanation focuses on contraception. The United States consensually (agreed to by many) argues that teenagers should not have sex. This value, however, interferes with teenagers' use of contraception because birth control implies sexual activity. Other countries are more concerned with preventing teenage pregnancy and therefore emphasize the proper use of contraception. The discrepancies of American values seem to bring about the rise in illegitmacy.

Analysis of these school-related issues on teen sex suggests a relatively equal contribution of conflict and consensus in the operation of the principle of social control and deviance. Only the accumulation of further evidence in support of theoretically derived hypotheses will make this claim more precise.

Student Drug Abuse

Another illustration of the principle of social control and deviance in the school is the issue of *drug abuse*. How does the concern over the increased misuse of drugs by youth indicate what society defines as deviant, how does it do so, and whose interests are served in this dynamic?

Evidence of the operation of the principle of social control and deviance is found in the definition of the problem as a national problem and in reports of the effectiveness of programs provided by the schools to prevent drug misuse. Drug abuse is considered a national problem and, according to a report by the President's Commission on Organized Crime (Rose, 1986), a threat to national security. Some research shows that it is relatively easy to increase drug knowledge, but difficult to modify attitudes; most studies have found no effects of drug education upon use (Hanson, 1980). Increasing effort has been expended examining the effectiveness of university-based prevention programs (Goodstadt and Caleekal-John, 1984). In response to evidence that chemical dependency is a lingering or growing problem, many universities have initiated programs of varying types and intensities to reduce the demand for illicit drugs (Bloch and Unger-leider, 1988). A review of 127 drug abuse prevention programs and found support for the efficacy of these programs (Schaps et al., 1981).

An annual national survey of high school seniors is conducted by the University of Michigan Institute for Social Research (Johnston et al., 1985). Findings on drug use among students showed that marijuana use declined slightly from 1975 to 1985; cocaine use increased from 1975 to 1985 by about ten percentage points; and about 65 percent of 1985 high school seniors reported using alcohol. Students using other illicit drugs such as heroin, opiates, tranquillizers, and amphetamines dropped slightly from 34 percent in 1981 to 27 percent in 1985. The increased use of cocaine is problematic and defined as deviant mainly because of the insidious way in which cocaine dependency develops and has debilitating effects on school and long-term life outcomes.

To account for this deviant behavior (with evidence that also happens to support cultural transmission theory through differential association) some researchers conclude that adolescents become susceptible to peer encouragement to try drugs as they advance through the grades (Huba and Bentler, 1980; Stein, Newcomb, and Bentler, 1987). R. Jessor, J. A. Chase, and J. E. Donovan (1980), analyzing data from the National Study of Adolescent Drinking Behavior, Attitudes, and Correlates, concluded that alcohol and marijuana use is probable when students have lower expectations for academic achievement coupled with greater tolerance of deviance.

As with teen pregnancy, delinquency (crime such as rape, vandalism, and larceny), and other youth problems, drug abuse is particularly a problem with lower-class youth in urban areas (Inciardi, 1980). This illicit use of drugs is explained by social class factors such as poverty and unemployment, and thereby also lends credibility to a structural strain theory by accounting for the gaps between means and ends, with consequent retreatist behavior.

Structural strain theorists account for drug abuse as deviant behavior in the same way they account for school misbehavior, that is, juvenile delinquency. Early theorists held that delinquency was a problem related to low SES. Robert Merton (1968) and R. A. Cloward and L. E. Ohlin (1960) proposed that the poor socialization of lower-class students or their academic deficiencies would lead to school failure that would subsequently lead to discipline problems. A. Cohen (1955) expanded this notion by theorizing that many students with these lower-class characteristics, when confronted with the middle-class values inherent in the schools, would become frustrated and fail. However, cultural transmission theory (Call, 1965; and Polk and Hafferty, 1966) found little class difference in the backgrounds of delinquents and nondelinquents. Other evidence suggested that it was not family status, but status prospects (student's educational and occupational outlook) that are important (Stinchcombe, 1964). That is, misbehavior at all class levels was lower among college-oriented students.

A focus on labeling theory and the hypothesis that schools, through various types of labeling, create the situation for failure, also has been a prominent explanation of deviance. Labeling theory argues that students who are labeled as inferior, who are treated as inferior, and who internalize the concept will in fact perform in an inferior manner. These students see school as unimportant to them and are thus likely to rebel (Pink, 1979). From this interpretation, the direction of causality is from academic failure to misbehavior. Other studies show a causal path from misbehavior to school performance (Coleman, Hoffer, and Kilgore, 1982; Purkey and Smith, 1983; DiPrete, 1981; Baker, 1985). These researchers argue that good discipline is a prerequisite for learning. T. DiPrete tested the two hypotheses concerning the relationship between school performance and misbehavior and found that the effect of misbehavior on grades was weaker than the effect of grades on misbehavior. Labeling and strain theories are more powerful in explaining deviance in this case.

In sum, while the schools have had to play an increasing part in the regulation of drug use, the evidence suggests that the school contributes to misbehavior as well as preventing it. Strain theory has explained why those students who come to the school with poor resources perform inadequately and retreat to taking drugs. Cultural transmission theory has partially accounted for the problem by explaining that permissive attitudes are the norm in the culture of poverty. Labeling theory has explained why students act the way they do by showing how they internalize a view of themselves as drug takers, a self-portrait that then is reinforced by others.

The analysis of drug abuse, as an illustration of the principle of social control and deviance in operation, shows a general societal consensus about the dysfunctional nature of illicit drug use,. But these same mechanisms that define deviance and employ methods to exact conformity to the norms seem to contribute to the replication of the *underclass.*

School Violence

The class of phenomena known as school violence is interpretable, sociologically, as a deviance. Since the early 1960s, violence in concentrated poverty neighborhoods has become a growing problem (Viadero, 1987): assaults on teachers, vandalism (such as false fire alarms, bomb threats, window breaking, and theft of teaching materials), rape or attempted rape. These behaviors are accompanied by problems that are characteristic of poverty neighborhoods, such as the infiltration of schools by teenage gangs and high rates of truancy and absenteeism. Efforts at social control have included the provision of security systems, safety corridors to provide access to and from the street, intensification of counseling services, basic skills programs, and organizational modifications (Ianni, 1980; Marvin et al., 1976). (See Levine and Havighurst [1989] for further review of literature on school violence.)

Perhaps the theory that best accounts for school violence is structural strain theory. The existence of widespread violent behavior in schools is almost exclusively an inner city school condition, which suggests that students who do not have adequate means to accomplish the goals society has defined as important resort to violence. Cultural transmission theory also explains how the culture of povery reproduces itself in its members. The degree to which this phenomenon depicts the nature of the principle of social control and deviance as coercive rather than functional is suggested by D. Levine and R. Havighurst's comments (1989)—unless radical improvements are made in the education available to students in poor neighborhoods, and unless systematic national efforts attack both the structural and cultural causes of underclass status, the typical difficulties of teaching and learning in low-status schools will continue to be compounded in concentrated poverty schools. Unfortunately, they note, achievement in these schools may continue to be extremely low even after substantial sums of money are spent to conduct compensatory education programs there.

Special Education as the Medicalization of Deviance

Social control and deviance also is illustrated in special education as the *medicalization* of deviance; in this case, deviants are treated as sick people rather than punished as bad people (Conrad and Schneider, 1980). The manner in which organized medicine has influence as an agent of social control—with psychiatrists defining the norms, labeling those who deviate from the norms, and ensuring that the deviants conform—became visible when one form of deviance, hyperactivity, came to be known as a disease and a drug was serendipitously found to cure it. Hyperactive children had been considered disruptive in classrooms when their behavior is considered a discipline problem. When researchers discovered Ritalin (a stimulant drug) produced a calming effect on these children, physicians formulated a label for the new "disease": hyperkinesis (literally, "overenergetic"). Although some hyperkinetic disorders result from factors such as neurological damage or imbalances in brain chemistry, most of them have no known physical causes. Even when a deficit is found, the children's behavior is deviant only in the social context. That is, differences do not matter as much as how they are valued. It is doubtful, however, whether deviant behaviors are medical problems in a scientific sense.

The evaluation (diagnosis) of students for special education programs constitutes an observation of medicine as an agent of social control, with psychiatrists defining the approved norms, labeling those who deviate from them, and trying to guarantee that the deviants conform. Misbehavior is now a disease or medical disorder as opposed to criminal; persons are not *bad*, but *sick*.

For example, the *Diagnostic and Statistical Manual of Mental Disorders, III-R* (American Psychiatric Association, 1987), attempts to differentiate between children whose attention deficit disorder is accompanied by hyperactivity from those whose attention deficit disorder appears in the absence of hyperactivity. Some researchers suggest that attention deficit disorder is due to deficits in the neural system (Hynd et al., 1989).

The medicalization of deviance is exemplified in the case of the New York City public school system. Children diagnosed as having attention deficit disorders are labeled as emotionally handicapped and are placed in special learning environments. Unfortunately, once they are placed in a special education program, approximately only 4 percent of these students are subsequently fully mainstreamed into a general education program (New York City Board of Education, 1986). Long-term educational and occupational opportunities for these special education students are limited. In 1986, of the 936,231 students enrolled in the New York City public school system, 117,469 students were in programs of the Division of Special Education (New York City Board of Education, 1986). Historically the goal of the system has included the provision of educational services to students with handicapped conditions in settings that assist students to realize their potential for full participation in society (Mulkey, 1988). To achieve this, a "least-restricted environment" has been provided for students with handicapping conditions to encourage them to participate to the maximum extent appropriate with peers who are not handicapped. More recently, a state mandate for functional grouping has been instituted, with the premise that classrooms should contain students with similar instructional needs instead of similar handicaps.

The crucial point is that the principle of social control and deviance operates, not surprisingly in this case, both functionally and coercively; further, the principle benefits from interpretation of several theories: structural strain, control, cultural transmission, and labeling. Purportedly, the system defines what is normal and what is deviant on the basis of functional importance; moreover, in United States education, acceptable standards are decided on the basis of "academic achievement criteria" that rule out any nonmeritocratic factors that might impinge upon equality of opportunity. Those who argue that elements of power dictate who shall have more or less are correct to question whose interests are served by the definition of what is an acceptable standard in the first place.

Summary

This chapter has been devoted to showing the utility of a sociological analysis for examining issues of social control and deviance in the school. The principle of social control and deviance was discussed as it operates in issues concerning school discipline: school and classroom approaches to student discipline; dropping out of school; adolescent sexual behavior, pregnancy, and motherhood; student drug abuse; school violence; and special education as the medicalization of deviance. The use of the principle as a conceptual tool for understanding these issues has entailed queries about why certain behaviors are defined as deviant in the school context and whose interests are served by these definitions and efforts to reinforce them. The evidence on school disciplinary strategies is mixed, but lends support to a "labeling" explanation of deviance. Moreover, the labels seem to benefit some groups more than others. Disciplinary strategies that encourage unthinking conformity to the status quo appear to be social class based; authoritarian techniques are favored by low-status schools. Research on high school dropouts indicates that SES creates a disadvantage for students of inner city schools, but anti-dropout interventions sometimes encourage persistence. Structural strain theorists explain dropout behavior as a rejection of culturally approved goals and culturally approved means; cultural transmission theorists explain that the school does not provide the skills necessary for students to survive in the lower-class subculture; control theorists explain that students deviate because their ties to the community at large are weak; and labeling theorists account for deviant behavior as the outcome of the successful definition the school gives to dropouts. Adolescent sexual inactivity, according to control theorists, is a response to the suppression of behavior that threatens the maintenance of society and its individuals; the social control of adolescent sexual activity is intended to exact conformity to formal educational requirements. Cultural transmission theorists explain that what is commonplace in the subculture of poverty is deviant in mainstream culture. Attitudinal differences among whites, blacks, and blacks in racially homogeneous schools characterize different normative contexts (for example, contemporary black youth are relatively accepting of early coitus and out-of-wedlock parenthood). Structural strain theorists explain that the poor are unable to obtain respectable status through mainstream channels and find other sources of achievement, such as through teen motherhood; having a baby at an early age reduces the future opportunities of the young mother. The principle of social control and deviance, as it operates in the case of teen pregnancy, suggests a consensus of values about the dysfunctional nature of teen sex, but it also perpetuates the deviance by defining an alternative for groups who cannot attain success by status quo avenues. Evidence on drug abuse lends credibility to the variety of theoretical interpretations of the operation of the principle of social control and deviance and suggests that the school contributes to misbehavior as well as prevents it. Cultural transmission theorists conclude that through differential association, adolescents become susceptible to peer encouragement to try drugs. Structural strain theorists explain why those students who come to the school with poor resources perform inadequately and retreat to taking drugs. Labeling theorists explain why students internalize a view of themselves as drug users, a self-portrait that then is reinforced by others. The analysis of drug abuse shows, for the most part, a societal consensus about the dysfunctional nature of illicit drug use, but these same mechanisms that define deviance and employ methods to exact conformity to the norms seem to contribute to the replication of the *underclass*. Structural strain theorists explain school violence as students' reaction to their inadequate means of meeting societal expectations. Cultural transmission theorists see school violence as part of the normative structure of the culture of poverty. Organized medicine is an agent of social control in the case of special education practices so that misbehavior is associated with a student who is "sick," not "bad." Theoretical interpretations of the medicalization of deviance suggest that the principle of social control and deviance operates both functionally and coercively.

Vocabulary

control theory
cultural transmission theory
labeling theory

principle of social control and
    deviance
structural strain theory

Questions

1. What kind of behaviors go on in schools that can be explained by the concept (principle) and theories of social control and deviance?

2. How can the issue of student drug abuse be understood from a sociological perspective ?

References and Suggested Readings

Agnew, R. "A Revised Strain Theory of Delinquency." *Social Forces,* (1985) 64:151–7.

American Psychiatric Association. *Diagnostic and Statistical Manual of Mental Disorders, III-R.,* 3rd Ed., revised, Washington, DC: American Psychiatric Association, 1987.

Anyon, J. "Social Class and the Hidden Curriculum of Work." *Journal of Education,* (1980) 162:67–92.

Baker, K. "Research Evidence of a School Discipline Problem." *Phi Delta Kappan,* (1985) 66:482–7.

Ballantine, J. *The Sociology of Education: A Systematic Analysis.* Englewood Cliffs, NJ: Prentice-Hall, 1989.

Bauer, G. "Restoring Order to the Public Schools." *Phi Delta Kappan,* (1985) 66:488–91.

Bernstein, B. *Class, Codes and Control.* Boston: Routledge & Kegan Paul, 1975.

Bloch, S. and S. Ungerleider. "Targeting High-Risk Groups on Campus for Drug and Alcohol Prevention: An Examination and Assessment." *International Journal of the Addictions,* (1988) 23:299–319.

Buie, J. "Pregnant Teenagers: New View of Old Solution." *Education Week,* (1987) 6:32.

Burch, S. "Commission Reports on Children at Risk." *Black Issues in Higher Education,* (1988) 4:15.

Call, D. "Delinquency, Frustration, and Non-Commitment." Unpublished Ph.D. dissertation, University of Oregon, 1965.

Chase-Lansdale, P. and M. Vinovskis. "Should We Discourage Teenage Marriage?" *The Public Interest,* (1987) 87:38–48.

Cloward, R., and L. Ohlin. *Delinquency and Opportunity: A Theory of Delinquent Gangs.* New York: Free Press, 1960.

Cohen, A. *Delinquent Boys: The Culture of the Gang.* New York: Free Press, 1955.

Coleman, J. *The Adolescent Society.* New York: Free Press, 1961.

Coleman, J., T. Hoffer, and S. Kilgore. *High School Achievement: Public, Catholic and Other Private Schools Compared.* New York: Basic Books, 1982.

Conrad, P. and J. Schneider. *Deviance and Medicalization: From Badness to Sickness.* St. Louis: Mosby, 1980.

Cryan, J. and J. Smith. "The Hick'ry Stick: It's Time to Change the Tune." *Phi Delta Kappan,* (February 1981) pp. 433–35.

DiPrete, T. *Discipline and Order in American High Schools. Report to the National Center for Education Statistics.* Washington, DC: National Center for Education Statistics, 1981.

Doyle, W. "Classroom Organization and Management." In M. Wittrock, ed., *Handbook of Research on Teaching.* New York: Macmillan, 1986.

Ekstrom, R., M. Goertz, J. Pollack, and D. Rock. "Who Drops Out of High School and Why? Findings from a National Study." *Teachers College Record,* (1986) 87:356–73.

Fortenberry, R. and B. White. "Districts Grapple with Dropout Problem." *The School Administrator,* (1987) 44:11–13.

Furstenberg, G., Jr., J. Brooks-Gunn, and S. Morgan. *Adolescent Mothers in Later Life*. New York: Cambridge University Press, 1987.

Gallup, G. "19th Annual Gallup Poll of Public Attitudes toward the Public Schools." *Phi Delta Kappan*, (September 1987), pp. 17–30.

Glasser, I. "School for Scandal: The Bill of Rights and Public Education." *Phi Delta Kappan*, (December 1969) pp. 190–4.

Glickman, C. and R. Tamashiro. "Clarifying Teachers' Beliefs about Discipline." *Educational Leadership*, (1980) 37:463–4.

Goodlad, J. *A Place Called School*. New York: McGraw-Hill, 1984.

Goodstadt, M. and A. Caleekal-John. "Alcohol Education Programs for University Students: A Review of their Effectiveness." *International Journal of the Addictions*, (1984) 19:721–41.

Hamilton, S. *The Interaction of Family, Community, and Work on the Socialization of Youth*. Washington, DC: William T. Grant Foundation Commission on Youth and America's Future, 1988.

_____. "Raising Standards and Reducing Dropout Rates." *Teachers College Record*, (1986) 87:410–29.

Hanson, D. "Drug Education: Does It Work?" In F. Scarpitti and S. Datesman, eds., *Drugs and the Youth Culture*. Beverly Hills, CA: Sage, 1980.

Havighurst, R. *The Public Schools of Chicago*. Chicago: Chicago Public Schools, 1964.

Hirschi, T. *Causes of Delinquency*. Berkeley, CA: University of California Press, 1969.

Hogan, D. and E. Kitagawa. "The Impact of Social Status, Family Structure, and Neighborhood on the Fertility of Black Adolescents." *American Journal of Sociology*, 90:825–55.

Howell, F. and L. McBroom. "Social Relations at Home and at School: An Analysis of the Correspondence Principle." *Sociology of Education*, (1982) 55:40–52.

Huba, G. and P. Bentler. "The Role of Peer and Adult Models for Drug Taking at Different Stages in Adolescence." *Journal of Youth and Adolescence*, (1980) 9:449–65.

Hynd, G., et al. "Attention Deficit Disorder With and Without Hyperactivity: Reaction Time and Speed of Cognitive Processing." *Journal of Learning Disabilities*, 22:573–9.

Ianni, F. "A Positive Note on Schools and Discipline." *Educational Leadership*, (March 1980) pp. 454–8.

Inciardi, J. "Youth, Drugs, and Street Crime." In F. Scarpitti and S. Datesman, eds., *Drugs and the Youth Culture*. Beverly Hills, CA: Sage, 1980.

Jackson, P. *Life in Classrooms*. New York: Holt, Rinehart and Winston, 1968.

Jaffe, F. and J. Dryfoos. "Fertility Control Services for Adolescents: Access and Utilization." *Adolescent Pregnancy and Childbearing: Findings from Research*. Washington, DC: United States Government Printing Office, 1980.

Jessor, R., J. Chase, and J. Donovan. "Psychosocial Correlates of Marijuana Use and Problem Drinking in a National Sample of Adolescents." *American Journal of Public Health*, (1980) 70:604–13.

Jones, E., et al. *Teenage Pregnancy in Industrialized Countries.* New Haven, CT: Yale University Press, 1986.

Jones, R. and L. Tanner. "Classroom Discipline: The Unclaimed Legacy." *Phi Delta Kappan,* (March 1981) pp. 494–7.

Johnston, L., et al. *Use of Licit and Illicit Drugs by America's High School Students 1975–84.* Ann Arbor: University of Michigan Institute for Survey Research, 1985.

Levine, D. and R. Havighurst. *Society and Education,* 7th Ed. Boston: Allyn & Bacon, 1989.

Mann, D. "Can We Help Dropouts: Thinking about the Undoable." *Teachers College Record,* (1986) 87:307–24.

Marvin, M., et al. *Planning Assistance Programs to Reduce School Violence and Disruption.* Washington, DC: United States Department of Justice, National Institute for Juvenile Justice and Delinquency Prevention, 1976.

McNeil, L. *Contradictions of Control: School Structure and School Knowledge.* New York: Routledge and Kegan Paul, 1986.

Mensch, B. and D. Kandel. "Dropping Out of High School and Drug Involvement." *Sociology of Education,* (1988) 61:95–113.

Mergendoller, J., et al. "Task Demands and Accountability in Middle-Grade Science Classes." *The Elementary School Journal,* 88:251–65.

Merton, R. *Social Theory and Social Structure.* New York: Free Press, 1968.

Moore, K., M. Simms, and C. Betsey. *Choice and Circumstance.* New Brunswick, NJ: Transaction Books, 1986.

Mulkey, L. "Using Two Instruments to Measure Student Gains in Reading Achievement When Assessing the Impact of Educational Programs." *Evaluation Review,* (1988) 12:571–87.

Myers, D., A. Milne, K. Baker, and A. Ginsburg. "Student Discipline and High School Performance." *Sociology of Education,* 60:18–33.

National Commission on Excellence in Education. *A Nation At Risk: The Imperative for Educational Reform.* A Report to the Nation and the Secretary of Education, United States Department of Education, April 1983.

Chancellor's Memorandum 15, 1985–86. New York: New York City Board of Education, 1986.

Pallas, A. *The Determinants of High School Dropout.* Baltimore: The Johns Hopkins University Center for Social Organization of Schools Report No. 364, 1986.

Pink, W. *An Exploration of Relationships Between Academic Failure, Student Social, Conflict, and School Related Attitudes.* Washington, DC: National Institute of Education, 1979.

Polk, K. and D. Hafferty. "Adolescence, Commitment, and Delinquency." *Journal of Research in Crime and Delinquency,* 3:82–96.

Purkey, S. and M. Smith. "Effective Schools: A Review." *Elementary School Journal,* (1983) 83:427–50.

Reinhard, B. "Sex, Drugs, and Dropping Out: Governors Come Face to Face with Real World." *Education Daily,* (1987) 20:3–4.

Reiss, I. "Premarital Sex as a Deviant Behavior: An Application of Current Approaches to Deviance." *American Sociological Review*, 35:78–87.

Rose, E. "Drug Education Programs Widespread, but Vary Greatly in Content." *Education Week*, (1986) 5:7.

Rumberger, R. "High School Dropouts: A Review of Issues and Evidence." *Review of Educational Research*, (1987) 57:101–21.

Schaps, E., R. DiBartolo, J. Moskowitz, C. Palley, and S. Churgin. "A Review of 127 Drug Abuse Prevention Program Evaluations." *Journal of Drug Issues*, (1981) 11:17–44.

Select Committee on Children, Youth, and Families. *Teen Pregnancy: What is Being Done?* Washington, DC: United States Government Printing Office, 1986.

Sonenstein, F. *Risking Paternity: Sex and Contraception Among Adolescent Males.* Washington, DC: Urban Institute, 1985.

Stein, J., M. Newcomb, and P. Bentler. "An 8-year Study of Multiple Influences on Drug Use and Drug Use Consequences." *Journal of Personality and Social Psychology*, (1987) 53:1094–1105.

Stinchcombe, A. *Rebellion in a High School*. Chicago: Quadrangle Books, 1964.

Thornton, A. and D. Camburn. "The Influence of the Family on Premarital Sexual Attitudes and Behavior." *Demography*, (1987) 24:323–40.

Udry, J. "Biological Predispositions and Social Control in Adolescent Sexual Behavior." *American Sociological Review*, (1988) 53:709–22.

Udry, J. and J. Billy. "Initiation of Coitus in Early Adolescence." *American Sociological Review*, (1987) 52:841–55.

Viadero, D. "More and More Students are Juggling Conflicting Demands of School and Work." *Education Week*, (1987) 6(34):1,17.

Wehlage, G., R. Rutter, and A. Turnbaugh. "Dropping Out: How Much Do Schools Contribute to the Problem?" *Teachers College Record*, (1987) 87:374–92.

Wilcox, K. "Schooling and Socialization for Work Roles: A Structural Inquiry Into Cultural Transmission in an Urban American Community." Unpublished Ph.D. dissertation, Harvard University, 1978.

Zabin, L., M. Hirsch, E. Smith, R. Street, and J. Hardy. "Evaluation of a Pregnancy Prevention Program for Urban Teenagers." *Family Planning Perspectives*, (1986) 18:119–26.

Notes

[1] Some issues of social control and deviance are not presented in this chapter (for example, teenage suicide and juvenile delinquency, etc.). Standardized testing, for example, as a mechanism of social control and deviance is treated in the chapter on stratification (Ch. 7) because the failure to meet testing standards has severe consequences for life outcomes. In the present case, as an illustration of the principle of social control and deviance, test performance is a standard of what is deviant and various rewards and punishments are used to bring about compliance and conformity to this standard. Mention of testing also appears in Chapter 10 to illustrate the principle of social change in the case of testing as part of the educational accountability regressive social movement.

[2]The rate of pregnancy for unwed teenage mothers compared to all unwed mothers in the United States has increased significantly from 15 percent in 1960 to 54 percent in 1983 (Select Committee on Children, Youth and Families. *Teen Pregnancy: What is Being Done?* Washington, DC: United States Government Printing Office, 1986). Families headed by young mothers are seven times more likely to be living below the poverty level than are other families and the teenage pregnancy rate (and out-of-wedlock births) in the United States is higher among black females than among white females (P. Chase-Lansdale and M. Vinovskis. "Should We Discourage Teenage Marriage." *The Public Interest,* (1987) 87:38–48). K. Davis (in "A Theory of Teenage Pregnancy in the United States." in C. Chilman, ed. *Adolescent Pregnancy and Child-Bearing: Findings from Research.* Washington, DC: United States Government Printing Office, 1980) and other researchers believe that racial oppression and discrimination have produced social conditions conducive to high illegitimacy rates among black Americans.

CHAPTER
10

Social Change

Changes in the Rules for Living Together

The frustrating thing about being human is that we so often feel like sheep; we must be social and take others into consideration if we are to survive as individuals. How then do the children in the photograph above develop a sense of responsibility to the group and to those with whom they live, yet maintain some semblance of individuality? Does loyalty to the group preclude initiating changes in the rules of the group? The operation of the principle of social change does not change—neither does the principle of institutions, in the case of education; education is a universal activity for preparing each generation for its place in the social system. But what does change is the form of education. And our investigation is of how, why, and in what ways the form of education changes. Democracy, freedom, and self-determination were advocated by *progressive* thinkers during the eighteenth century and by the first half of the 1900s these ideas affected the domain of formal education. Today, many people believe this approach should be discarded. This chapter concludes with an introduction to the idea that we do not have to be "just sheep"; Chapter 11 explains how we can locate, actually *realize,* individual freedom and discusses the implications of individual freedom for social change in education.

Outline

The Principle of Social Change

Social change refers to the alteration of social structure (behavioral prescriptions).[1] Sociologists especially like to talk about variations in behavioral prescriptions, and this idea presumes sameness, a fixed point or structure around which something varies. For example, almost all societies are the same in that they have some version of a formal educational system, but the exact form varies. When, then, does change occur in society—how, why, and in what ways?

Issues of Social Change in Education: Educational Movements

Educational movements in early European and American education exemplify how the principle of institutions guarantees that every generation prepares its young for a place in society, although the form of education varies. Formal education (not at home) was part of Greek and Roman society. These societies did not depend on formally educated populations: instead, the young were instructed in crafts and military skills. In the Middle Ages, religion influenced other institutions in society, including education, and the concept of *original sin* encouraged the use of authoritarian discipline. The Renaissance led to a secular and liberal education. The Reformation was a return to God-centered education. The Enlightenment of the eighteenth century emphasized the development of reason as an avenue to progress. Educational movements in the United States have included the public school, progressive education, the essentialists, humanistic education, alternative education, and back-to-basics movements (Ballantine, 1989).

Theory and Research on Social Change in Education

Explaining Social Change

As is true of the other principles of sociology, the operation of the principle of social change is lawlike in its function, but its description is less precise and determinate and its operation requires a variety of explanations. Sociologists theorize that social change results from the interaction of a number of factors, including physical environment (the rules for living in the arctic regions vary from the rules for living on a tropical island); cultural innovation (discovery, invention, and diffusion); population; technology; and social movements (collective social action by large numbers of people) (Olsen, 1968).

Theory on Social Movements

One major cause of social change is the phenomenon known as *social movement*. Social movement is usually an effort to resist and ameliorate a perceived injustice ranging from such issues as the abolition of slavery to the introduction of compulsory schooling, from the legalization of women voting to the use of birth control devices. When dissatisfaction exists in a society and the availability of resources permits, social movements of four types may come about.

The first type of social movement is a *regressive movement*. This is a social movement that attempts to restore things to the "way they used to be." The Moral Majority movement exemplifies this type of attempt to bring about social change by replacing what its members perceive as permissiveness with fundamental morality. In the second type of social movement, a *reform movement*, the existing social order is viewed as more or less satisfactory, but some reforms in specific aspects of the society are necessary. An antinuclear movement is illustrative. A *revolutionary movement* is a third type of social movement that results from pervasive dissatisfaction with the existing social order and works to design anew the entire society in accordance with a new plan or ideology. The birth of the United States came about from a revolt over the English colonial system. *Utopian movements*, the fourth type of social movement, seek to establish an ideal life or society. Some religious cults illustrate this type of movement.

Other Accounts of Social Change

The understanding of the operation of the principle of social change is advanced by knowledge of social movements as one of several sources of change. However, this knowledge does not explain how or why change takes place in the forms it does; for this purpose, functionalist, conflict, sociocultural evolution, and levels of change theories have also been used to account for social change.

Functionalist theory views society as consisting of interdependent parts, each of which helps to maintain the equilibrium of the entire social system. It focuses on social order rather than on conflict; it accounts for social change by arguing that society changes in the direction of greater complexity while maintaining its balance by integration of its parts or institutions. Strains to the system introduced by social change stimulate adjustment that return the system to stability and the new system contains different social arrangements than the one that preceded it. Conflict theory views social change as resulting from tension between competing interest groups in society over values and scarce resources.

Sociocultural evolution theory can be thought of as a focus on one aspect of functionalist theory; it interprets the operation of the principle of social change as the tendency for societies to grow more complex through time; adaptation in the rules occurs to accommodate, say, an agricultural versus an industrial or postindustrial structure of subsistence. (Refer to Chapter 4 for a more detailed discussion of these theories.)

By employing the functionalist view of social change as an adjustment of a system to strains through time and the conflict view of social change as coming about through revolution and struggles over the unequal distribution of resources, Rolland Paulston (1977) analyzes *educational change*. From the equilibrium paradigm of the structural-functionalists, educational change entails functional and structural requisites toward continued homeostasis or equilibrium, human capital, and national development. The conflict paradigm and Marxist theories seek the elimination of educational privilege and elitism.

Theory on Levels of Social Change

According to Fred Newmann and Donald Oliver (1967), social change has led to a deterioration of community in education. At the *individual level*, depersonalization and powerlessness have resulted from the machine replacement of tasks formerly carried out by humans. At the *organizational level*, fragmentation and the breakdown in the connectedness of human relations have resulted from specialization and differentiation. At the *societal level*, the general ideological stance in favor of instrumental values and esteem of technology have replaced humanistic ideals.

Ronald Corwin (1975) comments on the importance, at the individual level, of the teacher's role in bringing about change through feedback on educational issues such as new curriculum materials and teaching strategies. Matthew Miles (1975) identifies, at the organizational level, ten indicators of organizational health that make change successful: goal focus, communication adequacy, optimal power equalization, resource utilization, cohesiveness, morale, innovativeness, autonomy, adaptation, and problem-solving adequacy. Ann Lieberman and David Shiman (1973) state that for school change to take place the *whole school system* and community must be involved.

J. Victor Baldridge and Terrence Deal (1975) discuss five sources of change; they focus on the importance of the individual's proposing, adopting, or rejecting change; organizational change occurs by changing individual attitudes. This goals and saga perspective is an individual's effort to change based on his or her saga (belief) in some aspect of the organization's past. The *technological perspective* means implementing technological innovations that are used to assist with the procedures, processes, and activities needed to accomplish the system's objectives. The *environmental approach* involves including parents, students, teachers and teachers' unions, the community, and state, local, and federal governments in considering the implementation of change. The *structural perspective* includes the organizational structure as a facilitator or consequence of change.

E. G. Guba (1968) conceptualizes seven strategies for implementing educational change by individuals who hold positions in the school system. The *values* strategy requires that the adapter, or person who will implement and employ the new interventions, be persuaded to adopt the change by an appeal to his or her values. The *rational* strategy requires evidence and convincing logic to persuade the rational adapter of the utility of the innovation. In the *didactic* strategy, the adapter has the values, motivation, and economic resources, but is untrained; this strategy attempts to teach the adapter how to implement the change. In a *psy-*

chological strategy, the adapter is persuaded to feel accepted and involved in the proposed change. An *economic* strategy requires financial reward or deprivation to the adapter for supporting or not supporting the change. The *authority* strategy requires getting the adapter to change his or her relationship to someone in authority. The *political* strategy requires that the adapter be persuaded to accept the change on the basis that it is good for him or her.

Another avenue of educational change that is perhaps also a way of talking about an individual contribution to social change, or to an educational social movement, is through the role of the sociologist. The sociologist is a teacher and a researcher. In the teaching role, sociologists make available a distinctive way of understanding education and the forces, in this context, that cause our behavior. Research results in knowledge about education that is not available elsewhere. This information has been derived using scientific standards of observation and can be used by policymakers to inform their decisions (Gross, 1959).

For example, James Coleman (1966) was commissioned by the United States Department of Health, Education, and Welfare to investigate the educational opportunities for black and white children in the public school system. The results of this study were significant in school-related civil rights decisions. In the specific role of evaluation researcher, the researcher role focuses on assessing the effectiveness of interventions and programs proposed to ameliorate undesirable situations and thus to serve as a standard for change, to illuminate whether change has taken place, and to document the nature of program outcomes (Boocock, 1980).

The previous discussion has examined a variety of theoretical investigations of how the principle of social change operates in schools. Sources of change include demographic, environmental, and technological influences; other sources of change emphasize social movements, levels of change, evolution in the valued means of subsistence, conflict over resources, or the integration of or adjustment to strains put on the present system. An examination of the empirical documentation on some of the school movements will help us to decide which of these explanations of how social change operates are most viable.

The Public School Movement

The public school movement occurred in the early nineteenth century. Until this time, secondary schooling was available only to an elite who eventually went on to university training for the church or commerce (Ballantine, 1989). Industrialists needed ways to educate children from rural areas, to assimilate immigrants, and to relieve children from child labor. The dynamics of this movement suggest that the principle of social change operates in this case as a reform movement and as functional for society's needs for a mass and standardized education. Diverse languages impeded communication in industrial labor relations. The change is also explained, in this case, by demographic and technological factors such as the number of immigrants available and needed to perform machine-related skills.

The Progressive Education Movement

The progressive education movement ranged from the 1920s to the 1930s and was a reform movement that aimed, as did the public school movement—along with other, wider societal efforts—to assimilate immigrants into an industrial system. Concentration was on life skills that included sex, marriage, parenting issues, finances, and other practical skills. Repercussions from the progressive education movement appeared as the *open classrooms movement* or *open schools movement*. Open classrooms emphasized cooperation, not competition, freedom of movement and use of materials, and warmth and acceptance of students by teachers. Open schools were compared with traditional schools in a study conducted by James McPartland and Joyce Epstein (1977). The results of this study suggested that openness of instructional approach is of no importance in terms of student academic achievement. William Cockerham and Audie Blevins (1976) also considered the significance of open versus traditional education for special groups of students (Native Americans and white rural) and claimed that open education is beneficial for Native American children.

The Essentialists

In the 1950s, a movement (labeled the essentialists movement by Theodore Brameld [1977]) opposed progressive education and its emphasis on life skills, instead advocating the view that the school should promote the learning of basic intellectual skills. This movement fits the reform category of our typology of social movements and suggests that the principle of social change operates, as it did in the progressive education movement, to accomplish two dimensions of need that appear *functional* for industrialization. Elements of other sources of social change are visible: technology clearly has its influence in the development of an industrial economy; sociocultural evolution theory is supported from the perspective that the changes in means of subsistence are ultimately reflected in educational preparedness.

Humanistic Education

The essentialists movement was a reaction against the progressive education movement just as the progressive education movement was a reaction to Victorian authoritarianism. The humanistic education movement of the 1960s and 1970s was a response to residual authoritarianism existing in the schools and to a revival of the child-centered progressives (Ballantine, 1989). American education was described as *inhumane* (Silberman, 1970). Advocates of this movement insisted that attention be given to both affective and cognitive development. Teachers employed teaching strategies that encouraged values clarification (Simon, 1972), moral development, and student-focused activity. Jeanne Ballantine notes that this movement was greatly influenced by the client-centered therapies of such psychologists as Carl Rogers and Abraham Maslow; the work of Lawrence Kohlberg on the stages of moral development was also influential.

Alternative Education

The alternative education movement seems to fit the revolutionary type of social movement because it resulted from broad discontent across all institutions in the society. Schools were defined as free and open and encouraged love, openness, informality, parental and community involvement, and integration of all types of students. Schooling was viewed as a process that should be humane, aimed at fostering creativity, shared responsibility, and self-reflection with a deemphasis on failure, competition, and authoritarianism (Graubard, 1972).

English Primary Schools

The English primary school, characterized by the open primary school model with a focus on individualized instruction, stressed a broad curricular approach to basic skills in reading, writing, and mathematics, in conjunction with a program that included arts and crafts, history, physical education, geography, music, and science. The Plowden Report (1967) showed that the open education approach was successful in educating primary children. The report's findings influenced education in the United States by encouraging a commitment to individualized education and an emphasis on reading, writing, and mathematical skills. The social change spawned in education in the United States by the English primary school movement exemplifies and documents a revolutionary social movement as a source of change.

Free Schools

The free school movement also illustrates how the principle of social change appears in education as a revolutionary social movement. In 1921, A. S. Neill founded Summerhill in England (1960), a free school where students in primary through secondary levels attended on a voluntary basis and were unrestrained in their activities. Free schools in the United States, modeled after Summerhill, appeared in the 1960s and 1970s. This movement is viewed by Ballantine (1989) not as a reaction against repressive school structures, outdated curricula, or ineffective teaching methods, but against the school as an instrument of the mainstream culture. Advocates of free schools saw the public school as corrupt (for example, Kozol, 1972) and immune to reform. The free school was seen as an alternative school, a means of political revolution.

Pedagogy for the Oppressed

Revolutionary social movement in education and an alternative mechanism of schooling is illustrated in the method put forth by the Brazilian educator Paulo Freire (1970). He attempted to facilitate literacy among the peasants with techniques that raised the consciousness of the peasants about their oppressed social status. The school was in this situation an agency of political revolution.

Deschooling

Another revolutionary movement in education was Ivan Illich's (1971) attempt to liberate the illiterate poor through education. Illich saw the school as a coercive institution and argued for deinstitutionalization of schooling. He believed education does not have to take place in school. Notice that Ilich, Freire, and Neill illustrate the theory on level of change; in each case, a single individual was responsible for mobilizing efforts toward change.

Overall, alternative schools, especially the free schools, seemed to serve a variety of students seeking escape from their problems in public school (for example, boredom and academic failure). The impact of this education social movement was seen in the 1970s, when alternative public schools were developed for students who were performing marginally in the public school system.

Back-to-Basics

The back-to-basics movement is a regressive movement and a reaction to the alternative education movement. Critics of open education, career education, compensatory education, mainstreaming, tracking and ability grouping, and individualized instruction claimed that alternative education did not keep its promises in advancing moral and quality education (Egerton, 1976). Back-to-basics proponents argued for the elimination of open classrooms and the replacement of classes in art, music, and physical education with classes emphasizing discipline and basic skills. It is comprised of submovements such as private schooling and accountability (standardized testing and effective schools).

Private Schooling

One version of the back-to-basics movement is the emergence of private schools (Ballantine, 1989). The distrust of public school's capacity for good standards and discipline led to the development of an assortment of private schools. Religious sectarian schools were developed by fundamentalist Christians, Catholics, Baptists, and other sponsors. Military academies, elite preparatory schools (for example, Choate, Phillips-Andover, Groton, Lawrenceville), and schools for the gifted and handicapped are other types of private schools that represented conflicting beliefs about the role of education (Ballantine, 1989).

Accountability Movements

Accountability, an educational trend that is a version of back-to-basics reform, stresses the management of objectives, cost-effectiveness audits, systems analysis, performance contracting, voucher plans, community control, consumer education, critrion-referenced testing, competency-based teacher education, and program evaluation (Ornstein, 1977).

Standardized Testing

Another indicator of a regressive social movement is the widespread use of standardized tests. The decline in standardized test scores on the Scholastic Aptitude Test and the College Boards has been cited as a major reason for the back-to-basics ideology. Why scores have declined is unclear. Two explanations are that fewer high school juniors are taking the practice tests, and teachers are doing less coaching (Ebel, Rogers, and Baron, 1976).

Effective Schools

One concern of the back-to-basics regressive educational movement has been to hold schools accountable for student achievement. Interest in educational productivity was motivated in part by societal concerns for the quality of schooling as reflected in the level of competence of high school graduates (National Commission on Excellence in Education, 1983). The study of *educational productivity* developed into the study of school effects in the tradition of the Coleman Report (Coleman, et al., 1966). Maureen Hallinan (1985) states that although researchers have examined the association between school resources and student achievement since the 1950s, the Coleman Report motivated additional interest because it contradicted the commonly held belief that school resources affect not only educational outcomes but also the vested interests of school personnel. A number of studies were conducted on selected school variables and student achievement (net of family background) in which class size, student-teacher ratio, number of specialized staff, and expenditure levels were the attributes of interest. These studies showed that when the effect of student background is removed the impact of school resources is small (Hanushek, 1978; Lau, 1978). Other school effects studies examined contextual and compositional variables and their relation to student outcomes. Social class composition of a student body, for example, has a stronger effect on student performance than other school-level variables (Coleman, 1966). Later studies (for example, Hauser, 1970) argue that the amount of variance in achievement accounted for by contextual variables was too small to matter and that the research failed to specify social psychological processes that affect educational aspirations. John Goodlad (1984), in an examination of schools in thirteen communities, reported on the importance of the school principal in affecting student achievement.

A New Explanation of Social Change

Although this chapter is not comprehensive in its illustration of social change as manifested in educational social movements, it does provide, via the application of the principle of social change, a sociological framework for integrating and interpreting the vast array of human behavior in the context of education. In the educational context we are led to a general theory of the nature of the principle of social change. Elements of conflict and consensus operate independently of evolution from simple to complex; no single theory seems able to account simultaneously for social change as we have observed it in education. Moreover, these explanations have been inadequate in their account of precisely where and how social change begins. Of the explanations that we have examined, theory on levels of social change seems to carry the most explanatory power. The massive social systems we create cannot change themselves except in the predictable ways we have designed them to change; only people can initiate changes, and change starts with *one* person. One person is the impetus for a complex social system to turn a corner and begin in a different direction (Babbie, 1988).

The idea that all social change begins with one individual cannot be overemphasized. Furthermore, the question must be asked, is it possible that the individual is the major source of social change? That is, can the consciousness or level of awareness of one individual as *self-preserving* or *preserving of selflessness* determine the nature of social change?[2] P. Sorokin (1937) examined societal change through time and suggested that societies vary based on the type of reality perceived by their members. Ideas (consciousness) can be *sensate* (sense experience and science), *ideational* (spiritual and religious), or *idealistic* (rational, or an integration of sensate and ideational). However, in his consideration of broad social determinants of human action, Sorokin disregards the significance of one individual's ideas. Yet, regardless of the nature of societal change through time as represented in models such as Sorokin's, apparently the individual can transcend these determinants at any point in history; the individual can realize individual freedom (that part of self-consciousness that is independent of all social identification), and act back on society to initiate change. This does not mean that a person is free to make the world whatever she or he likes. However, the individual does have the freedom to stand outside of society, to be a beholder of society, to be "attached" to it in a different manner, and to change society from the perspective of self-giving versus self-preserving as the first determinant of behavior. The person then affects society—he or she is in the world, but not of it.

The preceding explanation, an evolutionary model of social change, is similar to Comte's Law of Human Progress (1896). He argues that the evolution of society has paralleled the evolution of the human mind; each of our leading conceptions, each branch of our knowledge, passes successively through three different theoretical conditions: the theological or fictitious, the metaphysical or abstract, and the scientific or positive. Each successive stage in the evolution of the human mind grows from the preceding one. Comte also argued that the stages of development and progressive emancipation of the human mind paralleled stages in the development of social organization, of types of social order, and of the material conditions of human life. While Comte shows that social structure is related to the evolution of the human mind through an emancipation from one stage to the next, he asserts that the change in the development of mind is from theological to scientific. However, what if the theological is the last stage in the development of consciousness? If so, then mind (belief) thus interprets the direct experience of reality, an awareness of being that frees the individual from solely a social identity and empowers that individual to affect society rather than be pummeled, or affected by it. This highest state of consciousness replaces solely economic and other types of motives with a belief that interprets experience outside of society as the antecedent, exogenous, causal link to social change.

The next chapter speculates about the varied outcomes of social change for society, depending on the level of awareness of the individuals who propose change, and introduces a theory that when individuals are free from society, then their proposed changes foster growth toward society as an ideal community. The theory also suggests that the level of consciousness of the individual who proposes the change determines (a) whether society is the cause, that is, the unquestioned determinant of the behavior of its members, (b) whether society is the effect, to the degree that consequential change in society is self-preserving, or (c) whether society is the effect, to the degree that the outcome of the change is others-preserving, that is, the ideal community. In its discussion of the relation between the individual and social structure, this final chapter addresses the enduring question, "How much does society tell us what to do and how much do we tell society what to do?"

Summary

This chapter has examined education sociologically by applying the *principle of social change*. The discussion has focused on social movements as a major source of change and has presented functionalist, conflict, sociocultural evolution theories and theories on levels of change to explain why these social movements take the form they do. Educational movements in the United States (with a few exceptions) have been analyzed using these movements as illustrations of the operation of the principle of social change: public school, progressive education, essentialists, humanistic education, alternative education, and back-to-basics. The chapter concludes with a proposition for a new theory of social change and the view that it takes just one individual to change the world.

Vocabulary

accountability movement
alternative education
back-to-basics
deschooling
educational movements
effective school movement
English primary schools
essentialists
free schools
humanistic education
pedagogy for the oppressed

principle of social change
private schooling
progressive education movement
reform movement
regressive movement
revolutionary movement
social movement
sources of social change
standardized testing
theory on evolution of individual
consciousness
utopian movement

Questions

1. What kind of behaviors occur in schools that can be explained by the principle of social change and related theories?

2. What explanation (theory) best accounts for the process of the principle of social change as it operates in education? Why?

References and Suggested Readings

Babbie, E. *The Sociological Spirit: Critical Essays in a Critical Science*. Belmont, CA: Wadsworth, 1988.

Baldridge, J. and T. Deal, eds. *Managing Change in Educational Organizations*. Berkeley, CA: McCutcheon, 1975. pp. 25–32.

Ballantine, J. *The Sociology of Education: A Systematic Analysis*. Englewood Cliffs, NJ: Prentice-Hall, 1989.

Biehler, R. *Psychology Applied to Teaching*, 3rd Ed. Boston: Houghton Mifflin, 1978.

Boocock, S. *Sociology of Education: An Introduction*, 2nd Ed. Boston: Houghton Mifflin, 1980.

Brameld, T. "Social Frontiers: Retrospective and Prospective." *Phi Delta Kappan*, (October 1977) pp. 118–20.

Cockerham, W. and A. Blevins. "Open School vs. Traditional School: Self-Identification Among Native American and White Adolescents." *Sociology of Education*, (1976) 49:164–9.

Coleman, J., et al. *Equality of Educational Opportunity*. Washington, DC: United States Department of Education, 1966.

Corwin, R. "Innovation in Organizations: The Case of Schools." *Sociology of Education*, (1975) 48:31.

Comte, A. *The Positive Philosophy of August Comte*, Vols. 1–3. H. Martineau, trans. London: Bell, 1896.

Ebel, R., V. Rogers and J. Baron. "Declining Scores: Two Explanations." *Phi Delta Kappan*, (December 1976) pp. 306–13.

Egerton, J. "Back to Basics." *The Progressive*, (September 1976) p. 24.

Freire, P. *Pedagogy of the Oppressed*. New York: Herder & Herder, 1970.

Goodlad, J. *A Place Called School*. New York: McGraw-Hill, 1984.

Graubard, A. *Free the Children: Radical Reform and the Free School Movement*. New York: Pantheon Books, 1972, pp. 9–10.

Gross, N. "Some Contributions of Sociology to the Field of Education." *Harvard Educational Review*, (1959) 29:275–87.

Guba, E. "The Process of Education Improvement." In P.R. Gaulet, ed., *Educational Change: The Reality and the Promise*. New York: Citation, 1968, pp. 149–50.

Hallinan, M. "Sociology of Education: The State of the Art." In J. Ballantine, ed., *Schools and Society: A Reader in Education and Sociology*. Palo Alto, CA: Mayfield, 1985.

Hanushek, E. "A Reader's Guide to Educational Production Functions." Paper presented at the National Invitational Conference on School Organization and Effects, San Diego, CA, January 27–29, 1978.

Hauser, R. "Context and Consex: A Cautionary Tale." *American Journal of Sociology*, (1970) 75:645–64.

Illich, I. *Deschooling Society*. New York: Harper & Row, 1971.

Kozol, J. *Free Schools*. Boston: Houghton Mifflin, 1972.

Lau, L. "Educational Production Functions." Paper presented at the National Invitational Conference on School Organization and Effects, San Diego, CA, January 27–29, 1978.

Lieberman, A. and D. Shiman. "The Stages of Change in Elementary School Settings." In C.M. Culver and G.J. Hoban, eds., *The Power to Change Issues for the Innovative Educator*. New York: McGraw-Hill, 1973, pp. 49–71.

McPartland, J. and J. Epstein. "Open Schools and Achievement: Extended Tests of a Finding of No Relationship." *Sociology of Education*, (1977) 50:133–44.

Miles, M. "Planned Change and Organizational Health: Figure and Ground." In J. Baldridge, and T. Deal, eds., *Managing Change In Educational Organizations*. Berkeley, CA: McCutcheon, 1975, pp. 224–47.

National Commission on Excellence in Education. "A Nation at Risk: The Imperative for Educational Reform: Final Report." *Education Week*, April 27, 1983.

Neill, A. *Summerhill*. New York: Hart, 1960.

Newmann, F. and D. Oliver. "Education and Community." *Harvard Educational Review*, (1967) 37:66–8.

Olsen, M. *The Process of Social Organization*. New York: Holt, Rinehart and Winston, 1968.

Ornstein, A. *Foundations of Education*. Skokie, IL: Rand McNally, 1977, p. 70.

Paulston, R. "Social and Educational Change: Conceptual Frameworks." *Comparative Education Review*, (1977) 21:372–3.

The Plowden Report (Central Advisory Council for Education). *Children and their Primary Schools*. London: H.M. Stationery Office, 1967.

Silberman, C. *Crisis in the Classroom*. New York: Random House, 1970.

Simon, S. *Values Clarification: A Handbook of Practical Strategies for Teachers and Students*. New York: Hart, 1972.

Sorokin, P. *Social and Cultural Dynamics*. New York: American, 1937.

Notes

[1] Further conceptualizations of the principle of social change, such as fads and crazes, are not included in our discussion. If you are interested, most introductions to sociology have information on other aspects of social change that also have relevance and applicability to the social analysis of education.

[2] Chapter 11 contains a more extensive discussion on distinctions between individual consciousness that is self-preserving versus preserving of selflessness. The conversion of a self-preserving consciousness to a preserving of selflessness consciousness is a realization that we do not need to take thought for our well-being. This does not presuppose that we do away with rational action, but that rational action, when it is grounded in a basic trust in

life (a *sacred canopy* [Peter Berger. *The Sacred Canopy: Elements of a Sociological Theory of Religion*. New York: Doubleday, 1967]), permits the individual to affect society as opposed to being affected by society. The same effortless belief that we exercise when we count on the sun rising and setting, this relaxed and peaceful orientation to being in the world, results in a state of individual freedom and the capacity to be in society, but not of it.

Enduring Questions

How Does Education Influence Your Life?
Can You Influence Education?

By now we are able to apply the sociological insight for obtaining an understanding of why the students in the photograph above are acting the way they are. When once we saw *a collection of individuals*, we now see *members of a group*. The social nature of the human being is somewhat peculiar and hilarious because in compelling us to give ourselves to the group, we have the opportunity to realize what is uniquely individual and our own. We now confront enduring questions about human freedom and social determinism. Ralph Turner (1988), for example, has commented that sociologists talk much about society's effects, but very little about the effects of the individual on society. In examining the children in the photo above, how much of what they do and are is determined by social institutions such as education, and how much say do they, as individuals, have in influencing education?

Outline

*T*he preceding chapters comprise a careful analysis of one aspect of our human behavior as "social" behavior. Our individual orientation to group living makes us create and follow rules such that collective agreements preserve the well-being of each group member. We refer to our social orientation as "the principles of sociology"; their objectified form is "society."

In this discussion, education has emerged as a social phenomenon in which the principle of institutions operates to guide human action and interaction to ensure the survival of the group and its members. Our adventure has resulted in a distinctive articulation of what education is about. But we have not yet completed our sociological investigation.

What now surfaces are the enduring questions:

- How much do I affect education? Or am I simply a product of education?

- Do I have any freedom from the social determinants of my behavior?

- Who am I and am I ever more than the statuses society provides for me—student, teacher, mail carrier, corporate manager?

- Do I base my life on the probabilities that I will be poor and uneducated because my parents were poor and uneducated? Does going to college make a difference in my life—if so, how much and why?

- Why choose school at all—how might things be otherwise?

- If I need to live cooperatively through the construction of rules that promote the well-being of all, and in the process become a person in response to the way the cooperative plan dictates, then what does it mean to be an individual in the process?

- If everyone does his or her "own thing," how do we preserve order?

- Just what is the interrelationship between individual freedom and social order that permits the activity of both, and in what fashion?

Enduring questions deserve an attempt at enduring answers. The full development of the human being requires *first*, but not *finally*, being a social being. Social being is a precondition for *freedom*. The stage of awareness of being human that must also be considered in a thorough sociological understanding of behavior is a higher level of awareness or consciousness that perceives reality, but not only scientifically. That is, it is a perception ultimately linked with another understanding of reality. This is the realm of *individual freedom*, as opposed to the *social scientific* realm. Sociology is a stage in consciousness (*scientific* and *collective*) that in a developmental fashion precedes and is a precondition for the consciousness of individual freedom (Mulkey, 1990). Sociology is thus one way of seeing the world, but by restricting our vision to this one way, it inhibits its own understanding and role in the development of being human. A Zen student, while watching the flag waving in the wind said, "See, the flag is waving." Another student said, "No, the wind is waving." The Zen Master said, "No, the mind is waving." As long as we persist in restricting ourselves to one view of reality, we will be excluded from the realm of human freedom, both in our knowing about it and our experience of it (LeShan, 1976). So, sociology can be a scientific understanding of human behavior, but in this way, it limits its own capacity to explain human action. When it incorporates a dialogue with philosophical and religious understanding, it then interprets as well as makes possible the total human experience.

In Retrospect: The Sociology of Education

Why do people act the way they do in the context of what we think of as "education"? Our review of analytical tools—the sociological framework and method (scientific)—coupled with the assumption that humans are social beings showed that people consider their behavior in light of others who live in the same group (society). Immanuel Kant (1963) says that persons are inclined to associate because only in this way can they develop their natural endowment. This consideration is a biological predisposition to make and follow rules in six basic ways, hence the principles of sociology: the principles of institutions, socialization, stratification, organization, social control and deviance, and social change. Society exists in its own right and cannot be found in the individual, but the individual is a representation of society. Society is, in objectified form, the collective reflections of its individual precursors (the *essential sociality* or social nature of the individual).

Education is a social phenomenon made possible through the joint operation of the principles of sociology. Education is a fundamental response to the principle of institutions, whereby society prepares each generation with the knowledge and skills necessary for survival in the system. Ongoing and contemporary issues in education are illustrations of each principle of sociology. For example, school programs in bilingual education exemplify the principle of stratification as it operates in education; they are a response to the rule or societal expectation concerning how resources are allocated and that all persons be given the same opportunities in the system. Or, for example, issues about the school curriculum and pedagogy (what counts as valuable knowledge and what methods for the transmission of knowledge best replicate society in individual personality?) illustrate the principle of socialization. The operation of the principle of organization interprets issues about school bureaucracy. School and classroom disciplinary strategies are behavioral responses to the principle of social control and deviance. The principle of social change interprets the phenomena we commonly observe as educational movements.

Theories explaining how each principle operates were presented alongside research on the issues. Research on the issue of bilingual education, for example, tells us something about the nature of the principle of stratification in that it functions democratically (support for a theory of consensus) in this case, as opposed to replicating inequality (support for a theory of conflict).

Enduring Answers: The Role of Sociology

Seeing First and then Believing: Scientific Awareness of Reality

> Once observed mosquitoes swarming. In gray masses. Host upon host. Each preoccupied with its own spoor. Each different, distinct in details and shape. A horde emitting a common sound. Were they mosquitoes or people? I feel over-awed by quantity where counting no longer makes sense. By irrepeatability within such a quantity. By creatures of nature gathered in herds, droves, species, in which each individual while subservient to the mass retains some distinguishing features. ("Assemblage of Variants of a Certain Prototype," Magdalena Abakanowicz, her description of her sculpture at the Aldrich Museum of Contemporary Art, Ridge-field, Connecticut, February 11, 1990.)

Sociologists study how each individual is subservient to the mass for its sur-vival, how through cooperation, the regulation of self-interest, each member of the group preserves the group that in turn preserves each member. Major forms or rules for cooperation explain the behavior of individuals; but what does Abak-anowicz mean when she says each individual retains some distinguishing features? Sociology isolates and makes visible the social or group, the herd, the drove, the species, as determinant of our behavior. We are then able to think about what it is to be unique and individual. The social scientific insight of group influences on our behavior fosters in us the very achievement of what it is to be individual.

The Relation of Principles to Theoretical Logic: Determinism

The first step in distinguishing freedom from determinism is to communicate that as a mode of discourse (level of awareness, consciousness) science can be a restrictive way of thinking about our experiences as reality. Sociology is charac-terized, most fundamentally, by its logical and empirical investigation of human action; that is, it presumes that everything that happens has an antecedent or *cause*. However, *freedom* and *causality* belong to disparate frames of reference; scientific method cannot uncover freedom by the process of elimina-tion: that would amount to digging through the layers from effect to cause to antecedent effect and cause until one reaches a residual phenomenon that does not have a cause and is therefore free (Berger, 1963). Freedom is that which is uncaused; it is not, after all, subject to scientific demonstration. Peter Berger exemplifies this when he distinguishes *utility* from *beauty*. The two do not logi-cally exclude each other, but we cannot establish the reality of the one by dem-onstrating the reality of the other. We can show that a piece of furniture has a certain utility for human living, to sit on, eat on, or sleep in, let's say, but no matter what utility is proven, we do not get closer to the question of whether the furniture is beautiful. The utilitarian and the aesthetic modes of discourse are incommensurable. In terms of social scientific method, we are confronted with a way of thinking, an awareness that assumes *a priori* that the human world is a causally closed system. If a phenomenon cannot be explained causally by one set of sociological categories, we try another one. We will continue to formulate new causes, but we will not encounter freedom. Thus, there is no way of perceiving freedom except through a subjective inner certainty that disintegrates as soon as it is attacked with the tools of scientific analysis. We must step outside the scientific frame of reference to encounter freedom. An object or event that is its own cause is outside the discourse of science. Science cannot measure a phenomenon that is defined as free. What seems free within the individual consciousness will only find its place in scientific discourse as an implied or hidden link in the chain of causation.

A significant part of the scientific level of awareness of social reality are the principles of sociology. These are *laws* that operate universally as biological predispositions in each person to act socially or cooperatively through rulemaking and following. *Theories* are logical, causal arguments that specify the relationship between two events or things. They explain how sociological principles operate, and they seek credibility through research evidence (the empirical testing of the ideas). On the continuum of social scientific thought (Alexander, 1982), principles designate a degree of specificity or determinateness at the empirical level. Theories also designate a degree of specificity, but they are less determinate and more general. In this manner, we talk causally about general aspects of reality. For example, instead of thinking we saw seventeen students from Mulkey High School who were smoking marijuana, we would think about the association between academic performance and drug abuse; we would infer from our observation a more general interpretation of the event.

Sociology, by incorporating a dialogue with nonempirical reality, becomes a comprehensive account of human action. The principles of sociology are, in this way, instruments for the description of two types of society, one that is predominantly a *cause*, and thus binding and deterministic, and another that is an *effect*, a reflection of an optimal level of operation of individual freedom.

Believing First to See: Freedom Outside of Society

> Lévy-Bruhl says with truth that in primitive consciousness, the consciousness of the individual depends upon the consciousness of the group. But this is not the final truth about man. Society is a special reality, a degree of actuality. To regard man as exclusively a social being means slavery for man. The slavery of man to society finds expression in organic theories of society. . . . Society is presented as though it were personality of a higher hierarchical degree than the personality of man. But this makes man a slave.
> (Berdyaev, 1944 pp. 102–16)

Nikolai Berdyaev employs the metaphor of "slavery versus freedom" to convey the idea that, as a science, sociology has a dual role; its first function is to make visible the social dimension and determinants of our behavior. Its second function is, as a level of awareness, to lead us developmentally to a higher level or state of self awareness—one in which the individual is free from the determinism inherent in the operation of the *social self*. Individual freedom, then, is that *residual sense of self* that is recognized or realized after the development of the social self; George Herbert Mead (1934) would say it is the "I" that makes the "me" possible and in this realization, the individual no longer equates himself or herself with social roles. That is, persons become free from their attachment to social self as the only self, and their social roles become, alternatively, vehicles for the expression of self. The stockbroker, for example, would not "be" his investments, so that if the market crashed he would commit suicide; alternatively he would "do" investing.

The Evolution of Consciousness

Procedure for Realizing Freedom   Bertrand Russell's (1925) philosophical interpretation of the realm of individual freedom in relation to society as a determinant of human behavior provides a map for experiencing or realizing individual freedom. Russell explains the realm of individual freedom by making the distinction between what he calls the *finite self* ("self-preserving") and the *infinite self* ("preserving selflessness"). The finite self aims at dominion and gives only to those that serve its purposes. The infinite self exercises uncalculating love and regards the same objects and events of everyday life with a perception that goes beyond means to ends—means to help or hinder our own purposes. The infinite dimension of the person unifies the world with its own contemplation.

Here is Russell's algorithm for the *individual realization of freedom.* The transition from the self-serving self to the self-giving self requires an exercise or discipline of mind in moments of self-surrender when all personal will ceases and the individual experiences a sense of passive submission to the universe. After struggling for some particular want or need, the pursuit of the object that has absorbed our desire is relinquished. After this relinquishment there arises a state of suspension of the will when it does not seek to impose itself upon the world, but is open to every impression that comes to it from the world. At this point the universal good (love) that constitutes the will of our infinite self becomes the motivation of all that we do. This is the location of freedom; it is a place in consciousness. We no longer depend on, equate with, or defend a social or material definition of who we are; we simply come to sense that Self is already there to express itself through material and social forms. What Russell calls the *essence of religion* is the dimension of human personality where the boundaries of a false sense of self or ego are transcended through the realization of a new self, a self that feels safe and comfortable in the world without having to seek validation from another person or thing. Inge Bell (1975) and Bernard McGrane (1991) say that realization is a process of "desocialization," when persons become aware of their identification with social roles. Students, for example, realize they are not their grades. The "transcendent" state of awareness finds articulation by way of a variety of scholars, but the "experience" of the "freedom" from the total attachment to social roles is independent of thinking about it. McGrane makes provision for social self-reflection through a discussion of exercises in disidentification.[1]

The result of the realization in every individual of the true self (or freedom)—when no need exists to preserve self, and each individual operates in the mode of giving to preserve itself—is the emergence of an ideal society, one built on love (love supersedes the law) and the community of love (see the work of Josiah Royce, 1968). In this case society is *effect*, the product of a level of consciousness attained by individual members of the group, where love (selflessness) knows exactly how to act toward the other without the law. The principles of sociology would operate, in this state, as instruments in the construction and expression of the ideal, loving community.

Socialization and Alienation   Peter Berger (1967), like Russell (1961), also provides insight for the realization of freedom through the evolution of consciousness when he points out that through the very process of becoming socialized we are alienated from that part of self that is the true self. He says that the true self (consciousness, ground of being, freedom) precedes socialization. Objectivation (as discussed in Chapter 6) is the production of a real social world external to the individuals inhabiting it; internalization causes the social world to occupy the status of reality within the consciousness of these individuals. Furthermore, he says, internalization carries an additional feature of great importance: It is a duplication of consciousness in terms of its socialized and nonsocialized components. By this he means, first, that consciousness precedes socialization. Second, consciousness can never be totally socialized. Socialization, then, is always partial. A part of consciousness is shaped by socialization into the form that becomes the individual's socially recognizable identity. As in all products of internalization, a dialectical tension exists between identity as socially (objectively) assigned and identity as subjectively appropriated. Even more important, he says, the duplication of consciousness brought about by the internalization of the social world results in the setting aside, congealing, or estranging of one part of consciousness from the rest. In other words, internalization entails self-objectivation; that is, a part of the self becomes objectivated, not just to others, but to itself, as a set of representations of the social world. This social self coexists in a state of uneasy accommodation with the nonsocial self-consciousness upon which it has been imposed. Morris Rosenberg (1988) concurs that self-objectivation results in self-alienation. The self-alienated person is one who is separated from his or her existential experience—a direct experience of self as opposed to that experienced through the haze of self-objectivation (Tiryakian, 1968). In the process of running with the herd (in social conformity) we lose contact with the irreducible and everpresent ground of being, or self.

Another way of putting this is to say that humans escape themselves insofar as part of themselves becomes shaped by socialization. The essential self is "blocked off" because "others" determine the very nature of identity in the individual's consciousness. This dialectical relationship between the individual and society is seen by Berger as a form of alienation from the true essence of individual self or consciousness. Berger (1967) comments that primitive and infantile consciousness is aware or conscious of society in alienated terms, as facticity, as necessity, as fate, as reality, as given. When in the evolution of consciousness society is grasped as a human product, this awareness or act of consciousness becomes a precondition for finding the experience of human freedom, and what follows is the capacity to act as a subject back on society (being in the world, but not of it) (*The Sacred Canopy*, pp. 85–87).

Other thinkers, particularly humanistic psychologists such as Viktor Frankl (1978) and Roberto Assagioli (1964), interpret the alienated self as the *repressed spiritual unconscious.* This is a sort of early development in consciousness, a cognitive fall from grace, when a separate, "self-in-charge" consciousness, the "pride of life," becomes dominant as the individual's self-awareness. Assagioli, like Russell, argues that *individual freedom* is an experience that lies outside scientific knowing—it is an existential experience, a direct awareness of pure self-consciousness (as in the experience of a color like red or blue). Modern social science, he declares, has denied that we can have a direct experience of the self. He stresses the need for a person to develop the higher psychic functions, the spiritual dimension. The social self is not the pure self or self-consciousness and the goal of human living is to disidentify, disassociate from the *content* of consciousness rather than from consciousness itself. Some people get their identity from their feelings, others from their thoughts, others from their social roles; but this identification with a part of the personality destroys the freedom which comes from the experience of the pure *I*. The exercise in disidentification and identification involves practicing awareness and affirming, "I have a body, but I am not my body." "I have emotions, but I am not my emotions." "I have a job, but I am not my job." Systematic introspection can help to eliminate all partial self-identifications. Assagioli says that we are socially conditioned by the past but we have the power to disown it. We have to change society, but from within ourselves first. He says that we should pay far more attention to the higher unconscious and to the development of the transpersonal self; he is interested not only in the basement of the human being, but in the whole building. An elevator is built that can allow a person access to every level of his or her personality; the need for finding these levels of being are as real as social needs.

Self-Preservation or Selflessness   Sociology is a study of cooperative living, but as a scientific understanding, it is itself a stepping stone (in individual awareness) to cooperation that results from love rather than from the imposition of law. Using sociological jargon, "consensus" and "conflict" are theoretical concepts used to characterize the operation of the principles of sociology; they represent the tensions in consciousness between law and love. Love makes society an *effect*; the law makes society a *cause*. Love does not need to be told how to act; the law is for those who are aware of themselves as personality in society and are not yet aware of themselves as society in personality. The law regulates social self-interest for those who have not attained the fuller understanding that self-defense is unnecessary for a Self that is never threatened in the first place. Love interprets society as an avenue, an instrument for the expression of individual freedom; the law interprets it as the sole determinant of human action.

Past theoretical interpretation of the relationship between individual consciousness and societal forms have been offered by Karl Marx (1930), Emile Durkheim (1950, 1953), and Max Weber (1976). Marx espoused the theory that societal economic conditions determine individual consciousness; Durkheim posited society in a causal relationship to individual consciousness such that the individual is a representation of society. Only Weber showed that the conditions of individual consciousness determine social relations. He said that religious factors are antecedent to economic interests, as illustrated in the case of the Protestant ethic and the spirit of capitalism; this suggests that an experience outside of society that can affect society. The further implication is that we must consider both the antecedent role of consciousness and the various orientations of consciousness when investigating the relationship of subjective consciousness to social structure.

A self-giving orientation in consciousness generates a loving community in which the law is subsumed by love. Anything less than self-giving consciousness explains the tensions between degrees of self-interest (between consensus and conflict). The more that society is based on individual consciousness that self-preserves the more it is coercive in its objectified nature. Laws are needed to ensure the well-being of each individual because each is self-concerned. The more society is based on love (self-giving consciousness), the more it is a representation or the effect of loving consciousness. For example, a group must decide how to distribute resources, let's say food. Half the group is selfish types and the other half is selfless types. How would the principle of stratification operate when there is only enough food for half the group? Ideally, the self-giving types will give their food to the self-preserving types and by doing so the level of awareness of the selfish types will be raised to the level of the selfless types and the distribution of food among all will follow—an entirely different schema than might be implemented as the effect of consciousness at the level of law or morality. Moral consciousness is still self-preserving. An illustration of moral social action would have been the recommendation to divide the food among everyone. Another example is the police chief's efforts to equalize resources to prevent crime, a recommendation that reflects the chief's level of consciousness (as to self-interest). The effect of his consciousness follows as a characteristic of society. Law, *explicitly* in the form of social controls such as legislation or police action, or *implicitly* in all of society's structure (its prescriptions for behavior), either stabilizes society when its members are not self-realized as love or makes society a means of expression when its members are self-realized as love.

Social Constraint as a Precondition for Freedom   Here is another way of talking about the individual realization of freedom in relation to societal constraint via an evolution of individual consciousness. A *humanistic,* as opposed to a *scientistic,* sociology specifies sociology as not only the study of humanity but also as a struggle for humanity. In this latter perspective, sociology becomes a science as a level of awareness that itself becomes a stepping stone to the realm of individual freedom as a higher level of awareness. Freedom is possible after— and through—the recognition of society as constraint. A scientistic sociology denotes an emphasis on the traditional notion of the discipline as a logical and empirical endeavor. A humanistic perspective deters the sociologist from separating his or her sociological understanding from the rest of his or her existence in society. This means that sociology is an awareness, a form of consciousness that has consequences for an understanding not only of who we are, but also for being who we are. Sociology is not just a scientific activity that produces an understanding of how, why, and to what degree our behavior is influenced by others. It questions how much say we have in the matter. It is a total view that includes the degree to which logical and practical reasoning serve the achievement of, and are informed by, transcendental (nonempirical, nonrational) ends as well (Alexander, 1990). A humanistic sociology, contrasted to the more commonly occurring scientistic sociology, permits a fuller understanding of and participation in what it means to be human by acknowledging the mechanism whereby society and the individual, through empirical and nonempirical dynamics, create each other. This does not mean that sociology must leave the frame of reference of the empirical discipline; rather, it interprets and refers to, but does not constitute, religious, transcendent, spiritual experience.

Through *methodological atheism*, that is, through empirical reference to religious, transcendent, nonempirical consciousness (Berger, 1967), sociology can truly encompass the human condition. Within this frame of reference, the religious consciousness is dealt with only as such, as a human activity, and brackets have to be placed around the question as to whether the consciousness may not also be something else than, or refer to something else than, the human world in which it empirically originates (see LeShan [1976] and Russell [1925] for further discussion). The task of social theory is not to explain away "meaning systems," but to reveal how human identity is built on the powers of others: Through the meeting of religion and science persons can ground the meaning of their lives as firmly as possible under their own control (Becker, 1965). Whatever else it may be, the sociological formulation of the human condition must refer to transcendent consciousness as an empirical phenomenon if it is to really comprehend the individual and society. Berger further comments that all meanings are transmitted in social processes. Society provides for the very avenues that lead to our wondering contemplation of being and either buries our metaphysical quest or provides forms in which it can be pursued. Freedom is realized outside society, but must come full circle as actualized in society. Knowledge of society and social constraint is a precondition for freedom; freedom is possible because there is constraint. A humanistic sociology empowers individuals to be in the world and not of it, and the study of humanity is also a struggle for humanity.[2]

Sociology and Educational Change

The introduction of the notion of enduring questions does not imply that the issue of human freedom is unresolved—quite the contrary. The enduring questions confront us every time we feel constrained by society, every time we feel its institutions, like education, defining who we are and determining what we do. These questions are reminders to find our freedom in that part of us that lies outside society. Society is within us, but only part of us, and the authentic self is always there to be realized. It is always there beholding and participating in society, and changing it to be a reflection, an effect of the consciousness that creates it.

Individual Freedom and Social Change

The previous chapter explains general dynamics of the principle of social change and discusses that social movements take various forms, contributing to functional integration or to shifts in power in the society, or simply reflecting the evolution of means of subsistence. Although we know these as sources of change, we can postulate some new theory on social change that might help us to decide, where, as individuals, we can introduce such change. Individuals can initiate two types of social change. One type is based on self-interest and the other is based on selflessness. The effects are observed in society as cause in contrast to society as effect. The scientific version of reality interprets schools, for example, as enhancing life chances or as reproducing inequality. When change begins as an idea that is based on what benefits you, rather that on what you can give, the effect is reflected "as" society and "in" society. Change emanates in individual consciousness from a self-preserving orientation—perhaps even in the direction of moral good. This is distinguished from reform through love and not law. The love supersedes law. Love doesn't need the law; love generates values and knows automatically how to act toward the other. Ideally, if each person thinks of the other, then there is no need for the law; these persons are "in" society, but are not "of" society.

Society is a reflection of one or many individuals' level of self-awareness. The principles of sociology operate, then, to create society and change society; society is the expression of ideal or nonideal forms of cooperation (these forms being dependent upon individual levels of awareness). Ultimately and potentially, sociology is less about the study of groups and is more an understanding which itself is the basis of finding the essence of what it means to be an individual and fully human. Sociology shows us our bondage and by doing so, we conceive the notion of freedom. Then are we free to change society.

Individual Freedom and Institutional Change

Although the institutions that we create take on their own existence and ensure their own survival (even at our expense), challenge to an institution must begin with an individual. The answer to the question of how you can change the world, how you can change society, how you can change a big institution like education, is fraught with irony. We have spent much time talking about sociology as the power of others to influence our behavior and of the impersonal mechanism of society, a system that isn't human, that functions to shape what we come to think falsely are our own lives. But this is a lie—maybe just something about which we have been unaware until now. Institutions such as education, which we create to ensure our own survival, can also make us lose our sense of what it means to be an individual if we do not understand their role in fostering the development of subjective freedom. The good news is that such institutions are amenable to change beginning, as you might have guessed, with the individual. It takes just one person to change the world, as Rosa Parks did by refusing to give up her seat in a bus; she initiated a revolution in American race relations.[3]

In the closing chapter of *The Sociological Spirit: Critical Essays in a Critical Science*, Earl Babbie (1988) asks "If massive social change is possible, where and how does it begin?" and "What's the impetus for a complex social system to turn a corner and begin lumbering mindlessly off in a different direction?" The answer, he says, is ultimately the individual. He states that the systems we create cannot change themselves except in the predictable ways we have designed them to change. Only people can initiate those changes, and it usually starts with *one person*. Some of the largest changes in education—desegregation and busing—started with one person. Babbie recounts how on December 1, 1955, Rosa Parks, who was a seamstress in Montgomery, Alabama, was riding the public bus home after a hard day's work. When the bus driver called out for those black persons who were seated in the first rows of the black section to stand up to let the white passengers sit down (because the bus was becoming crowded with rush-hour commuters), she refused to give up her seat. She violated the established conventions of society, the rules of what seemed to most people as the way things had to be. Parks was arrested and jailed for her defiance, but the local black clergy believed she had been treated unjustly. The protest started with ideas about boycotting the bus system: if a sizable proportion of the black community gave up riding the buses for one day, they might have some effect. The black boycott of the Montgomery bus system, with Martin Luther King, Jr. chosen as organizer, originated in the consciousness of one person—Rosa Parks. Even though police had beaten and jailed supporters of the boycott, it continued and gained a widespread audience. In November, 1956, less than a year after Rosa Parks defied the conventions, the United States Supreme Court declared racial segregation in public facilities unconstitutional.

Opportunites for Change

Now that we have located the realm of individual freedom and have discussed its potential for social change, we can think about schools of the twenty-first century. Change can be the effect of individual consciousness that is either self-preserving or selfless, with selfless orientation resulting in changes that bring about various approximations of the ideal society. What kind of changes, then, can one effect in education once consciousness considers the other instead of itself for its well-being?

In the epilogue of her *Sociology of Education*, Jeanne Ballantine (1989) discusses schools in the early twenty-first century. Projections for education are a basis for thinking about the relation of the individual to educational institutions and the potential for social change that begins with the individual. Projections are based on knowledge of present socioeconomic conditions, the prospect of new technologies, and commission and task force reports. Ballantine discusses information available on demographic trends, students, teachers and schools.

In general, we can anticipate longer school weeks and overall terms (210 days), an earlier school-starting age, more educational requirements, reeducation of the total work force to match changing occupational demands, more home schooling, more business and school collaboration, higher pay for teachers, more computer-assisted instruction, and student placement in businesses for job training. By taking a detailed look at the present and projected conditions of education in society, we have a context in which social change can be enacted.

Demographic Trends

Demographers provide information on trends and projections that affect education. Public school enrollments declined (a decrease of 3,500,000 students from 1975 to 1982) (National Center for Education Statistics, 1983, 1984, 1985). Since the low point in 1983, enrollments have increased gradually from year to year, with a projected increase to continue into the mid-1990s. Primary school enrollments were lowest in 1985 and high school enrollments were projected to be lowest in 1990 (National Center for Education Statistics, 1983, 1984, 1985). Middle- and upper-class families are having fewer children while lower-class families are having more. One in five high school students is nonwhite (National Institute of Education, 1978). One in two black and one in three Hispanic children live in poverty. The Hispanic population increased 30 percent between 1980 and 1987, five times the increase for all other racial and ethnic groups combined. Half of these Hispanic children finish high school and half of the families have a single parent (United States Bureau of the Census, 1987). To accommodate these statistics, schools are teaching an increasing number of children from poverty backgrounds and from non-English-speaking households. Asian refugees, immigrants, and illegal aliens comprise increasing proportions of the minority population. English as a second language will be an increasingly important part of the curriculum. The percentage of children from poor families in urban areas is increasing while city tax bases are declining. Many children will live in single-parent households part of the time before they become 18 years old and an increasing number of mothers of school-aged children who are working will require after-school care for their children (Neill, 1979). The number of service sector and skilled high-tech jobs is increasing and rapid technological changes will lead to the need for reeducation and high school graduation (Office of Technology Assessment, 1988).

The consequences of these demographic changes to education (Hodgkinson, 1985) are projected as follows: more children entering school from poverty households; more children entering school from single-parent households; more children from minority backgrounds; a smaller percentage of children who have had Head Start and similar programs, even though under current regulations more are eligible; a larger number of children entering school who were premature babies, leading to more learning difficulties in school; more children whose parents were not married (now 12 of every 100 births); more *latch-key* children and children from blended families as a result of remarriage of one original parent; more children from teenage mothers; fewer white, middle-class suburban children, with day care becoming a middle-class norm as more women enter the work force; a continued decline in the level of retention to high school graduation in almost all states; a continued drop in the number of minority high school graduates who apply for college; a continued increase in the number of black middle-class students in the entire system; increased numbers of first-generation Asian-American students; increased numbers of Indonesian students, and with increasing language difficulties; continued high dropouts rates among Hispanics, currently about 40 percent of whom complete high school; a major increase in part-time college students and a decline of about one million in full-time students; a major increase in college students who need both financial and academic assistance; increased percentage of workers with a college degree and a continued increase in the number of college graduates whose jobs do not require a college degree; continued increases in graduate enrollments in business; increased undergraduate enrollments in arts and sciences courses but not majors; increased numbers of talented minority youth choosing the military as their educational route, both due to cost and direct access to high technology; major increases in adult and continuing education outside of college and university settings (by business, government, other nonprofit organizations such as United Way, and by for-profit franchise groups such as Bell & Howell Schools and The Learning Annex).

Students

Projections show that the student population will include toddlers, adults, and older citizens as well as those of traditional school age. In general, the school district will make provision of learning experiences and training for students from three to twenty-one and for adults from twenty-one to over eighty. Students could be in school on an extended day and year basis, with options available. For example, students might attend school seven hours a day and 210 days or more a year, depending on their needs and ability to handle tasks; select a variety of courses, both required and elective, in academic, vocational, or enrichment programs; work from an interactive computer-videodisc learning station at home or school; work on a job and go to school; enter apprenticeships with master teachers; have opportunities for expanded time in a science laboratory or music, art, or vocational class; have opportunities to be tutored individually or in small groups.

Teachers

Projections about teachers (Cetron, Soriano, and Gayle, 1985) indicate that teaching will become an increasingly multidimensional job. Computer-managed information on teachers will determine which jobs will be taken by which teachers. Teaching jobs may be defined in terms of specific services: learning diagnostician; information gatherer for software programs; courseware writer; curriculum designer; mental-health diagnostician; evaluator of learning performances; evaluator of social skills; small-group learning facilitator; media-instruction producer; home-based instruction designer; home-based instruction monitor.

Schools

Factors affecting future schools (in relation to work) are projected as follows: minority populations will become the majority in most grade schools in the nation's large and middle-sized school districts; computers will be available to students in prosperous districts on a 1:4 ratio; federal grants will provide a major portion of the funding for job training and equipment (including computers) in poor school districts; women, particularly married women, will enter the work force at a faster rate than any other group within the population; more businesses will be involved in schools, including apprenticeship training; older citizens (over 55) increasingly will become students in public schools, job-training programs, and community source programs; a core nine-month program will be offered in elementary and high schools, shifting electives to later in the lengthened day and to summer sessions; teachers' salaries on an annual basis will be raised to within 10 percent of other professions requiring college degrees.

Summary

This chapter has introduced some enduring questions and some enduring answers. In delineating sociology as a field of study (and sociology of education as a subfield of study), we come to see that it is not only a study of what it is to be human, but it is also part of the struggle of becoming human. It is foremost a *science*, a particular *level of awareness of reality* that itself has consequences for our behavior because human action is not a response to genes, but to awareness—*consciousness* of reality and how to act in it. The consequences of scientific awareness for human behavior can be *bondage, slavery*, and *determinism* through *society as a cause*. But this consciousness can be, alternatively, a precondition for a new awareness that develops and makes possible a total state of *individual freedom* through *society as effect*. The application of this understanding has been illustrated in the consideration of the role of the individual in initiating change in education.

Specifically, each of this chapter's discussions, though somewhat overlapping, attempted to emphasize a particular aspect of the issue of *individual freedom* and *social determinism* from the perspective of *evolution of individual and subjective consciousness*. The first focused on the nature of science as a limited form of awareness of reality and how it can potentially, through its laws and theories, result in a limited understanding of human behavior. The second discussion brought our attention to how one finds individual freedom outside scientific consciousness, but bases it on scientific consciousness. As part of this second discussion, we were presented with a method for the *individual realization of freedom*. Then we got a glimpse of the evolution of consciousness at the level of *socialization as alienation*—how, in the very process of becoming socialized, we are alienated from the place of freedom in our individual consciousness. Finally, the association between individual consciousness and societal forms was discussed in terms of the relationship of freedom to determinism and of *humanistic* and *scientistic* sociologies (sociology as a level of consciousness that itself has consequences both for *understanding* and for *being*). Education determines us, and in knowing this, we are free to recreate education. Individual freedom does not imply that we revolt against society, but rather that we evaluate it from a disinterested, nonself-serving perspective. Some things we will think should remain the same; others might require our proposal and impetus for change. When "designs for order" emanate from individuals who are in the world, but who are not of it, the situation is much like the child who doesn't worry about whether its mother has enough money in her handbag, but solely concerns itself with holding her hand. When advocated changes are grounded in disinterestedness, then we will not need to concern ourselves with the actual changes proposed because we will know that they will be sound. We can regard proposals for changing educational institutions as reflections of varying degrees of individual self-interest or self-giving. Despite society's apparent capacity to act in its own right, separate from individuals, ultimately it takes just one individual to override its influence. Society in its changing forms is the effect of change in individual self-awareness.

Vocabulary

alienation

evolution of consciousness

finite self

freedom

humanistic

infinite self

society as cause

society as effect

Questions

1. What is the relationship between the individual and society (discuss individual freedom and social determinism)?

2. Can one person influence society, particularly the institution of education?

References and Suggested Readings

Abakanowicz, M. "Assemblage of Variants of a Certain Prototype." Sculpture at the Aldrich Museum of Contemporary Art, Ridgefield, CT, February 11, 1990.

Alexander, J. "Prolegomena to a Theory of Social Institutions: Commentary: Structure, Value, Action." *American Sociological Review*, (1990) 55:339–45.

_____. *Theoretical Logic in Sociology (Volume One): Positivism, Presuppositions, and Current Controversies.* Berkeley, CA: University of California Press, 1982.

Assagioli, R. *The Act of Will.* New York: Viking, 1973.

Ballantine, J. *The Sociology of Education: A Systematic Analysis.* Englewood Cliffs, NJ: Prentice-Hall, 1989.

Babbie, E. *The Sociological Spirit: Critical Essays in a Critical Science.* Belmont, CA: Wadsworth, 1988.

Becker, E. *Escape from Evil.* New York: Free Press, 1965.

Bell, I. *This Book Is Not Required, An Emotional Survival Manual for Undergraduates.* 2nd Ed. Fort Bragg, CA: Small Press, 1975.

Berdyaev, N. *Slavery and Freedom.* New York: Charles Scribner's Sons, 1944.

Berger, P. *The Sacred Canopy: Elements of a Sociological Theory of Religion.* New York: Doubleday, 1967.

_____. *Invitation to Sociology: A Humanistic Perspective.* New York: Doubleday, 1963.

Cetron, M., B. Soriano, and M. Gayle. *Schools of the Future: Education into the Twenty-first Century.* New York: McGraw-Hill, 1985.

Durkheim, E. *Sociology and Philosophy.* New York: Free Press, 1953.

_____. *The Rules of Sociological Method.* New York: Free Press, 1950.

Frankl, V. *The Unheard Cry for Meaning: Psychotherapy and Humanism.* New York: Simon and Schuster, 1978.

Hegel, F. "Introduction." In C. J. Friedrich, ed., *The Philosophy of Hegel.* New York: The Modern Library, n.d., p. 34.

Hodgkinson, H. *All One System: Demographics of Education, Kindergarten through Graduate School.* Washington, DC: Institute for Educational Leadership, 1985.

Kant, I. *Kant on History.* Indianapolis, IN: Bobbs-Merrill, 1963.

LeShan, L. *Alternate Realities: The Search for the Full Human Being.* New York: Ballantine, 1976.

Marx, K. and F. Engels. *The German Ideology.* New York: International, 1930.

McGrane, B. *Society, Self and Desocialization: An Introduction to Buddhist Sociology.* Orange, CA: Sociology Department, Chapman University.

Mead, G. *Mind, Self and Society.* Chicago: University of Chicago Press, 1934.

Mulkey, L. "Comments on a Critique of a Classic." *Teaching Sociology,* (1990) 18:510–15.

National Center for Education Statistics. *The Condition of Education: Statistical Report.* Washington, DC: United States Department of Education, 1985, pp. 18–9.

National Center for Education Statistics. "Private Elementary and Secondary Education, 1983: Enrollment, Teachers, and Schools." *NCES Bulletin* 85–102b. Washington, DC: United States Department of Education, December, 1984.

National Center for Education Statistics. *Projections of Education Statistics to 1992–93.* Washington, DC: United States Department of Education, 1985.

National Center for Education Statistics. *Statistics of Public Elementary and Secondary Day Schools.* Washington, DC: United States Department of Education, 1983, 1984, 1985.

National Institute of Education. *Declining Enrollments: The Challenge of the Coming Decades.* Washington, DC: United States Department of Education, 1978.

Neill, S. "The Demographers' Message to Education." *American Education,* (January/February 1979).

Office of Technology Assessment. *Technology and the American Economic Transition.* Washington, DC: United States Department of Education, 1988.

Rosenberg, M. "Self-Objectification: Relevance for the Species and Society." *Sociological Forum,* 3:548–65.

Royce, J. *The Problem of Christianity (Volume I): The Christian Doctrine of Life.* Chicago: Henry Regnery, 1968.

_____. *The Problem of Christianity (Volume II): The Real World and the Christian Ideas.* Chicago: Henry Regnery, 1968.

Russell, B. *Mysticism and Logic and Other Essays.* London: Longmans, 1925.

Russell, B. "The Essence of Religion." *The Basic Writings of Bertrand Russell.* New York: Simon & Schuster, 1961.

Teilhard de Chardin, P. *The Future of Man.* New York: Harper & Row, 1964.

Tiryakian, E. "The Existential Self and the Person." In C. Gordon and K. Gergen, eds., *The Self in Social Interaction.* New York: Wiley, 1968.

Turner, R. "Personality in Society: Social Psychology's Contribution to Sociology." *Social Psychology Quarterly,* (1988) 51:1–10.

United States Bureau of the Census. "The Hispanic Population in the United States: March 1986 and 1987." Series P-20, No. 416, *Current Population Surveys.* Washington, DC: United States Department of Commerce.

Weber, M. *The Protestant Ethic and the Spirit of Capitalism.* New York: Scribner's, 1958.

Notes

[1]See Bernard McGrane's *Society, Self and Desocialization* (Orange, CA: Sociology Department, Chapman University, 1991) for exercises that make the everyday world a strange place. The perceived orderliness of social life becomes a remarkable accomplishment—not seeing a new thing, but a new way of seeing things. The "exercises" in social deconditioning invoke the individual's ability to behold or look at its social sense and dimension of self.

[2]Varied ideas of an *evolution of individual consciousness* are found in the works of F. W. Hegel, "Introduction," in *The Philosophy of History* (Carl J. Friedrich, ed., New York: The Modern Library, 1954) and Pierre Teilhard de Chardin, *The Future of Man.* For Hegel, the history of humankind is the history of the gradual unfolding of the Spirit; this is a history marked by stages in which the Absolute Spirit evolves into its own. Humans slowly arrive at true self-consciousness. Teilhard de Chardin similarly posits a historical evolution of consciousness. These conceptions of progress focus on growth in society as a whole, and de-emphasize the significance that an individual can have in changing the course of history by moving from the level of law and morality to the level of love and freedom.

[3]The illustration of Rosa Parks is one of society perceived as effect. Rosa Parks did not take society for granted; she challenged the givens. We assume her action was spontaneous and not part of a planned protest. We do not know, however, whether her individual level of awareness was one of self-preservation or selflessness. Recall that both levels of consciousness produce society as effect as opposed to society as cause.

Name Index

Subject Index